D1103955

Famous Chefs & Fabulous Recipes

Famous Chefs & Fabulous Recipes

LESSONS LEARNED AT ONE OF THE OLDEST COOKING SCHOOLS IN AMERICA

Lisa Abraham
with Catherine St. John

To: Sheila,
Keep on Learning!
Keep on Cooking!

Catherine St. John

11/5/12

RINGTAW BOOKS
AKRON, OHIO

16   15   14   13   12   5   4   3   2   1

LIBRARY OF CONGRESS CATALOGING IN PUBLICATION DATA

Abraham, Lisa.

  Famous chefs and fabulous recipes: lessons learned at the Western Reserve School of Cooking / Lisa Abraham; with Catherine St. John.

      p. cm.

  Includes index.

  ISBN 978-1-931968-88-1 (cloth : alk. paper)

1. Western Reserve School of Cooking (Hudson, Ohio) 2. Cooking. 3. Cooking—Study and teaching—United States. 4. Cooks—United States. 5. Cookbooks. I. St. John, Catherine. II. Western Reserve School of Cooking (Hudson, Ohio) III. Title.

TX365.W47A27 2011

  641.5092—dc23

2011031188

The paper used in this publication meets the minimum requirements of American National Standard for Information Sciences—Permanence of Paper for Printed Library Materials, ANSI Z39.48–1984. ∞

Photo of Zack Bruell by Epstein Design Partners.
Photo of John Desmond by Tomas Tyner.
Photo of Naomi Duguid by Laura Berman.
Photo of Fred and Linda Griffith by Barney Taxel.
Photo of Giuliano Hazan by Andrea Hillebrand.
Photo of Scot Jones by Julie Aronson.
Photo of Wendy Kromer by Lexie Cataldo.
Photo of Emily Luchetti by Jeffrey Gleason.
Photo of Deborah Madison by Laurie Smith.
Photo of Nick Malgieri by Quentin Bacon.
Photo of Alice Medrich by Dave Lauridsen.
Photo of Roland Mesnier courtesy of The White House.
Photo of Betty Rosbottom by Pete Parry.
Photo of Roger Thomas by Ernest J. Aranyosi.
Photo of Joanne Weir by Greg Habiby.

This book is dedicated to the chefs who have taught here, the students and to Zona Spray, who started it all.

Contents

Acknowledgments

It was my husband, Carl, who first came up with the idea of writing a book about the cooking school. I thought it wouldn't be that hard—we had all the school's brochures and the recipes from the last forty years. It turned into quite a task and I thank Carl for all of his hours of scanning recipes into the computer. Without his encouragement, I am not sure I would have ever taught cooking, let alone purchased my own cooking school. His support throughout our twenty-two-year marriage has meant the world to me.

To Zona Spray, for believing in me enough to make me a part of her school and for hiring me as a teacher. Even though I only worked with Zona for a few years, I tried to absorb all that she had to offer.

I'm not a writer, so I needed to find someone who was. Lisa Abraham and I had come to know each other through the school and through her work as food writer for the *Akron Beacon Journal*. It was only natural to go to her with this project. She has poured her heart and soul into this book, and perhaps a little blood, too. So thank you Lisa, for spending all those long hours pouring over the piles and piles of recipes and tracking down all the chefs who have taught at the school over the years.

The staff at the school and store have been the best staff anyone could ask for. To Nancy Neal for taking such great care of the store, The Cookery, and making sure we have all the greatest and latest cookware and gadgets on the market. To Mary Jones, for being a jack of all trades—teaching classes, working the store and fixing a leaky sink all at the same time. We would not have found all of these recipes without the help of Kathy Myers. Kathy has been my right hand since buying the school in the spring of 2007, and she spent countless hours in the basement office finding everything we needed.

There are too many people to thank individually, so thanks to all of the staff, teachers, students and loyal customers. Without all of you, we would not still be here after forty years to offer you the best in culinary education and the tools with which to create. Thanks also to everyone at the University of Akron Press for believing that our story was worth telling.

To Ed Schiciano, who has been the school's accountant for many years and was for a time its owner, thanks for making it possible to carry on a forty-year tradition in Hudson.

To my kids, Allison and Lorenzo, you have grown up at the school and put up with me and my work schedule for many years, but hopefully you have enjoyed eating the fruits of my labor.

Finally, thanks to my parents, Larry and Ruth White, who brought me up in a house that was built around the kitchen. Every meal was made with love, which fostered my love of cooking and gave me a place where I could discover myself.

Catherine St. John
Owner, Western Reserve School of Cooking

First, to Catherine St. John, for giving me the opportunity to tell the wonderful story of her school, for putting up with all of my quirks (and delays) and for two years worth of invaluable help, not to mention a few suppers. To her husband, Carl St. John, and their children, Allison and Lorenzo, for their support throughout this project, especially for many recipes scanned (thanks Carl!). To Kathy Myers for countless hours spent digging through forty years worth of files and catalogs. To Zona Spray, without whose vision this school would never have been, and without whose cooperation this book would not be nearly as complete.

To all of the amazing chefs who have shared their gifts at the Zona Spray Cooking School and the Western Reserve School of Cooking. Thanks for being so willing to share your time, your stories and your wisdom. Your personal stories, as much as your recipes, make this book a true treasure.

To all of the fine folks at the University of Akron Press, for their help, support and patience (especially their patience). To Thomas Bacher for saying yes to our idea sight unseen, to Amy Freels for her editing skill, to Julie Gammon for getting the word out and to Carol Slatter for her assistance.

To friends, too numerous to name, for their support, well-wishes and prayers, which helped to make this book a reality. To my family at the *Akron Beacon Journal*, particularly those in the Features Department, for being a constant source of support and friendship during some very trying times.

To my real family, including the best in-laws a girl could ever ask for, John and Ellen Jayne Hart, my siblings and siblings-in-laws and a host of nieces and nephews, for their kind words and good cheer.

To my parents, Tim and Mary Catherine Abraham, for their never-ending love, pride and life-long support. Without my Dad's love of books and my Mother's skills in the kitchen, I would never have ended up writing about food.

Finally, and most importantly, to my dear husband, Richard Hart, who has patiently endured. Your kind ways and gentle love lift and inspire me every day. You really are the best husband in the world.

Thank you, thank you, thank you all!

Lisa Abraham

Foreword

O nly two hours remained before people would arrive for class. I hurriedly propped up a still-wet handmade sign against the back staircase at Hudson's Little Church on the Green. Thirty minutes earlier, before racing off that sunny September morning to teach the school's first class, I had suddenly realized that no one—except Hudsonites—would find 1 East Main Street. And who would think to walk to the back of the church and down the basement stairs without direction?

Looking for a solution, I spied a flimsy two by four-foot plywood board in my garage. It wasn't ideal, but at least the shape could accommodate four words. I grabbed a two-inch paint brush, cracked open a small can of black paint and scrawled the school's name, vertically, not horizontally, down the board. It looked like child's play.

Thirty-eight people came to class that morning, forty years ago. There have been many changes during those four decades: the most important was a move across the Green to the school's current location, 140 North Main Street. The new address brought instant visibility; though enlarging the teaching space demanded major structural overhauls. Since those earliest years, thousands of people have ventured through the school's doors. And each student and teacher have marked the school's history with a story. Put together, they could fill a book with behind-the-scenes fascination and intrigue. Not as gripping as 007, but close.

From the beginning, the school's goal was to help people understand cooking, its logic and why things happen in the pot. Recipes were little more than examples of cooking techniques, with a bit of food chemistry thrown into the mix. Used together, they help cooks identify cause and effect—knowledge that spurs creativity and helps purge kitchens of costly mistakes.

The earliest classes were filled with home cooks. But when young chefs from Paris started arriving to teach, bringing exciting nouvelle cuisine dishes and revolutionary cooking tricks, the mix of students changed, as did the times. Consumers were now demanding increasingly sophisticated food and they were willing to spend hours in the kitchen. Boning a turkey, stuffing it and roasting it for Thanksgiving proved to be one of the school's most popular participation classes. Students flew in from Chicago to learn the technique. It was a green light for all things French, but it didn't last.

During the 1980s, while the United States dominated the art world, food writers cried for an American cuisine. But what was it? No one knew exactly. But it initiated a flurry of creativity among local chefs. They competed with one another, improved their menus, honed dishes until they were art forms on a plate and searched for ever-changing, innovative ideas. Restaurant owners and chefs came to classes, hoping to soak up the creative juices, as foreign chefs practiced their skills with such perfect timing and fluidity that watching them perform was as good as the ballet.

Over the years, people behind the scenes kept the pulse of the school beating. Food editors from the *Cleveland Plain Dealer, the Sun News* and *Akron Beacon Journal*, including food writers from Kent, Hudson and as far away as Canton and New Philadelphia, helped spread the word about classes. It didn't matter if a class was for beginning cooks, wait staff or chefs, as long as there was a story, food editors covered it.

The school has outlived many, if not all, of those earliest writers who watched over the little nascent school. But know this—the school exists today because of them. They gave us the courage to be adventurous, and they quietly guided food lovers to our doors, keeping us alive financially. Another huge thank you goes to the numerous Cookery and school employees; and posthumously, I fear, to more souls than I want to count. And of course, there were the students. Many came to improve the food shared at family tables.

Others became leaders in the commercial food world. Some became writers, wrote cookbooks or opened highly successful restaurants. A remarkable number returned to the school as teachers. And there are those who came and never left, building the business—both in front of the house and behind the stove.

From my seat, looking back over the years, the school offered a fascinating kaleidoscope of ever-changing experiences, opportunities and connections. Only a few weeks ago, I met two young opera singers in Sarasota, Florida. One was a twenty-four-year-old apprentice, on his way up the grueling singing ladder. He grew up in Hudson, lived catty-corner to the high school. The other was Hak Soo Kim, performing as the principal tenor in Sarasota's opera production, *La Cenerentola (Cinderella)*. Alone and fresh from Korea in the 1990s, Kim had attended Hudson's Western Reserve Academy, where he had discovered that his voice might be more than choir quality, and the food in Hudson made him homesick for rice and kimchee. "Oh, yeah...that cooking school...my mom went there," and, "Yes...oh yes...I remember that place," they reminisced, smiles widening. I felt like a mom who hadn't been forgotten.

Zona Spray Starks

Famous Chefs & Fabulous Recipes

The Recipes

Chapter 1

The History of the Zona Spray / Western Reserve School of Cooking

Enter the unassuming doorway of 140 North Main Street in Hudson, Ohio, and step into the storefront jammed with pots and pans. Walk past the stacks of books, the wall of aprons and whisks, into the back room, where you will come to rest on hallowed ground.

In this tiny kitchen, with its rows of chairs squeezed tightly together, the food world's royalty have come to share their knowledge and teach their craft. Their images, collected over forty years, festoon the back wall and gaze upon the new generation of students who come to the Western Reserve School of Cooking. It is one of the oldest continuously-operating cooking schools in the country. The lessons taught here can be quantified—there are files, records and course books of class schedules. But the lessons learned here are immeasurable.

This unpretentious culinary artery has provided lifeblood to chefs, restaurants and home cooks throughout the globe, all from this tiny enclave south of Cleveland. Thousands of recipes, hundreds of chefs and thousands of students have passed through the doors over the past forty years.

French chefs Jacques Pepin and Madeleine Kamman, baking elite Nick Malgieri and Alice Medrich, crafters of California cuisine John Ash and Hugh Carpenter, and members of the newest generation of television's celebrity chefs, Alton Brown and Michael Symon, all have taught in this small kitchen, with its well-worn equipment hanging in plain sight.

The list of chefs is large and lofty, and seems to be missing only Julia Child. School founder Zona Spray still keeps the letters—apologies from Child for not being able to accept the invitations to teach at the school—tucked inside a drawer in her home outside of Sarasota, Florida. One can imagine Spray's determination in trying to schedule Child as a guest, particularly considering that Spray counted Child among her friends; the pair would get together every time Child came though Cleveland. Child's hectic schedule never permitted anything more. "It wasn't for lack of trying," Spray recalled.

It was that same kind of determination that Spray summoned to open the school some forty years ago. In 1971, Spray realized that she could rent space in Hudson's Little Church on the Green for the cooking classes that she had been hosting in the basement of her home in Twin Lakes, just outside of Kent,

Ohio. The rent was reasonable, just $5 an hour, and Spray found that students who wanted to learn how to cook were everywhere.

"It was pretty incredible," Spray recalls of her early days. The church had a kitchen in its basement and Spray used that space for her classes. Right away she had more than thirty people sign up, paying $20 each for her to teach them how to cook. "I discovered they were so ripe for learning," Spray says of her early clientele.

For two years, she stayed in the church basement, her students mostly housewives and sometimes their children. The classes were hands-on and extremely technique-oriented—Spray has never been about teaching recipes. While the thousands in the school's collection would suggest the contrary, they do bear witness to the students' desire to take something tangible home for practice after their classes were over. For Spray it was never about the recipe, but always about teaching her students how to cook.

Knowing how to follow a recipe and knowing how to cook are two entirely different things. It can be likened to the old adage, give a man a fish and he'll eat for a day; teach a man to fish and he'll eat for a lifetime. In Spray's case, if you gave a housewife a recipe for fish, she could make one dish, but if you taught her how to sauté, she could fix endless meals. Spray knew that basic cooking techniques—how to braise, how to sauté, how to chop, how to make a pan sauce—needed no recipe, yet provided the foundation for cooking nearly everything. Techniques give body to the creative soul of the chef and skills open up the portal through which the culinary muse can dance.

"Even during my great-grandmother's time, cooking was technique-oriented and cooking by ratio. That's been around for a long time. Even the Eskimos cook by ratio and have for centuries." Spray would know—in 1939 she was born in an Eskimo village in Shungnak, Alaska, high above the Arctic Circle. Her parents, Delmer and Teresa Boyer, were teachers employed by the federal government to educate native Eskimos, years before Alaska became a state. When World War II began, Alaska became too dangerous a place to remain, due to its proximity to Russia and Japan. The family returned to their Oregon home in 1944, where Spray had her schooling and later graduated from the University of Oregon with a degree in sociology. It was there she met her future husband, Lee Spray, who was studying for a career as a university professor. They married and stayed in Oregon while he earned his doctorate degree.

Lee Spray's first job was in Louisiana. Zona, just twenty-four-years old, became acquainted with her neighbor, Katie Buelle, at the time a well-known Creole cook. "She and I cooked night and day for about two years," Spray recalled. "We worked on her books and did a number of things." During the same time period, Spray gave birth to her son, Eric.

After Spray's two-year immersion in Creole cooking, her husband took a teaching job at the University of Chicago and the young family moved north, where daughter, Deirdre, was born. Spray's interest in cooking, piqued by her days with Buelle, led her to enroll in the Antoinette Pope Cooking School. The classes were demonstrations, and Spray attended faithfully, sitting among the rows of watching students. She graduated from the program, but Spray's desire for cooking knowledge still wasn't satisfied. She wanted more and she wanted to do something more than watch.

Spray obtained an apprenticeship at the Dumas Père l'Ecole de la Cuisine Française in Chicago, operated by renowned master chef John Snowden. Snowden was unusual at the time, an African-American, he was not French, but was French-trained from the time he was a young boy. He had won several gold medals at the Culinary Olympics and Spray was impressed by his credentials. Moreover, his classroom consisted of twelve stoves. The training required students to cook, every day, all day and Spray was anxious for the opportunity to do more than watch. Snowden could be cruel and barked at his students for the slightest mistakes, not afraid to humiliate them in front of the others when things went wrong. As a woman, Spray was already considered handicapped. In the 1960s, restaurant kitchens were still the domain of men, and Spray's diminutive size—just 5'2", about 100 pounds—didn't give her any advantages. But she was eager for more information; she wanted to know why things worked the way they did and Snowden was a master of kitchen chemistry. "He was very chemically-oriented and very technically-oriented. This was 30 years before a lot of books on technique ever started coming out. He was a real technician," she said. Later, Spray would enroll in college chemistry courses to continue to satisfy her curiosity about why things happened the way they did.

Her training with Snowden was difficult, but Spray kept her focus, despite the environment, and even recalls the time fondly. "That's really where I consider I got my training," she said. It is also where Spray began to nurse the idea that one day she too would teach cooking.

A third move was in the offing for the Spray family, this time to Toronto, Ontario, Canada, where Lee Spray took a job at York University. It was here that Spray began to teach for the first time, giving lessons out of her home and later teaching at the local YWCA, where she also taught classes in art history. In 1970, a fourth and more permanent move soon followed, as Lee Spray accepted a teaching post at Kent State University and the family moved to Ohio. By this time, Spray's children were in school and she knew that she could devote more time to a career. The family settled in a home in Twin Lakes, outside of Kent, and Spray once again began teaching cooking classes from her home kitchen. Soon after, she discovered Hudson's Little Church on the Green.

Spray was able to easily attract many chefs to come and teach with her, as it was the era before the birth of the celebrity chef. Chefs who wanted to sell books outside of New York and make names for themselves nationally had to travel. The two years she spent in the church basement solidified her own reputation as the source for cooking lessons in Northeast Ohio. But Spray knew that if she wanted to grow, her school needed a permanent location. She found The Cookery, a cookware and gift shop owned by the chef at Hudson's prestigious Western Reserve Academy and his wife. Spray purchased the business in 1973, converted the back room to a kitchen and the Zona Spray Cooking School found its official home. Spray taught cooking, sold cookware and began building a stable of regular teachers, some of who remain at the school to this day.

Kathy Lehr began taking classes from Spray in 1977. A grade-school teacher at the time, Lehr wanted to study bread-making, but eventually worked her way through Spray's professional series of classes and earned a chef's certificate. These classes are typically taken by students who want to work as chefs, not home cooks looking to learn how to prepare new dishes. Over the years, Lehr formed a longtime friendship with Spray, whom she affectionately refers to as "Zoner," and began to teach at the school as well. "She gave me, more than anything, a really wonderful basis for how I teach today," Lehr said. After years of devotion to her craft of bread-making, Lehr is now regarded as a national expert and teaches throughout the country. Spray remains one of her favorite instructors. "When she taught, she had the history and the knowledge that goes with the lesson, the whole history, the stories—I think that's what I loved so much about learning from her," Lehr said.

Food Network Iron Chef Michael Symon of Cleveland, also remembers Spray's passion for food and knowledge. "She knew everything about food and was a little bit of a history book about food," he said. He remembers the school as being ahead of its time in the American culinary landscape. "Now there are cooking schools all over the place. There was nothing really like it at the time and it preceded—by a lot—the kind of food movement that has happened."

It was perhaps Spray's degree in sociology that made her such a keen observer of how the world, in particular the food world, was evolving. Blessed with the ability to pick a winner and spot trends early, she had Chicago chef Rick Bayless and his wife Deann as guest teachers in the early 1990s, just as Bayless was beginning to burst onto the culinary scene.

In the late 1970s, Spray noticed another trend—one that struck directly at her business. In a time when Americans were beginning to travel abroad more frequently, Spray noticed that American women were heading to France to study at the Ecole de Cuisine LaVarenne in Burgundy. After two weeks they would return home and start their own cooking schools. Spray was incredulous. What could these women possibly learn in two weeks that would qualify them to teach others? "How can you possibly open a cooking school and know nothing?" Spray wondered.

She set out for France to find out. The move would have a lasting impact on Spray's school and help establish it among the international cooking set. LaVarenne was run by the internationally-acclaimed cooking teacher Anne Willan. A native of England, Willan had graduated from Le Cordon Bleu in

London, and had worked as a chef at the Palace of Versailles before moving to the United States in 1973. She worked as an editor at *Gourmet* magazine and later as the food editor of the now-defunct *Washington Star*, before moving back to Burgundy, where she opened LaVarenne in 1975. Spray arrived at LaVarenne in the summer of 1978, and during her first visit, ended up teaching. The wife of one of the instructors had delivered a baby prematurely and the child did not survive. Since the instructor was unable to teach, an administrator at the school asked Spray if she would co-teach the sessions with him. Spray learned little new about cooking techniques during her time in France, but was blown away by the ingredients she encountered. At the time, the United States was still a culture steeped in iceberg lettuce. No one was eating or even cooking with the variety of greens Spray experienced. "The cheeses, the butters, no one had ever even heard of at the time," she said. "I certainly learned a lot about food." She returned for a six-week stint in 1979, and worked as a chef's assistant.

During her time at LaVarenne, Spray forged friendships with Willan and many of the chefs who taught there. In the evenings, Spray tested recipes with chefs like Ireland's John Desmond and Steve Raichlen, who was steeped in French training long before he became America's barbecue guru. Spray issued an open invitation for the chefs to visit her school, and in the summers when teams from LaVarenne would travel to the U.S., Hudson, Ohio, became a regular stop between the New York and Chicago scenes.

In the early 1980s, Cleveland chef Parker Bosley began taking classes from Spray. He recalls the era as a heady time in culinary circles. The region was just beginning to wake up to food and all of its possibilities and Spray was leading the way. "She was pre-Williams-Sonoma. Zona's was where you could find a great knife or a copper pot," he said.

Bosley met French chef Michel Pasquet at Spray's school in 1983, and arranged an apprenticeship with him at his Paris restaurant; he also studied at LaVarenne. In the early 1980s, he regularly taught classes for Spray, before opening his namesake Cleveland restaurant, Parker's New American Bistro, in 1986. Bosley became Cleveland's first and most vocal proponent of the sustainable foods movement, a role he continues today. A farm boy from rural northern Trumbull County, Ohio, Bosley was ahead of his time in his quest for sourcing local produce and meats for his restaurant, which closed upon his retirement in 2006. Bosley's voice may never have emerged if not for Spray and the opportunities he had at her school.

Over the years, Spray's school grew, as did her business acumen. Bosley recalls that Spray always had an eye on the bottom line. Her interest in succeeding financially was an asset to her professionally, because she was always willing to take a chance on something new. "She was receptive to many kinds of food and teaching and to all kinds of people. She always got the cookbook authors and those people who were the hot names to come to do a class," he said.

Filling the seats in a class and keeping the business viable was always a concern for Spray, who, after divorcing in 1986, supported herself with the school. She had purchased the building in 1979 and at one time, was operating the school, The Cookery, a deli and carry-out, a sit-down restaurant and a catering business, all out of the first floor.

Spray routinely hosted the visiting chefs at her home, and while some saw the move as a way for her to save on hotel bills, most of the chefs fondly recalled the experience. Returning to Spray's home after their evening classes, Spray would uncork wine and cook a late supper for her guest. Cookbook author Giuliano Hazan said Spray's school was always one of his favorite places to teach, in part because of his late-night dinners and conversations with Spray. She also made an effort to be a good ambassador for the Cleveland area, often taking visiting chefs to see the current exhibit at the Cleveland Museum of Art or the Rock and Roll Hall of Fame. New York-based pastry chef Nick Malgieri, a frequent teacher at the school, felt Spray's hospitality made the experience enjoyable. "Zona considered the people who came to the school her friends, and that's why people would come back," he said.

Spray was also notorious for watching the budget. Nancy Neal, who has worked at the school in various capacities since 1992, when Spray hired her as a dishwasher, said Spray's frugality was legendary. "You didn't waste a thing," Neal said. Bones went into the stock pot and dried bread became breadcrumbs. But Neal said what she learned from Spray about being organized and not wasting food stayed with her and helped her to feed her family of four children on a lot less than what her friends were spending. Like many of the people who worked for Spray, there was an intimidation factor, at least at first. "Most people were quite in awe of her, but I guess I was a little afraid of her," Neal said.

Catherine St. John, who trained at the Tante Marie Cooking School in San Francisco, recalls the time in 1994 she approached Spray about the possibility of teaching at her school. A mother with a young daughter, St. John had relocated to Ohio, her husband's home state, a few years earlier and knew of Spray's reputation. St. John said Spray had a larger-than-life presence, not only because of her immense cooking knowledge, but because of how she conveyed it and how she conducted herself. Plenty of people were intimidated by Spray, but everyone respected her, she said. St. John felt her training in classical French techniques gave her a foundation similar to Spray's and the two got along well. Spray remembers St. John as one of the hardest workers she ever hired, one who came with excellent references.

During the 1990s, Carole Ferguson, an Akron native, worked for AT&T in nearby Boston Township. One of the closest places for lunch was downtown Hudson and Ferguson remembers that more often than not, she would end up eating at Zona Spray's. Ferguson felt drawn to the school and the cooking environment. Her dream was to win the lottery so that she could make Spray an offer she couldn't refuse. Ferguson never won the lottery, but an opportunity for early retirement did come her way. In 1996, AT&T offered workers a chance to retire early. Ferguson fit the requirements and left the company. She began making lists of what she wanted to do in retirement and "go to cooking school" was at the top, so Ferguson enrolled at Zona Spray. She finished the three levels of professional courses and at her class graduation dinner, she and Spray discussed her future plans. Ferguson recalls how Spray said to her, "Perhaps you'd like to buy my cooking school," and from that point on, it became Ferguson's goal. "I had been in love with the place forever," Ferguson said.

Ferguson hired an accountant and a lawyer, obtained a small business loan, invested most of her retirement savings and on April 12, 1997, Ferguson became the school's new owner. The move was a surprise to some, but Spray had been teaching for twenty-six years at that point and longed for more free time to travel.

"I had taken it as far as I could. I didn't want to franchise and I didn't want to keep doing the same thing," Spray said. Spray stayed around for a period of transition, but after her 1998 remarriage to Grant Starks, the pair eventually retired to Florida.

The school's identity had been so wrapped up in Spray that it was hard for some to imagine the school without her. Ferguson set out to blaze her own trail with the school, which began with the very bold move of changing the name to the Western Reserve School of Cooking. Ferguson said she felt the school needed a new identity, with Spray no longer involved, and felt using Western Reserve in the name truly reflected Hudson's role as one of the earliest cities in the Connecticut Western Reserve. Moreover, she was tired of customers coming into the shop and asking her "What's a Zona Spray?" Ferguson established a website for the school and got involved with the International Association of Culinary Professionals (IACP), an organization that encompasses chefs, cooking school owners and food writers. Through the IACP network, she made contact with up-and-coming young chefs and found they were still willing to come to Hudson, even without Spray's presence. In the Ferguson years, Pam Anderson, John Ash and Colette Peters all came to the school for the first time. By 2002, Ferguson had even begun teaching classes. Unfortunately, while she had a passion for the school, Ferguson did not possess the business acumen that had kept Spray going for so long. In 2004, when she was on the verge of losing the school, her accountant, Ed Schiciano of Twinsburg, who had helped to broker her purchase from Spray, stepped in and bought the store.

Despite losing most of her retirement savings, Ferguson is not bitter about what she lost or what she put into the business. "I never regretted it. I loved every day of it. The cooking school is really the jewel of Main Street," she says, "I've had a really good life and the best part was the cooking school. Going to cooking school was a dream come true, much less owning the school. It was the best seven years of my life."

For his part, Schiciano admits he stepped in for sentimental reasons. He had worked for Ferguson, and Spray before her, and didn't want to see the school close. An avid cook, he was aware of the school's history and felt it could be saved with time and care. He put Nancy Neal in charge of running the day-to-day operations and while he wasn't making money, the school was breaking even and surviving. Schiciano describes himself as a "caretaker owner." He watched the books, paid down the debt and basically stayed out of the way, hoping that one day someone would step forward to purchase it.

By 2007, Schiciano had grown weary of his role of caretaker. He was on the verge of closing the school when one day in the spring, St. John and her husband, Carl, stopped by his office. St. John remembers his first words to her were, "What took you so long?" Purchasing the school was something that St. John had been considering for ten years, from the time Spray originally sold it, but the timing hadn't seemed right. Like Schiciano, St. John didn't want to see the school close and felt she could find a way to make it profitable again. St. John has a dual approach; she shares Ferguson's enthusiasm for attracting big-name chefs to teach, but also embodies Spray's practicality. She's not afraid to make changes and cut costs when needed to keep the school on strong financial footing.

Like Spray, St. John is in the classroom every week, teaching fundamental cooking techniques. But unlike Spray, her students have expanded far beyond the Hudson housewife set. St. John's classes have a wide mix of men and women, from middle-aged laid-off workers looking for a fresh start, to young students who have found her professional certificate program a less expensive way into the job market than one of the larger, out-of-state cooking schools.

The course offerings have changed, too, to reflect the times. Most classes are now participation classes, not lectures, and the course book is filled with classes more relevant to this generation—barbecuing, pressure cooking and even couples classes. As a way of developing a new revenue stream, St. John has developed programs for corporate team-building exercises and cooking retreats. It's rare that a French chef comes to town these days. It's not that St. John would dismiss the idea, but she knows that American cuisine has come into its own over the past twenty years and it is reflected in her clientele's course selections. John Ash, Hugh Carpenter and other leaders of the California cuisine movement will fill her classroom, along with younger members of America's culinary guard—chefs like Molly Stevens and Wendy Kromer, who are leading the way into America's food future. Spray sees the sale to St. John as an excellent move and said while she could have never predicted in 1994 that St. John would one day be the school's owner, she is not surprised by it either. "She has very much blossomed there," Spray said.

Even with the perspective of forty years, Spray doesn't necessarily share the sense of awe that others have when gazing upon the images of the chefs who hang over the kitchen. The famous ones who chopped, braised, baked, sautéed and gave thousands of lessons on food, they are colleagues and friends to her. She never set out to create anything grand. The chefs she played host to were there, in part, to satisfy her own selfish desire to learn more, as much as they were for her students and her business. "I was just doing what I had a passion for," Spray said. "I was drawn to the cooking. I love food. I love to eat."

Zona Spray

Zona Spray has spent most of her lifetime teaching other people how to cook. When asked which recipes, of the thousands in her collection, she wanted to share, she offered a small collection of classic, unpretentious foods—a simple soup, roasted chicken, mashed potatoes and parsnips. Yet contained within each recipe are the skills that Spray has worked so tirelessly to teach her students over the years: chopping, roasting, braising and building layers of flavors, using the freshest ingredients and right equipment for the job. These recipes are her lessons.

Soup Bonne Femme (Soup of the Good Woman)

As the story goes, this soup was made on laundry day, when women hauled water to the laundry tubs, heated it, scrubbed the clothes, hauled more water, rinsed the clothes and hung them out to dry. Exhausted, but with dinner yet to prepare, women could quickly make this soup and serve it with an excellent crusty country bread for a satisfying supper.

1 teaspoon butter or oil	milk, cream or sour cream, as desired
1 small onion, sliced	salt and pepper, to taste
1 clove garlic, bruised (optional)	nutmeg, to taste
1 medium potato, sliced	cayenne, to taste
water or light chicken stock (enough to barely cover potatoes)	chives or other fresh herb for garnish

In a saucepan, add butter, onion and garlic and cook gently, until translucent, but not colored. Add potato, season, barely cover with water or stock and cook until tender.

Purée soup finely for a smooth-textured first course or leave small chunks in soup for a more rustic texture. Add stock or milk and thin to soup consistency. Season to taste with salt, pepper, nutmeg and cayenne.

Garnish with a fresh herb and a little sour cream, if desired. Serve with crusty bread.

Makes 2 servings.

Tilapia with Tomatoes and Basil

Only one skillet is needed in this braised dish and like all fish, you can have dinner on the table within minutes. If basil isn't available, use fresh parsley.

1 tablespoon olive oil	1 tablespoon chopped chives
⅓ cup diced onion	2 sorrel leaves, diced
2 garlic cloves, minced	salt and pepper, to taste
⅛ teaspoon red pepper flakes	1¼ pounds Tilapia fillets (3 fillets)
⅛ teaspoon salt	5 to 10 torn basil leaves
1 (whole) 3-inch diameter tomato or 2 plum tomatoes, diced with seeds	grated zest of 1 lime
	juice of half a lime
15 basil leaves, torn into ½-inch pieces	

In a 10 or 12-inch skillet (large enough to hold all 3 fillets), add olive oil. In separate areas of the oil, add onion, garlic, pepper flakes and salt. Heat on medium-low until garlic begins to turn golden.

Distribute diced tomato, basil, chives and sorrel over pan contents and season with salt and pepper. Lay fillets on top in a single layer.

Sprinkle salt and freshly ground pepper over fish. Toss 5 to 10 torn basil leaves over fish. Cover, braise gently on medium-low heat, simmering until fish is white and tender when pierced with a metal skewer.

Uncover; grate lime zest over fish. Squeeze fresh lime juice over all. Adjust salt and pepper if needed.

Serve over rice, with a green vegetable. (Broccoli and chard are good because of the textural contrast.)

Makes 3 servings.

Note: Sorrel is a lemony-flavored herb. Leaves are 3 to 5 inches long. It grows like a weed in the garden and is wonderful in many dishes. If you don't have it, add some lemon zest or a squeeze of lemon just before serving the dish. Though this dish has lime in it, the combination of lemon and lime is excellent.

Slow Roast Chicken and Vegetables

For years I've preached the merits of breaking down proteins with low heat. But until I had to be out of the house for two hours, with friends waiting for dinner upon my return, I hadn't tested the theory with a whole chicken. It was delicious and juicy; try it.

1 whole fryer chicken, liver reserved

handful of fresh thyme (about 16 sprigs)

salt

3 medium-size potatoes
(such as Yukon Gold),
washed and quartered lengthwise

1 large onion, cut lengthwise into 10
pieces

3 large carrots, cut into 2 by ½-inch
strips

8 large garlic cloves, unpeeled

3 tablespoons olive oil

salt and pepper

Preheat oven to 400 degrees.

Remove giblets and vent fat from chicken. Sprinkle salt inside cavity. Put liver and fresh thyme inside. Tie a string around legs and tail. Place, breast up, in a 9 by 13-inch heavy au gratin pan.

Arrange vegetables around chicken, or mound in one end of pan. Drizzle all with olive oil. Toss vegetables in oil. Smear oil over chicken (use your hands; it's efficient) and rub ¼ teaspoon salt over skin. Sprinkle vegetables with salt and pepper Pop pan with chicken and vegetables into oven and immediately turn heat to 250 degrees and leave alone for two hours.

After two hours, chicken should be done; thigh meat will feel soft to the touch. If vegetables are not quite tender, or you want chicken to be beautifully browned, raise heat to 400 degrees. Toss vegetables in juices; spoon some juices over chicken. Return to oven for about 10 minutes, until chicken is browned and vegetables are tender.

Remove chicken from oven; rest five minutes so juices distribute throughout the meat. Warm plates in oven while you're carving the bird and pouring dinner wine. Cut chicken into four pieces: breasts with wing attached and drumsticks with thigh attached. Arrange chicken and vegetables on plates. Sprinkle with salt and freshly ground pepper. Degrease juices and spoon over meat.

Makes 4 servings.

Note: Free-range chickens are preferred. If you don't have one large heavy pan, then use two smaller ones. Parsnips are excellent roasted with this mélange of winter vegetables; or substitute parsnips for the potatoes.

Parsnip and Potato Purée with Truffle Oil

Many people have been deprived of enjoying parsnips, a sweet root vegetable that blends beautifully with other root vegetables. Mashing parsnips with potatoes enhances the flavor of both vegetables.

3 medium potatoes (a starchy variety), peeled and chunked

2 parsnips, peeled and chunked

water to cover

½ cup hot whipping cream (optional)

4 tablespoons butter, or to taste

salt, pepper, nutmeg, to taste

1 tablespoon truffle oil

2 tablespoons minced chives

Put potatoes, parsnips and enough water to barely cover in saucepan. Boil; simmer until tender when pierced with a skewer.

Drain potatoes; reserve cooking water. Return saucepan to heat and shake pan until potatoes look dry and a little powdery.

Mash potatoes and parsnips while adding hot cream; use some of the hot cooking water to thin out as desired. Enrich with butter.

Add salt, pepper and freshly ground nutmeg to taste. (You should not taste nutmeg, but know if it is missing.) Add truffle oil and chives.

Mashed potatoes are best served immediately, but if you must make them ahead, set aside at room temperature with lid slightly askew. Reheat when needed.

Makes 6 servings.

Note: Add or subtract cream and butter to your taste. For the lightest purée, the liquid should be hot and butter should be room temperature. Use saved drained hot potato water in lieu of cream, if desired.

The Recipes

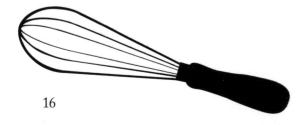

Chapter 2

Teachers of the Year, International Association of Culinary Professionals

....
John Ash
....

"Food is this extraordinary gift … to connect with our world every day."

J ohn Ash has been called the "father of wine country cuisine," but perhaps more appropriately, he should be called its Godfather. When Ash speaks about food, it is with a thoughtful, almost religious appreciation. His ethical convictions on food, how it is tended, how it is prepared and how it is shared are so deep that he uses Christian terms to describe it.

"Food is the sacrament, the communion, if you will, with the world around us, through the people around us," Ash says. Our literal breaking of bread, to him, is the profound expression of our humanity.

Ash learned to be a good steward of the earth at an early age. He was reared on his grandparents' ranch in Colorado, where the family was essentially self-sufficient, raising their own meat and vegetables, canning and preserving. About the only thing Ash recalls his grandmother purchasing from a store was coffee, and even then, she left nothing to waste. The top and bottom of the coffee can were turned into garden reflectors to keep the birds away, while the can itself was flattened and often used to replace a roofing shingle on one of the out buildings. Years later, Ash realized how his upbringing was a gift, because it taught him the importance of taking care of the earth that provides for him, the message at the very core of the organic and sustainable food movement of which he is an integral part. "We needed to take care of what was around us," he recalled.

Ash left Colorado for college, studying fine arts and later landing a job in San Francisco working in marketing for Del Monte. America in the late 1960s was all about big, mass-produced food. Ash recalls that one of his achievements at Del Monte was suggesting the company add basil to its line of stewed tomatoes, a move considered gourmet at the time. He also had a role in the company's early version of pudding cups, which became a national lunchbox staple. The pudding was actually a way to use B grade milk, which was deemed fine for cooking, but not for bottling. Del Monte was able to get the milk for free, so finding a use for it was a very profitable solution.

Six years into his career in big food, Ash decided it was time to see the world and left to spend time in Europe. In France and England, Ash was absorbed by the food culture and attended some cooking schools, including LaVarenne in Burgundy. Heading back to San Francisco in the mid-1970s, he began working in catering while doing freelance art illustration on the side. He also began to take a serious look at his region. California's Napa Valley had all the attributes of the French wine country, yet what was considered the best restaurant at the time was still serving canned vegetables as a side dish. Ash saw the opportunity for something new and in 1980, opened John Ash & Company in Santa Rosa. It was the first restaurant in California wine country that focused on serving fresh, locally-grown, seasonal food; dishes created to compliment the region's wines. He also found a host of farmer-partners in the region who could supply what he needed for his restaurant.

Books, television shows, a radio show and work as a cooking teacher have filled the more than thirty years since Ash opened his namesake eatery. His first book, *From the Earth to the Table: John Ash's Wine Country Cuisine* is in its second printing, and his latest work, *John Ash Cooking One-on-One: Private Lessons in Simple Contemporary Food from a Master Teacher*, won a 2005 James Beard award.

Over the years, Ash has become a prominent voice in the sustainable food movement. He is on the board of the Chef's Collaborative, a national network of chefs who promote local and sustainable foods, and he is a member of the Board of Advisors of Seafood Watch, an initiative of the Monterey Bay Aquarium, which seeks to educate the public on how to select ocean-friendly seafood.

Ash first arrived at the Western Reserve School of Cooking in 1998, on an invitation from then-owner Carole Ferguson. When he teaches, wine and sustainable seafood often are on his menu. While he seeks to educate his students on how wine should always be an integral part of the meal, he is careful to make sure that students realize that the wine is part of the fun and enhances the meal. "If you've got good food and good wine, how bad can it be? You can get a nice bottle of wine for $6.99."

In 2008, the International Association of Culinary Professionals named Ash its Cooking Teacher of the Year. Ash said he tries to impart to his students the importance of being mindful and thoughtful about the food that they eat. "Food is this extraordinary gift that God has given us to connect with our world every day," he said.

Grilled Spiced Spring Lamb Chops with Butter Braised Spinach

In America we are finally beginning to use and appreciate the world of spices. This simple recipe puts together both savory and sweet spices to flavor the lamb. It's equally delicious on chicken or rich fish like tuna.

For the spice mixture

1 (3-inch) cinnamon stick

1 tablespoon whole coriander seeds

1 tablespoon cumin seeds

2 whole allspice

2 tablespoons sweet paprika

½ teaspoon cayenne (or to taste)

2 teaspoons kosher salt

2 teaspoons brown sugar

⅓ cup olive oil

2 tablespoons finely chopped garlic

2 trimmed 8-bone lamb racks, frenched and cut into 2-bone chops (about 2½ pounds total)

1 cup finely chopped parsley

3 tablespoons finely chopped mint

sea or kosher salt

Butter Braised Spinach (recipe follows)

Break cinnamon stick into small pieces and add to a coffee or spice grinder with the rest of the dry spices and grind until very fine. In a separate bowl, mix together oil and garlic and stir in spice mixture. Coat lamb well with mixture and then with parsley and mint. Cover and marinate for at least 2 and up to 8 hours in refrigerator.

Grill lamb over moderately hot coals until rare to medium rare. Let stand for 3 minutes or so and prepare spinach. To serve: cut each double chop into single chops. Place spinach on warm plates, top with chops and serve immediately.

Makes 4 servings.

Butter Braised Spinach

3 tablespoons butter

1 tablespoon olive oil

10 cups baby spinach (gently packed)

fresh lemon juice

salt and freshly ground pepper

In a large sauté pan heat butter and olive oil over moderately high heat. Add spinach and toss quickly to wilt, about 1 minute. Be careful not to overcook or spinach will weep. Season to taste with drops of lemon juice, salt and pepper. Serve immediately.

Achiote Roasted Sea Bass and Fresh Citrus Salsa

Annatto seeds, which are the basis for achiote, are used extensively in Mexico, especially in the Yucatan. They contribute not only a bright orange-red color, but also a subtle flavor. You can buy prepared achiote pastes in markets that are perfectly fine to use. A quick recipe is to add ⅓ cup fresh lime juice to a 3½-ounce package. El Yucateco brand is my choice and is widely available in Mexican markets. A recipe to make your own follows, which will yield far superior results.

6 (6 ounce) portions of fresh sea bass or halibut fillets

Achiote paste (recipe follows)

3 tablespoons olive oil

2 cups mixed young savory salad greens, such as arugula, watercress, mizuna or spinach

Citrus salsa (recipe follows)

cilantro sprigs and avocado slices, if desired, for garnish

Preheat oven to 425 degrees. Smear achiote paste on both sides of sea bass and marinate for at least 30 minutes.

Heat oil in a large heavy skillet and cook fish in a single layer for a minute or two, to color nicely. Turn and finish cooking in the oven for another 3 or 4 minutes, depending on thickness. Be careful not to overcook.

Toss greens with salsa and arrange attractively on plates. Place fish on top. Garnish with avocado and cilantro; serve immediately.

Makes 6 servings.

Achiote Paste

2 tablespoons finely ground annatto seeds (sometimes labeled as achiote)

1 tablespoon olive oil

1 tablespoon pure chile powder such as ancho

2 tablespoons chopped fresh garlic

1 teaspoon whole allspice (about 5), toasted and ground

½ teaspoon ground cinnamon

2 teaspoons honey (or to taste)

2 teaspoons oregano, preferably Mexican

1 teaspoon salt

⅓ cup or so fresh orange or tangerine juice (enough to make a smooth paste)

Place all ingredients in a blender and blend until very smooth. Add orange juice a bit at a time to facilitate the making of the paste. Makes approximately ½ cup.

Citrus Salsa

4 large navel oranges, peeled and sectioned

½ cup peeled, seeded and diced fresh cucumber

¼ cup diced sweet red onion

⅓ cup diced jicama (optional)

1 to 2 teaspoons finely chopped serrano chile

1 tablespoon minced crystallized ginger

2 tablespoons fresh lime juice

1 tablespoon brown sugar or to taste

3 tablespoons finely chopped cilantro and/or mint

Cut orange sections in half crosswise and gently stir in rest of ingredients. Allow to sit for at least one hour for flavors to develop. Correct seasoning to your taste.

Curried Wild Mushroom and Tomato Chowder with Parsley Pesto

Remember that curry powders vary in strength and flavor profile. Choose the one you like and taste carefully to decide if you want more.

1 pound fresh wild or flavorful cultivated mushrooms, such as shiitake or oyster

5 tablespoons olive oil

1 ounce dried porcini or forest blend mushrooms, soaked in warm water until soft

1 large white onion, finely diced

1 tablespoon finely chopped garlic

1 tablespoon finely minced, peeled ginger

1 tablespoon (or more) good curry powder, or to taste

1 can (28 ounces) diced tomatoes in juice (Muir Glen fire roasted preferred)

4 cups rich chicken or vegetable stock

1 cup dry white wine

1 teaspoon whole fennel seed

salt and freshly ground pepper, to taste

Parsley Pesto (recipe follows)

Clean fresh mushrooms (discard stems from shiitake if using) and slice thickly. Heat 3 tablespoons oil in a heavy bottomed soup pot and sauté mushrooms over moderately high heat until lightly colored, but still holding their shape. Remove mushrooms and set aside.

Drain dried mushrooms, reserving soaking water and chop. Add remaining oil to pot along with dried mushrooms, onion, garlic, ginger, curry powder and cook over moderately high heat until just beginning to color. Add tomatoes, stock, wine, fennel seed and reserved mushroom soaking liquid (strained if gritty) and simmer for 10 minutes. Season to your taste with salt and pepper. Add cooked fresh mushrooms and serve in warm soup bowls swirled with a dollop of pesto.

Makes 6 to 8 servings.

Parsley Pesto

1 quart gently packed parsley leaves, woody stems discarded

1 tablespoon chopped poached or roasted garlic

1 to 2 tablespoons lightly toasted pine nuts or blanched almonds

2 teaspoons finely grated lemon zest

⅓ cup freshly grated Parmesan, pecorino or Asiago cheese

⅓ cup or so olive oil

salt and freshly ground pepper

Plunge parsley leaves into a pan of lightly salted boiling water for five seconds. Immediately drain and plunge into a bowl of ice water to stop cooking and set bright green color. Drain and squeeze out as much water as possible.

Add parsley to a blender along with garlic, nuts, zest and cheese. Purée, adding oil slowly to facilitate. Correct seasoning with salt and pepper.

Store, covered, in refrigerator for up to 5 days or freeze for up to 3 months.

Pesto can be added to a vegetable or chicken stock to make a delicious sauce or soup base.

Makes about 1 cup.

Hugh Carpenter

"Look upon cooking as an act of democracy."

He has taught more than 100,000 students in his lifetime, written fifteen cookbooks and is one of the most celebrated American cooking teachers of our time. But what makes Hugh Carpenter so amazing is that he did it all without ever having taken a single cooking lesson.

Carpenter is blessed with an innate sense of flavor, which became evident the minute he started cooking for others in the 1970s. "I have a natural affinity for flavors. Who knows where it came from? It was never any problem for me. I had no one to show me. I just started cooking and I enjoyed it," he recalls.

A California native, Carpenter went East for college, where he majored in Far Eastern Studies and Chinese language. He began cooking at a Chinese professor's house, along with three classmates. They cooked only Chinese food, dining together most nights during Carpenter's junior and senior years at Dartmouth College. The experience with Asian foods and flavors would follow him throughout his career. Even when his cooking branched out into other areas—Mexican and barbecue—his commitment to flavor only deepened.

Carpenter believes most of us suffer from flavor-deprived diets without knowing it. When he cooks, whether at home or in the classroom, he tries to create dishes that are bursting with flavor—garlic, chiles and Asian sauces—and he is always looking at other cuisines to add impact to his dishes.

Carpenter had been cooking for his family for years and the Asian submersion in college had only helped his natural culinary ability. In 1972, after dropping out of graduate school he returned home to Santa Barbara and opened a small catering business. It was a chance career, at a time before food was glamorized on television. Carpenter's business grew and he began to teach cooking. After a few years, he was in such demand that he abandoned catering to teach cooking full-time.

In the 1980s, Carpenter started traveling to cooking schools across the country, awakening the American palate to the flavors of the Far East. His first book, *Pacific Flavors*, and the fourteen that have followed, have been in collaboration with his photographer wife, Teri Sanderson. It was a tour for *Pacific Flavors* in 1988 that brought him to the Zona Spray Cooking School for the first time. He has been a frequent guest, teaching at the school more than ten times.

When he teaches, Carpenter tries to achieve three things—to produce food that tastes so good that it gets the students excited, to communicate new information so that students learn something and don't just review what they already know, and to entertain the class and be enthusiastic about the subject matter. "If you combine those three elements, then the classes are going to be successful," he said.

In 1990, Carpenter and Sanderson moved from southern California to the Napa Valley in search of a more rural life and a better quality of life. The next year, they hosted their first Camp Napa Culinary, a six-day cooking school that featured lessons from Carpenter mixed in with vineyard, winery and kitchen tours in the region. The classes were a hit and Carpenter now hosts the camp every year. He also offers similar sessions at a camp in San Miguel, Mexico.

In 2010, the International Association of Culinary Professionals named Carpenter its Teacher of the Year. "Teaching is really my passion," he says. When he teaches, the lesson he most wants to convey to his students is that cooking is an experience that is meant to be shared. "I think that you should look upon cooking as an act of democracy and part of that democratic act is sharing the food with family or friends gathered around the table, but more importantly it is to get people involved in one way or another."

Whether it's a student at his camp or a guest at his own table, Carpenter gives everyone a job to do—setting the table, folding napkins, watching the grill—something to get them involved in the meal. "We want to have our dinners be more of *we* events than *I* events. *I* events are boring and dull and not very exciting. *We* events are much more fun. The more one can get people to participate in and interact with and have more contact with the food, the eating experience is even that much more pleasurable," he says.

BBQ Shrimp Packed with Serrano-Herb Butter

2 pounds large to jumbo raw shrimp,
  shells on

½ pound salted butter, at room
  temperature

4 cloves garlic, peeled

3 Serrano chiles

½ cup (packed) cilantro sprigs,
  including stems

grated skin of 2 limes

2 limes cut into wedges

Using scissors, cut along top ridge of shrimp shells. Devein without dislodging shells.

Cut butter into small pieces. Using a food processor, mince garlic. Stem chiles. Cut chiles into small pieces. With garlic still in food processor and machine on, drop chiles into food processor. When minced, add cilantro and mince again.

Add grated lime to food processor. Add butter to food processor and run machine until butter-herb-chile becomes a smooth mix.

Cut 2 limes into wedges and set aside. Place herb butter underneath shrimp shells. I do this by putting a little herb butter on my index finger and smearing butter under the shell. The butter does not have to be under the entire shell—just a little bit on each side of the shrimp.

May be completed to this point up to 12 hours before barbecuing, with shrimp refrigerated.

Last Minute Cooking: Heat a barbecue to medium-hot. Add shrimp. Turn shrimp over several times. (Keep those shrimp moving!) Cook until shells blacken and shrimp are cooked through (to test for doneness, cut into shrimp). Serve with lime wedges. Each person shells the shrimp.

Option: Shell shrimp. Melt herb butter in a saucepan. Just before barbecuing shrimp, toss raw shrimp with melted butter. Barbecue shrimp, brushing on more melted butter during cooking.

Serves 8 as an appetizer.

Chiles Rellenos Stuffed with Corn, Pine Nuts and Cilantro

6 fresh Anaheim chiles
 or fresh poblano chiles

¼ cup pine nuts, toasted
 in a 325-degree oven

2 cloves garlic, minced

2 whole green onions, chopped

¼ cup chopped cilantro

2 ears corn, kernels cut off

½ cup currents or dark raisins

6 ounces soft goat cheese
 (or mozzarella or queso fresco)

½ teaspoon salt

½ teaspoon hot sauce

3 eggs, well beaten

½ cup unbleached white flour

2 cups flavorless cooking oil

salsa

Place chiles directly over a stovetop flame turned to high. Blacken chiles only partly so there are small amounts of green color still visible (or blacken on a cast-iron skillet). Transfer to a paper or plastic bag, close bag and let rest 5 minutes. Using a paper towel, rub off black skin. Make a slit lengthwise along the chile and carefully remove seeds.

In a bowl, combine pine nuts, garlic, green onion, cilantro, corn kernels, currants, goat cheese, salt and hot sauce. Using your fingers, mix until evenly blended. Stuff goat cheese mixture into chiles.

Dip chiles in beaten egg, gently roll in flour and transfer to a wire rack. Place a 14-inch frying pan over high heat. Add cooking oil. When oil becomes hot enough that the end of a wooden spoon dipped in oil begins to bubble around the tip, add half the chiles. Fry until golden on both sides and transfer to a wire rack. Repeat with remaining chiles.

Place salsa on a plate. Place chile on top of salsa. Serve.

Makes 4 servings.

Note: You can omit the battering and frying of the chiles, and instead roast them in a 350-degree oven for 15 minutes. You can also add ½ pound shredded cooked pork or chicken to the cheese filling.

Grilled Chicken Satay
with Peanut Glaze

For the chicken:

6 chicken thighs, boned and skinned

24 (6-inch) bamboo skewers

¼ cup thin soy sauce

¼ cup lime juice or lemon juice

2 tablespoons flavorless cooking oil, such as canola

For the peanut glaze:

½ cup peanut butter

¼ cup orange juice

1 tablespoon dark soy sauce (mushroom soy sauce)

2 tablespoons vinegar

2 tablespoons honey

2 tablespoons flavorless cooking oil

1 tablespoon dark sesame oil

2 teaspoons Asian chili sauce

4 cloves garlic, minced

2 tablespoons minced ginger

¼ cup minced green onion

Cut each chicken thigh into 4 strips. Push a skewer down each piece lengthwise, with tip barely showing. Combine soy, lime juice and oil. Rub on chicken. Stand chicken upright in a 4-cup, glass measuring cup and refrigerate.

Combine Peanut Glaze, stir well and set aside at room temperature.

Heat a barbecue to medium hot. Brush grill with oil. Lay a double layer of aluminum foil on grill. Add chicken skewers so that foil is under the exposed part of bamboo skewers. Grill about 2 minutes on each side until cooked through. Spoon a little peanut sauce along the length of each piece of chicken. Serve hot.

Serves 8 as an appetizer.

Giuliano Hazan

"Cooking is not a difficult, daunting task."

I f anyone was predestined to have a career in food, it seems it would be Giuliano Hazan. The only son of Italian cooking legend Marcella Hazan, he was raised by food royalty—the woman who taught a country saturated in red sauce and meatballs what Italian cooking is really about.

But Hazan had other ideas. He wanted to be an actor and director, and after graduating from Swarthmore College, spent two years studying with the Trinity Rep Conservatory in Providence, Rhode Island. Eventually, his lineage won out. He's now a top cooking teacher in his own right, with his own cooking school. In 2007, the International Association of Culinary Professionals named him its Cooking Teacher of the Year.

Hazan first taught at the Zona Spray Cooking School in 1993, shortly after his first book, *The Classic Pasta Cookbook*, was released. It went on to sell more than half a million copies worldwide. Hazan wanted to teach and used the IACP directory to contact cooking schools that might be interested in him as a traveling teacher. Spray was only too happy to set up a pasta class. He's been back to the school numerous times since and he continues to put it on his schedule, particularly because he has a keen appreciation for how cooking schools of its kind are a dying breed in the U.S.

When he teaches, Hazan said he tries to making cooking less intimidating. "It's something people can do on a regular basis, not just for special occasions. It's not a difficult, daunting task. You don't have to spend hours in the kitchen. It can be very simple and not take that long to make. Cooking for your family is one of the most loving things you can do. Hopefully I help people become more able to cook at home," he said.

Cooking at home was something so engrained in Hazan's upbringing that he almost took it for granted. "Food had always been important. It was always a part of my life."

He would sit in the kitchen and watch his mother cook and he believes he learned much of what he knows just from watching her. "I suppose I have been her longest running student. I had all the private lessons and I learned through osmosis. I liked to sit in the kitchen and watch."

Hazan was born in New York, lived in Italy for several years as a child and later spent summers there. When his mother opened her famed cooking school in Bologna, he was involved from the beginning, helping out with classes. In its last few years, he began teaching some of the basic curriculum and his mother's recipes.

He continued to teach cooking throughout his theater training and afterwards ran a small catering business of his own. He later gained restaurant experience in Atlanta and in Oregon, before he started writing, but has found teaching to be the most fulfilling. "Teaching was really what I felt the most passion for and I focused on that," he said. In 2000, Hazan and his wife Lael opened their own cooking school in Verona, Italy, where they go every year to teach.

"I always like to say I really didn't leave the theater. Cooking is kind of a performance and it is an art form. It might have been fun to become a movie star, but I don't think that would be very likely. I'm glad I did what I did," Hazan said.

Penne All'Arrabbiata

1 pound penne pasta

⅓ cup plus 1 tablespoon extra-virgin olive oil

½ teaspoon finely chopped garlic

2 ounces pancetta cut from a ¼-inch thick slice of pancetta, cut into thin strips

3 cups canned whole peeled tomatoes with their juice, coarsely chopped

¼ teaspoon crushed red pepper flakes

12 medium-sized fresh basil leaves

2 tablespoons freshly grated Pecorino Romano cheese

salt

Put ⅓ cup olive oil and chopped garlic in a large sauté pan over medium-high heat and cook until it begins to sizzle. Add pancetta strips and cook until browned but not crisp.

Add canned tomatoes, red pepper flakes and some salt (go easy on salt because pancetta is already rather salty). Lower heat and let simmer until tomatoes have reduced and separated from oil, approximately 35 minutes. Remove from heat and set aside.

Bring 4 quarts water to a boil, add about 1 tablespoon salt and penne and stir well.

Just before pasta is cooked, return sauce to a medium heat and add basil torn by hand into ½-inch pieces. When penne is cooked al dente, toss with sauce adding 1 tablespoon olive oil and grated Romano cheese. Taste for salt and spiciness and serve at once.

Makes 4 servings.

(Adapted from *The Classic Pasta Cookbook* by Giuliano Hazan.)

Pan-Roasted Pork Loin
with Fresh Leeks

3 or 4 medium leeks

2 tablespoons butter

salt

freshly ground black pepper

1 tablespoon vegetable oil

2 pounds boneless pork loin

½ cup dry white wine

Cut off root end of leeks and trim tough dark green tops of leaves. Cut leeks in half lengthwise (or in quarters if they are more than 1-inch thick) and then slice them crosswise into ½-inch chunks. Place leeks in a large bowl full of cold water, swishing them around to loosen any dirt that is clinging to them.

Lift leeks out of water and put them in a braising pan large enough to hold the pork. Add 1 tablespoon butter and ½ cup water, and season lightly with salt and pepper. Cover pan and place over medium heat and cook for about 10 minutes or until leeks have wilted. Pour leeks and any remaining liquid into a bowl and set aside.

Raise heat under pan to high and put in remaining tablespoon of butter and vegetable oil. When oil and butter are hot and butter is just beginning to turn color, put in pork. Brown meat well on all sides and season with salt and pepper.

Add wine and let bubble for about 30 seconds to allow alcohol to evaporate. Put leeks with their liquid back into pan, turn heat down to low and cover, leaving lid slightly ajar. Cook until meat is very tender when pierced with a fork, turning meat about every 20 minutes, for 1½ to 2 hours. If all of the liquid in pan has evaporated before roast is tender, add a little water.

When pork is done, uncover pan and transfer meat to a cutting board. If there is any excess liquid in pan, raise heat and cook until sauce has reduced. If there is no liquid at all left in pan, add a little water, raise heat and scrape cooking residues from bottom of pan with a wooden spoon to make a sauce.

Transfer pork to a cutting board and cut into thin slices. Put slices back in pan to coat them with sauce. Arrange slices on a platter and pour sauce over them. Serve hot.

Serves 4 as a main course or 6 as part of a multi-course Italian meal.

(Adapted from *How to Cook Italian* by Giuliano Hazan.)

Fusilli with Belgian Endive, Leeks and Roasted Peppers

1 pound long fusilli

1 red pepper

⅓ cup extra-virgin olive oil

1 teaspoon garlic, finely chopped

3 medium leeks, thoroughly washed in cold water

1 cup Belgian endive, finely shredded lengthwise

salt and freshly ground black pepper

Cut leeks in half lengthwise, then across, into pieces ¼-inch wide and set aside.

Roast red pepper over an open flame or under broiler until skin is charred on all sides. Place in a bowl and cover tightly with plastic wrap. After about 20 minutes, take pepper out, cut in half, remove core and scrape away charred skin and seeds. Cut into strips 1-inch long and ⅛-inch wide.

Put olive oil and garlic in a sauté pan over medium-high heat. When garlic just begins to change color, add leeks and Belgian endive; season with salt and pepper. Stir until well-coated with oil and garlic; turn heat down to medium-low and cover pan. Cook, stirring occasionally, until vegetables are very tender and almost creamy in texture.

Bring 4 quarts water to a boil, add 1 tablespoon salt and drop in fusilli, stirring until all pasta is submerged.

Uncover the pan with the vegetables, raise heat to medium-high and add roasted peppers. Cook, stirring often, for 2 to 3 minutes. Remove from heat and set aside.

When pasta is cooked al dente, drain well and toss with sauce. Serve at once.

Makes 4 servings.

(Adapted from *The Classic Pasta Cookbook* by Giuliano Hazan.)

Molly Stevens

"Taste your food."

I t's hard to imagine a loaf of bread could have life-transforming powers, but in the case of Molly Stevens it sent her on a journey across the Atlantic and into a world of food that previously didn't exist for her.

A native of Buffalo, New York, Stevens had cooked in high school and college, working in the kitchens of family-style restaurants, making the French fries or opening cans. Growing up, her family didn't eat out much, and the fare she ate at home was pretty typical American. "We never had cheese or seafood. We had fish sticks on Fridays and our cheese was yellow American," she recalls.

Time spent working for a caterer in high school was her first introduction to good food. She had earned an English degree at Middlebury College in Vermont and was working in a small restaurant in Montpelier when she purchased a sourdough baguette that had been baked in a wood-burning oven. It was a life-changing moment—Stevens sat in her car and ate the entire loaf. The bread was like nothing Stevens had ever had before. She sought out the baker, a retired anthropology professor from Goddard College, who told her about the bread ovens in France.

After college, Stevens eventually made her way to Paris. She knocked on the door of LaVarenne cooking school in Burgundy, but was turned away because she could not speak French. In the meantime, she found work in all sorts of places—kitchens where she served unpaid internships, babysitting, cooking for Americans. It was a difficult existence but Stevens was too proud to go home. She toughed it out, eventually learned French and went back to LaVarenne to train as a chef.

After more than two years at LaVarenne, Stevens met Dorothy Cann Hamilton, founder of New York's French Culinary Institute, when Hamilton had lunch at LaVarenne. Hamilton offered her a job; she moved back to the United States and began teaching in New York. The mid-1980s were an exciting time to be in New York. People were starting to get excited about food, especially French food. Stevens rode the wave for several years, but while on a ski trip to visit friends in Vermont, she met her future husband, Mark. Love sent her job hunting in New England. She joined the staff of the New England Culinary Institute, and moved back to Vermont permanently.

In 1995, after embarking on a career as a freelance teacher and writer, Stevens' reputation grew on a national scale. She has written, co-authored or edited more than fifteen cookbooks and her 2004 *All About Braising* won a James Beard Award. She is one of the most sought-after cooking teachers in the country and in 2006, was named Teacher of the Year by the International Association of Culinary Professionals, followed in 2007 by Teacher of the Year honors from *Bon Appétit*.

Stevens began teaching at Western Reserve School of Cooking in 2009, and said she is always impressed with the energy of the students, their desire to learn and their enthusiasm. She prefers teaching to writing, but believes the recipes she writes are an extension of her teaching. A good recipe, she said, gives a lot of information beyond just a list of ingredients, and will help a student become a better cook. "I try to think about a recipe as a learning opportunity. To become a really good cook, you are cooking without recipes. If a recipe teaches you enough technique, if you follow those recipes two or three times, you won't have to read the recipe because you will understand what is going on."

The one lesson her students won't learn from a recipe is the one she always stresses in class: "Taste your food." Stevens is always surprised that students will prepare an entire dish without ever tasting it along the way. She advocates tasting each ingredient individually, to help understand how their flavors will come together and to ensure proper seasoning. The more students become familiar with their ingredients and develop an appreciation for them, the more likely they are to cook from scratch. "Taste all of the raw ingredients from start to finish. It's amazing what you can learn," she said.

Pan-Roasted Barramundi Fillets

2 tablespoons extra-virgin olive oil	salt and freshly ground black pepper
4 (5 to 6 ounce) barramundi fillets	2 tablespoons unsalted butter

Heat 2 tablespoons oil in heavy large skillet over medium-high heat. Sprinkle fish with salt and pepper. Add to skillet and cook 30 seconds. Reduce heat to medium and add butter to skillet.

Continue to cook fish until edges appear opaque, occasionally basting with juices in skillet, about 4 minutes. Turn fish over. Cook until just opaque in center, about 2 minutes. Serve immediately.

Makes 4 servings.

Zinfandel Pot Roast with Glazed Carrots and Fresh Sage

I think of this as dinner-party pot roast. While the basic technique is the same as a regular Sunday night pot roast, the herb-flecked carrot garnish makes it dressy enough for company. If you like, use half parsnips and half carrots. The parsnips will cook in the same amount of time. Serve with buttery mashed potatoes, soft polenta, or savory bread pudding and a light salad of Bibb lettuce tossed with a creamy vinaigrette.

For the braise:

1 (3½ to 4 pounds) boneless beef chuck roast, preferably top blade roast

coarse salt and freshly ground black pepper

2 tablespoons extra-virgin olive oil

1 large yellow onion (about 8 ounces), coarsely chopped

1 carrot, coarsely chopped

1 celery stalk, coarsely chopped

2 garlic cloves, peeled and smashed

1 cup Zinfandel or other robust dry red wine

1 cup beef, veal or chicken stock

3 large leafy fresh sage sprigs, 3 to 4 inches each

2 to 3 leafy flat-leaf parsley sprigs, 6 to 8 inches each

8 to 10 black peppercorns

For the garnish:

1½ pounds small to medium carrots, peeled, or ¾ pound each carrots and parsnips, peeled

1 tablespoon extra-virgin olive oil

1 tablespoon unsalted butter

coarse salt and freshly ground black pepper

1 tablespoon red wine vinegar

pinch of sugar

2 tablespoons fresh sage

2 tablespoons chopped flat-leaf parsley

Heat oven to 300 degrees.

Using kitchen string, tie beef into a neat, snug shape. Season beef all over with salt and pepper. Heat oil in a large Dutch oven or other braising pot (5-quart works well) over medium heat. Add beef and brown on all sides, turning with tongs as you go, about 18 minutes total. Remove beef and set aside on a large plate or dish, to collect any juices that the meat releases. If there are any charred bits in pot, remove them with a damp paper towel, but leave behind any tasty-looking drippings.

Return pot to medium-high heat and add onion, carrot, celery and garlic. Season lightly with salt and pepper. Cook, stirring often, until just starting to brown, about 5 minutes. Pour in wine, scrape bottom with a wooden spoon to loosen any of the cherished cooked-on bits of caramelized beef juices and boil to reduce about one third, another 5 minutes. Return meat to pot and add sage, parsley and peppercorns. Cover with parchment paper, pressing down so that it nearly touches the meat and edges of paper overhang pot by about an inch. Set lid in place.

Transfer pot to lower third of oven and braise at a gentle simmer, turning roast once halfway through braising, until fork-tender, about 3 hours. Peek under lid after first 10 to 15 minutes to check that liquid isn't simmering too vigorously; if it is, lower oven heat by 10 or 15 degrees.

While beef braises, cut carrots crosswise in half, and cut halves lengthwise into sticks, about 3 inches by ½-inch. This typically means cutting thicker tops into quarters and skinnier tips in half. (If using parsnips, remove any woody core before cutting them into sticks.) Chop sage and parsley for garnish now as well. Set aside.

Remove pot from oven. Lift beef out with tongs or a sturdy spatula, set on a carving platter to catch juices and cover loosely with foil to keep warm. Strain cooking liquid, pressing down on solids to extract as much liquid as possible. Discard spent aromatics, and pour liquid into a medium saucepan. Let braising liquid settle; spoon off and discard as much fat with a wide spoon as you can easily. Measure out ½ cup of the juices for glazing carrots and set rest aside in a warm spot.

Heat oil and butter in a large skillet (12 or 13-inch) over medium-high heat. When quite hot, add carrots (and parsnips, if using), season with salt and pepper and cook briskly, shaking or stirring them, until lightly glazed and browned in spots, about 8 minutes. Add ½ cup braising liquid, cover partway, reduce heat to medium and simmer until tender but not at all mushy, 6 to 8 minutes. Uncover, raise heat and bring back to a boil. Add vinegar, sugar, sage and parsley, and cook until liquid is reduced to a glaze, about 1 minute. Taste for salt and pepper.

Heat remaining reserved cooking juices over medium-high heat, and boil for 1 or 2 minutes to concentrate their flavor. Taste. You may not need to add any salt or pepper, but do so if juices are lacking in flavor.

Remove strings from roast. For a platter presentation, arrange carrots (and parsnips, if using) around pot roast. Alternatively, slice roast into ½-inch thick slices and arrange slices on dinner plates along with carrots (and parsnips, if using). Spoon a bit of sauce over meat and serve immediately. Pass any remaining sauce at the table.

Makes 6 servings.

From *All About Braising: The Art of Uncomplicated Cooking* by Molly Stevens. Copyright © 2004 by Molly Stevens. Used by permission of W. W. Norton & Company, Inc.

Lime-Spiked Roasted Sweet Potato Purée with Brussels Sprout Chips

A uniquely delicious side dish for fish, poultry and pork. For a restaurant-style presentation, spoon the sweet potato purée onto warm plates and prop the fish (meat or poultry) alongside the purée. Drizzle the vinaigrette over everything and scatter the "chips" on top.

1 small shallot, minced (about 1½ teaspoons)

3 teaspoons fresh lime juice, divided

1¼ teaspoons finely grated lime zest

1 teaspoon white wine vinegar

½ teaspoon honey

3 tablespoons extra-virgin olive oil, divided

1¾ pounds red-skinned sweet potatoes

3 tablespoons unsalted butter, at room temperature

1 teaspoon chopped fresh thyme

pinch of freshly grated nutmeg

¼ cup warm whole milk

8 ounces brussels sprouts, leaves separated, cores discarded

Whisk shallot, 1 teaspoon lime juice, lime zest, vinegar and honey in small bowl. Whisk in 2 tablespoons oil. Season vinaigrette to taste with salt.

Preheat oven to 450 degrees. Pierce sweet potatoes in several places with fork. Place on sheet of aluminum foil and roast 30 minutes. Turn potatoes over and roast until soft, about 20 minutes longer. Let stand until cool enough to handle. Scoop flesh into processor; discard skins. Purée sweet potatoes until smooth. Add butter, thyme, nutmeg and remaining 2 teaspoons lime juice; process until blended and smooth. Add milk; process to blend. Transfer to baking dish or microwave-safe bowl. Season to taste with salt and pepper.

Place brussels sprout leaves on rimmed baking sheet. Drizzle with 1 tablespoon oil, sprinkle with salt and pepper and toss to coat. Spread leaves out in even layer. Roast until almost all leaves are brown in spots and crisp, tossing occasionally, about 15 minutes.

Divide sweet potatoes among plates. Drizzle vinaigrette over. Sprinkle brussels sprout chips over and serve.

Makes 4 servings.

Note: Vinaigrette and potatoes can be made 1 day ahead. Cover separately and chill. Bring vinaigrette to room temperature and re-whisk before using. If made ahead, rewarm sweet potatoes in low oven or microwave in 30-second intervals until heated through, stirring occasionally.

Joanne Weir

"I want to keep people in the kitchen."

With a great-grandmother who ran a restaurant and a mother who edited noted cookbook author Charlotte Turgeon's work, it's probably no surprise that Joanne Weir ended up as one of the country's most prominent cooking teachers. "It definitely is in my blood and in my soul," she says of her career in food.

Her teaching has spanned the globe—including nearly a dozen trips to Hudson, Ohio—and Weir is best known for her work teaching Mediterranean cuisine. She likes to say that she specializes in the cuisine of "any place that grows grapes."

Food was a strong part of her upbringing. Weir spent her childhood weekends visiting her grandfather's farm in the Berkshire Mountains in Cummington, Massachusetts, where a Saturday lunch outside under the maple trees might consist of rolls he made, chicken he had raised and butchered, potato chips he had fried and maple walnut ice cream made from syrup from his own trees.

While her career path may seem inevitable considering her lineage, Weir wasn't planning on a life in food when she studied art education at the University of Massachusetts in the 1970s. She was teaching high school fine arts in the Boston public schools when she felt a pull toward food.

Weir began to take classes from legendary French chef Madeleine Kamman at her Modern Gourmet school in Massachusetts, and later studied with her in France, where she was awarded a master chef's diploma. From there, Weir decided she needed restaurant experience, so she moved to California and spent five years working at Alice Waters' acclaimed Chez Panisse restaurant. Having studied with two of the best the food world has to offer, Weir had her choice of careers, but found that returning to the classroom was where she wanted to be.

She finds the need to immerse herself in her subject matter. Her study and travels abroad solidified her in olive oil-based cooking, and she continues to travel extensively in the Mediterranean, taking group trips abroad about six months of the year.

In 1994, her first book, *From Tapas to Meze*, was released and Julia Child named it as one of her top twelve favorite cookbooks of the more than 1,000 published that year. In 1996, she was the first-ever recipient of the International Association of Culinary Professionals' Cooking Teacher of the Year Award.

Weir, who makes her home in northern California, has studied wine and the wine regions of the world. She has hosted her own cooking show on public television, which focused on wine country cuisine, and has written three books on the subject.

Kamman, who was a frequent visitor to the Zona Spray Cooking School, helped Weir get booked there for the first time in 1990. In addition to a long-standing friendship with Spray, Weir said she enjoyed her classes in Hudson, where she said the students were always well-versed on food and the importance of good ingredients.

One of Weir's fondest memories of teaching at the school was the time she prepared a custard dish and, as the students were sampling it, a woman in the back row proclaimed it the best thing she had ever eaten, actually picked up her plate and licked it clean. "I thought that was so cool," Weir recalled.

Weir has been able to keep up her enthusiasm in the classroom because she is serious about wanting people to learn. "I want to keep people in the kitchen. Cooking isn't rocket science and I want people to feel that they can do it and I'm all about giving them the tools to do it," she said.

Venetian Tomato-Rice "Olives"

2 tablespoons extra-virgin olive oil

½ cup onion, finely minced

1 cup arborio rice

1¼ cups chicken broth

1¼ cups milk

⅔ cup sun-dried tomato paste

coarse salt and freshly ground black pepper

¼ cup finely grated Parmigiano-Reggiano

1 cup all-purpose flour

4 eggs

½ cup water

4 cups toasted fresh bread crumbs, finely ground

mixture of vegetable and olive oil for frying

Place chicken broth and milk in a saucepan and heat just to a simmer.

Heat 2 tablespoons olive oil over medium heat in a skillet. Add onions and sauté until soft, about 5 minutes. Add rice to skillet with remaining oil and continue to cook, stirring constantly for 2 minutes.

Add milk and broth to rice, along with half of the sun-dried tomato paste, salt and pepper. Bring to a simmer, reduce heat to low, cover and cook slowly until rice is cooked, about 20 minutes. If rice dries out during cooking process, add additional hot water. When rice is done, add remaining sun-dried tomato paste and Parmigiano-Reggiano. Remove from heat and cool completely.

Form mixture into small olive-size balls using less than a tablespoon of mixture for each one. Place on a baking sheet.

Place flour in a bowl. Whisk eggs and water in another bowl. Place bread crumbs in a third bowl. Roll rice olives in flour, egg and bread crumbs. Place on a baking sheet until you are ready to cook them. These can be prepared up to one day in advance up to this point.

In a deep pan, heat 1 inch of a vegetable and olive oil combination to 375 degrees.

Fry rice olives until golden on all sides, 60 to 90 seconds. Remove and serve immediately.

Makes 60 rice olives.

Baked Stuffed Artichokes

8 medium artichokes, about 4 pounds

14 salt-packed anchovy fillets

3 cups fresh sourdough breadcrumbs

½ cup plus 3 tablespoons extra-virgin olive oil

8 cloves garlic (2 whole and 6 sliced)

4 tablespoons chopped fresh Italian parsley

2 pounds (about 3 large) onions, thinly sliced

1¼ pounds mixed colored peppers, seeded and cut into small strips

small bunch fresh thyme

3 bay leaves

¾ teaspoon salt

¼ teaspoon ground pepper

3 tablespoons red wine vinegar

garlic mayonnaise (recipe follows)

½ cup water

⅓ cup niçoise olives

Choose artichokes that have about an inch of stem attached. With a serrated knife, cut through leaves of artichokes crosswise, removing about half of top part. Using a small knife, trim stems down to tender core and pare away tough leaves around the bottom. Scoop and scrape out the hairy chokes and set in a bowl of water that has had some lemon juice added to it.

Soak anchovies in several changes of cold water for 15 minutes. Drain and pat dry.

Toss breadcrumbs in 3 tablespoons olive oil and toast them for 15 minutes on a sheet pan until golden brown and crisp. Pound the 2 reserved garlic cloves and 6 anchovies to a paste in a mortar and combine them with breadcrumbs and 2 tablespoons parsley.

Warm ½ cup olive oil in a large sauté pan. Add onions, peppers, thyme, bay leaves, sliced garlic, salt, pepper and vinegar. Stew mixture for 15 minutes, stirring often, until vegetables have softened. Turn onions and peppers into a large enamel baking pan. Pack breadcrumb mixture into artichoke bottoms and invert them stem up onto bed of vegetables. Season artichokes and pour water over them. Cover with parchment and tightly with foil.

Bake at 350 degrees for 1 hour and 15 minutes or until artichokes can be easily skewered. While artichokes are cooking, make garlic mayonnaise.

Allow artichokes to cool until just warm. Serve artichokes directly from baking pan on individual plates with some of the onions and peppers. Sprinkle with remaining 2 tablespoons parsley and drape with remaining anchovies, cut lengthwise into thin strips. Strew olives around plate and pass garlic mayonnaise separately.

Makes 8 servings.

Garlic Mayonnaise

½ cup extra virgin olive oil

½ cup unflavored oil, sunflower, safflower, canola, vegetable or corn

1 egg yolk

1 teaspoon Dijon mustard

3 to 4 cloves garlic, minced

2 to 3 tablespoons lemon juice

salt and freshly ground black pepper

In a liquid measuring cup with a spout, combine olive and unflavored oils. In a medium size bowl, whisk egg yolk, mustard and 1 tablespoon of combined oil together until an emulsion is formed. Drop by drop, add olive oil to emulsion, whisking constantly. Continue to do this, drop by drop, in a steady stream, whisking, until all oil has been added. Do not add oil too quickly and be sure that emulsion is homogeneous before adding more oil. Add garlic and lemon juice to taste. Season with salt and pepper. Add 2 to 4 tablespoons warm water to mayonnaise, whisking constantly. This should be used the same day it is made.

Makes about 1¼ cups.

Crostini Rossi

1 slice country-style sourdough bread

3 tablespoons red wine vinegar

6 tablespoons extra-virgin olive oil

1 tablespoon capers

1 clove garlic, chopped

3 tablespoons chopped fresh parsley

2 teaspoons chopped fresh thyme

pinch of crushed red pepper

2 large tomatoes, peeled, cored, seeded and chopped

salt and freshly ground black pepper

8 slices sourdough bread, ¼-inch thick

Soak first slice of bread in vinegar for 1 minute and wring dry. Put bread in a large mortar and pestle with 3 tablespoons olive oil, capers, garlic, parsley, thyme, crushed red pepper and tomatoes. Pound to make a rough paste. Taste and season with salt and pepper.

Brush bread slices with remaining olive oil and bake at 400 degrees until golden on each side. Remove and spread crushed tomato mixture on top. Serve immediately.

Makes 8 servings.

Baked Ricotta

15 ounces ricotta cheese

3 tablespoons extra-virgin olive oil

¼ cup dry bread crumbs

1 egg, lightly beaten

¼ cup grated Parmesan cheese

½ teaspoon fresh thyme, chopped

salt and freshly ground black pepper

If ricotta is wet, drain for 2 hours in a cheesecloth-lined strainer in refrigerator. Oil a 6-inch soufflé dish with 1½ tablespoons olive oil and coat with bread crumbs. Tap out excess.

Combine ricotta, egg, Parmesan and thyme. Season to taste with salt and pepper. Pour mixture into prepared dish. Drizzle remaining olive oil evenly over top. Bake at 375 degrees for 35 to 40 minutes or until golden and firm on top.

Serve with crackers or crostini for spreading.

Makes 6 servings.

The Recipes

Chapter 3

A Little Something Sweet

Nancy Baggett

"With baking, you've got to be careful. The chemistry will reach up and smack you if you aren't careful."

It's hard to classify Nancy Baggett. She's a baker and trained pastry chef, who is capable on the savory side too. But she's actually a writer before either of those. That is probably why she has produced more than fifteen cookbooks in her career, which was born when she combined her two loves, writing and cooking.

Baggett was a natural in the kitchen. Growing up on a farm, the kitchen was always the hub of activity. Her family kept a large garden and would preserve their harvest, putting up hundreds of cans of tomatoes and other vegetables for winter. Baggett worked at her mother's side, learning to bake cookies, cakes and sweet rolls at an early age. By the time she was a young teen, her mother was working as a school teacher. On the nights her mother had to stay late for meetings, Baggett was in charge of getting supper on the table. She relished the responsibility. Even if her dinners were nothing more than cream soup casseroles, Baggett loved having her family eat the dinners she had prepared.

After earning an English degree at Hood College in her home state of Maryland, Baggett worked as a technical writer and editor, even working in government security developing manuals for intelligence-gathering equipment. It was very dry, technical writing, but the job had its perks—plenty of single engineers with whom she was working, including her future husband.

After their son was born, Baggett was looking for a way to work from home, and began writing freelance articles for a variety of newspapers. She became a regular in the *Baltimore Sun* and *Washington Post*. Baggett had been developing recipes and after securing her first book contract, she decided that she needed more training than the years of practice in her own kitchen, so she signed up for a pastry course taught by Roland Mesnier, longtime White House pastry chef. The classes helped to expand Baggett's skills and taught her many of the intricacies of presentation for pastry, which gave her work a more polished, professional edge. However, the class also solidified for Baggett that she is a baker, not a classical pastry chef, and that writing will always be a large part of her work.

Baggett began teaching at the Zona Spray Cooking School in the late 1980s, often coming to promote her current book, but also teaching classes on food writing and recipe writing. "Zona liked these classes better than anything else that I've taught for her. They were extremely popular," she recalled. "Deep in the hearts of most people is this feeling that they'd like to write a recipe from scratch."

These days, Baggett doesn't teach as often, spending most of her time developing recipes for new books. "If you write cookbooks, so much of your time gets spent developing your own recipes. A lot of the time I don't appear to be writing, I'm actually developing recipes. They all go together." Her goal is that her efforts will result in a recipe that is simple for her readers to follow easily and successfully.

Baggett's advice is to remember that unlike cooking, baking involves chemistry and the process must be respected. When dealing with ingredients like sugar and chocolate, there are ratios and formulas that need to be followed. "With baking, you've got to be careful. The chemistry will reach up and smack you if you aren't careful."

Spiced Almond Crisps

Janhagel, from the Netherlands

2 cups all-purpose or unbleached white flour

¾ cup granulated sugar

1 teaspoon ground cinnamon

¼ teaspoon ground allspice

¼ teaspoon salt

1 stick plus 5 tablespoons cold unsalted butter

1 egg white, beaten with 1 tablespoon water

1 cup unblanched sliced almonds

Preheat oven to 350 degrees. Generously grease and flour a 15 by 10-inch jelly roll pan.

Combine flour, sugar, cinnamon, allspice and salt in a food processor fitted with a steel blade. Process in on/off pulses for 6 to 7 seconds to mix ingredients. Cut butter into small pieces and sprinkle over flour mixture. Processing in on/off pulses, cut butter into flour until mixture resembles fine meal. Continue processing, gradually adding about 2 to 3 tablespoons cold water through feed tube in on/off pulses, until ingredients are cohesive and mixture begins to mass. Press into a ball.

Lay dough between 15-inch long sheets of wax paper. Using a rolling pin, roll out dough to form an evenly thick rectangle just slightly smaller than the jelly roll pan. (Patch or cut away any uneven places as needed to obtain the right dimensions.) Peel off top layer of wax paper. Turn dough over so underside is facing up; center and place directly on prepared jelly roll pan. Peel off second sheet of wax paper. Patch any tears using fingers.

Famous Chefs & Fabulous Recipes

Generously brush dough surface all over with egg white mixture. Sprinkle almonds over dough surface, patting down with fingers. Lay wax paper over almonds and press down firmly to embed almonds slightly. Using a sharp knife, cut dough into six 2½-inch strips horizontally and make five vertical cuts every 2 inches; for best appearance, measure and mark dough prior to cutting.

Bake for 20 to 25 minutes or until dough is golden and almonds are nicely browned. Remove pan to a rack and let cookies stand for about 5 minutes. Retrace cuts previously made in dough using a sharp knife. Separate rectangles and, using a spatula, transfer them to racks until completely cold.

Store cookies airtight in a single layer for up to a week. Freeze for longer storage.

Makes 36 1¾ by 2¼-inch rectangles.

Orange Meltaways

From England and Scotland

1½ cups all-purpose or unbleached white flour

¼ cup cornstarch

¼ teaspoon baking powder

1 stick plus 5 tablespoons unsalted butter, slightly softened

⅔ cup confectioners' sugar

1 large egg yolk

finely grated zest of 1 small lemon

finely grated zest of 1 large orange

2 teaspoons lemon juice

2 to 4 teaspoons orange juice, approximately

For the glaze:

¼ cup strained apricot preserves

½ teaspoon lemon juice

¼ teaspoon very finely grated orange zest

1½ to 2½ tablespoons granulated sugar

Preheat oven to 350 degrees. Grease several baking sheets and set aside. Sift together flour, cornstarch and baking powder.

In a large mixer bowl with the mixer on medium speed, beat butter for 3 minutes, until very light. Add confectioners' sugar and beat until very fluffy and smooth. Beat in egg yolk, lemon and orange zest, lemon juice and 2 teaspoons orange juice until mixture is well blended. Beat in dry ingredients until thoroughly incorporated. Let stand for 2 or 3 minutes. If mixture seems too stiff to pipe, beat in a bit more orange juice to soften just slightly.

Spoon mixture into a pastry bag fitted with a ½-inch or slightly larger diameter star tip. (For convenience, stand bag in a tall glass and turn down cuff about 3½ inches before filling. Turn cuff up again and twist top tightly to close.) Pipe 1½-inch shell shapes onto baking sheets, spacing them about 1½ inches apart. Let stand for about 5 minutes.

Prepare glaze by stirring together sieved apricot jam, lemon juice and orange zest. Bake cookies for 12 to 14 minutes or until edges are nicely browned. Remove sheets from oven and lightly brush tops with glaze. Generously sprinkle glazed cookies with granulated sugar. Return sheets to oven and continue baking for 4 to 5 minutes longer or until glaze starts to bubble and caramelize. Remove sheets from oven and let cookies stand for about 2 minutes. Transfer them to racks and let stand until cooled completely. Store cookies airtight in a single layer for up to a week. Freeze for longer storage.

Makes about 40 1¾ to 2-inch cookies.

Jam-Filled Butter Cookies

Hussar's Kisses, from Hungary

1½ cups (3 sticks) unsalted butter, at room temperature

¼ teaspoon salt

1 cup granulated sugar

3 egg yolks

2¼ teaspoons vanilla extract

⅛ teaspoon almond extract, generous

3¾ cups all-purpose white flour

½ to ⅔ cup red currant or red raspberry jelly

about ⅔ cup slivered blanched almonds

Preheat oven to 375 degrees. Grease several baking sheets. Cream butter until lightened in a mixer bowl with mixer on medium speed. Add salt and sugar and beat until light and fluffy. Beat in yolks, vanilla and almond extract. Gradually mix in flour to form dough.

Pinch off pieces and roll between palms into 1-inch balls. Space on baking sheets about 1½ inches apart. Press a deep indentation in the center of each cookie using knuckle or thumb. Bake cookies for 7 minutes. Remove from oven and fill indentations with about ½ teaspoon jelly. Sprinkle a few almond slivers over center of each cookie.

Return to oven and bake about 5 minutes longer or until cookies are just tinged with brown and jelly is melting. Transfer to racks to cool. Store cookies airtight in a single layer for up to a week. Freeze for longer storage.

Makes about 5 dozen 1¼-inch diameter cookies.

Eric Bedoucha

"Learn the basics."

Pastry Chef Eric Bedoucha was just fourteen when he decided that he did not want to go to school; he wanted to be a chef. His mother arranged a placement for him at a local charcuterie (pork butcher's shop) in his home city of Paris. Bedoucha laughs about it now, because he believes it was a strange place for a Jewish mother to send her son. But because the shop was supposed to be the best in the city, she wasn't daunted by the non-kosher environment; she wanted him to have the best training possible.

But it didn't take Bedoucha long to decide that pastry was where he wanted to specialize, not meats. As executive pastry chef and co-owner of Financier Patisserie, Bedoucha has expanded one shop in the heart of Manhattan's financial district into a growing chain of a dozen French pastry shops throughout the city. Before that, he worked at some of the finest hotels and restaurants in the city, including Maxim's, La Grenouille, Lutece, Bayard's and the Plaza Hotel.

At the Plaza in the 1980s, Bedoucha hired Pastry Chef Tina Körting, who has also become a longtime instructor at Western Reserve School of Cooking in Hudson. It was their friendship that brought him to the cooking school in 1997 to teach a class on French desserts.

Bedoucha was born in Algeria, when it was still under French control, and lived there for several years until his family moved back to Paris. The flavors of his youth, however—fragrant rose and orange blossom water, pistachios, almonds, pine nuts and dates—continue to inspire his dessert creations.

After training in France in the early 1980s, Bedoucha followed his American girlfriend to the United States. After a rocky start in Chicago, where he nearly called it quits and moved back to France, he eventually ended up at the Westin Hotel, where he worked as a pastry chef from 1983 to 1985, before moving on to New York's Plaza Hotel in 1985.

While he still goes to work in a chef's jacket and pants each day, Bedoucha said that since his pastry chain began its rapid expansion, his life these days is more about pushing paper and less about pushing flour sacks. His teaching is mostly confined to training his staff and surveying the skills of the people he hires. Bedoucha trained the old-fashioned way. He started out mopping floors, and from there moved to the flour room, later doing bench work, and eventually moving up from small confections like petit fours to cakes.

He said all students should strive to learn the basics—sugar dough, brioche dough, croissant dough and pastry cream—so their skills will translate to a wide variety of confections, not just one dessert or one recipe. "Learn the basics. If you don't know the basics, you don't know anything," he said.

Bedoucha gets discouraged by America's food television culture, which he believes has sent legions of young people into food, not because they have a passion for the craft, but because they want to be celebrities. "If there was no Food Network, the line in Hollywood would be a lot longer," he said.

Chocolate Cream

2 cups whole milk

2 cups heavy cream

10 egg yolks

⅓ cup granulated sugar

1¼ pounds (20 ounces) semi-sweet chocolate (64% cacao), chopped

In a mixing bowl, whisk together egg yolks and half the sugar. In a saucepan, combine milk, heavy cream and remaining sugar.

Scald milk mixture over medium-high heat and temper into egg yolk mixture. Return to heat and cook, whisking continuously, until thickened enough to coat the back of a wooden spatula. Strain mixture through a chinois (or fine mesh strainer) directly over chopped chocolate and mix until smooth.

Let cool. To be used as a filling for cakes or to fill chocolate tarts.

Makes about 4 cups.

White Chocolate Pistachio Mousse

6 ounces milk

2 teaspoons powdered gelatin

2½ teaspoons pure vanilla extract

6 ounces white chocolate

3½ ounces pistachio paste (available from specialty pastry suppliers)

2 cups whipped cream

In a heavy saucepan, combine milk and vanilla. Bring to a boil, remove from heat. Add gelatin, pistachio paste and chopped white chocolate. Stir until chocolate is melted.

Let cool completely and fold into the soft peaks of whipped cream.

Pour in to a plastic wrap-lined mold and chill for several hours before unmolding.

Makes 4 servings.

Flo Braker

"Just keep baking."

It's hard to imagine that one of the most celebrated bakers in America today, a woman who taught Julia Child a thing or two about baking, actually began her career because it was something a traditional homemaker could do at home.

It was the early 1960s and Flo Braker was married with two young children. In those days, a woman who worked outside the home carried a stigma—she was someone "who had to work," Braker recalled. Wives and mothers in her neighborhood didn't work; they cooked and cleaned and volunteered and, in Braker's case, baked.

First she baked her way through the *Better Homes and Gardens Cookbook* that she received in 1960 as a wedding gift. But a lot of the recipes didn't always work for her. A chocolate cake that turned out perfectly one time fell flat the next. Why? Braker sought answers in her kitchen. Her interest turned into obsession, and her obsession into her passion. Braker just kept on baking. She literally baked non-stop for more than eleven years, working her way through book after book, staying up late at night to experiment with new recipes, searching for knowledge and perfecting her techniques.

Looking back, Braker can trace the roots of her passion to age nine, when she received a chemistry set as a gift. Baking was essentially her grown-up chemistry kit—but it had the added bonus of providing her with something to share with her family and friends, and it kept her home with her husband and children.

Her first venture into cookbook writing came in the early 1970s, when Braker volunteered to put together a small recipe booklet as a fund-raiser for her children's school. At $1.50 a copy, it sold out in three weeks and was Braker's first official best seller. The project gave her confidence, so when a friend invited her to take some cooking classes, Braker accepted. After a few classes, she had the courage to ask the school's owner if he would consider letting her rent his school to teach her own baking classes.

Intrigued by her ideas, the school's owner, celebrated San Francisco cooking teacher Jack Lorio, asked Braker if she would consider teaching the classes with him. The six-week sessions with Lorio and Braker were a huge hit and helped to solidify Braker's reputation as one of the Bay area's most talented bakers.

Braker also started selling her confections, particularly her miniature desserts, for which she was becoming well-known. Braker has always loved tiny things, an affection she traces back to her childhood in Indiana, when her grandfather would come home from business trips in New York bearing boxes of fancy miniature cookies.

In 1985, ten years after she started teaching, Braker's landmark work, the *Simple Art of Perfect Baking*, was published. It caught the eye of none other than Julia Child, who invited Braker to Massachusetts to teach her and a group of her associates about baking.

It was the same year that Braker first came to Hudson, Ohio, to teach at what was then the Zona Spray School of Cooking. It's been more than a decade since Braker has been back to Hudson but she has fond memories of the school, the students and their appreciation for baking. "I adored those classes in Ohio," Braker recalled. "I have never met such bakers as I have in Ohio."

Tiffany's Heart with Chocolate Butter Glaze

For the cake:

2 ounces (½ cup, by weight) pecans

⅓ cup unsifted all-purpose flour

⅓ cup granulated sugar

⅓ cup light brown sugar, packed

3 eggs, at room temperature

1 teaspoon granulated sugar

3 ounces (6 tablespoons) unsalted butter

6 ounces semi-sweet chocolate

2 tablespoons water

1 tablespoon rum or framboise

1 cup fresh raspberries, at room temperature, for garnish

Chocolate-Butter Glaze (recipe follows)

Position rack in lower third of oven. Preheat oven to 350 degrees.

Trace the shape of an 8-inch heart-shaped pan on cardboard. Cut the heart from cardboard. Set aside until baked cake is unmolded.

Using a paper towel, grease bottom and sides of pan with solid vegetable shortening. Dust generously with all-purpose flour, shake to distribute, tap out excess and insert parchment liner.

Grind pecans until they have the consistency of cornmeal; you will need ¾ cup ground. Add flour to nuts.

Measure granulated and brown sugars, set aside.

Separate eggs, placing whites in a deep 1½-quart mixing bowl and yolks in a small bowl. Place 1 teaspoon granulated sugar near whites for whipping time.

Melt butter and chocolate in a small heavy-bottomed saucepan over very low heat. Stir in water and blend until smooth.

Transfer warm chocolate mixture to a 3-quart mixing bowl, and while still warm, stir in granulated and brown sugars. Cool for 5 minutes. Stir in egg yolks until incorporated. Add rum and blend. Pour in nuts and flour mixture and mix together.

With an electric hand mixer, whip egg whites on medium-low speed until small bubbles appear and surface is frothy, about 30 seconds. Increase speed to high, add teaspoon sugar and whip until soft, white peaks form, about 1 minute.

Scoop a third of the whites into chocolate mixture and stir-fold with a rubber spatula to lighten. Fold in remainder.

Scoop batter into prepared pan, smooth evenly with rubber spatula. Bake for 25 minutes, or until soft, but not liquid in the center. Do not overbake because chocolate will firm as it cools.

Remove pan from oven to a cooling rack for 15 to 20 minutes. Tilt and rotate pan, and gently tap on the counter to see if cake is releasing cleanly from the metal. If not, or if in doubt, run a small metal spatula between the cake's edge and metal rim, freeing sides and allowing air into the layer as it is rotated. Cover pan with cardboard, invert cake and carefully lift pan to remove. Peel off and discard parchment liner.

Prepare chocolate-butter glaze. Place 3 tablespoons into a 3-quart mixing bowl and set aside.

Place cake on its cardboard on a cooling rack over a jelly roll pan. Pour chocolate glaze onto the center and spread glaze with a flexible metal icing spatula. If necessary, place bowl with reserved glaze over warm water, just to liquefy it and until no warmer than body temperature. Pour raspberries on top. Gently slide a rubber spatula under the berries, and fold the two together. Repeat this three more times. The object is to partially coat some of the raspberries, but not all.

Carefully scoop the fruit on top of cake. Or lift chocolate-covered berries gently with your fingertips and place them individually on top.

Store and serve cake at room temperature—refrigeration changes its flavor and texture.

The cake may be baked ahead, cooled, wrapped in plastic wrap, overwrapped in foil and frozen up to 2 weeks. After defrosting, glaze as described above.

Makes 8 to 12 servings.

Chocolate Butter Glaze

4 ounces semi-sweet chocolate

2 ounces unsweetened chocolate

3 ounces (6 tablespoons) unsalted butter

Chop chocolate into matchstick-sized pieces with a chef's knife on a dry cutting board. Place butter and chocolate pieces in top portion of a 1½-quart double boiler, or a 1-quart mixing bowl that fits snugly over a saucepan or another mixing bowl. Fill bottom vessel half full with hot tap water (120 to 130 degrees) and place chocolate-butter bowl on top to melt.

You may put the double boiler on the stove over a very low flame if you wish, though only to maintain the water's temperature while melting mixture.

Stir occasionally to blend, until mixture is smooth, shiny and liquid. Remove from container of water, and use for glazing cake.

You may make this glaze ahead and store in an airtight container in refrigerator for up to two weeks. To liquefy, heat over water bath, being careful that water temperature doesn't exceed 130 degrees.

Makes 1 scant cup.

From *The Simple Art of Perfect Baking* © 2004 by Flo Braker. Used with permission.

Americana Banana Roll

Banana Sheet Cake (recipe follows)

1 tablespoon granulated sugar

For the filling:

¾ cup (6 ounces) heavy cream

2 tablespoons sour cream

1 tablespoon granulated sugar

1 teaspoon vanilla

3 tablespoons unsifted powdered sugar

Prepare Banana Sheet as directed below. Cool no more than 30 to 60 minutes under foil tent. Prepare to roll the cake. Slip a 12 by 15 by ½-inch baking sheet under foil-lined cake as though it were a large spatula. Sprinkle 1 tablespoon granulated sugar over cake's surface. Place two 18-inch strips of foil lengthwise on top of sugared cake, one overlapping the other. Place second baking sheet on top of foil. Invert cake and carefully peel baking foil from cake to avoid tearing the thin layer.

Combine filling ingredients in a deep 1½-quart mixing bowl and whip until some cream dropped from beater or whisk does not disappear on surface. Another test is to draw beater or whisk through the center of the bowl. If the track stays in place, you are ready to spread filling on cake. The cream will appear soft, shiny and smooth but stiffer than for most desserts. It will coat the cake layer, sticking to it and staying in place when rolled.

Lift cake on its two overlapping foil sheets off baking sheet so that a long side is parallel to the edge of your counter. The cake will be rolled lengthwise.

Spread cream evenly over cake with a rubber spatula, up to 1 inch before reaching the long end farthest from you. (Some filling will move to that end as you roll.)

Begin rolling by flipping cake edge nearest you over onto itself. With the aid of the foil that extends on either side, roll cake lengthwise until you reach the other end. With your hands, wrap some of the foil around the roll to assist you in rounding the shape as you work toward the other end.

Cut each end on the diagonal for eye appeal and sprinkle a light coating of powdered sugar over it to disguise any cracks. Lift onto a serving plate with a long and wide spatula or a baking sheet without sides.

Makes 8 to 10 servings.

Banana Sheet Cake

1 cup (100 grams) sifted cake flour

½ teaspoon baking soda

⅛ teaspoon baking powder

⅛ teaspoon salt

1 large egg, at room temperature

½ cup (1 large) mashed ripe banana

1 tablespoon sour cream

1 teaspoon lemon zest

5½ tablespoons (2½ ounces) unsalted butter, at room temperature

½ cup (100 grams) granulated sugar

Position rack in lower third of oven; preheat oven to 375 degrees.

Using a paper towel, lightly grease a small area in the center of a 12 by 15 by ½-inch baking sheet with solid shortening, and line pan with foil, leaving a 2-inch overhang at each short end (the dab of shortening will hold foil in place). Lightly grease foil with shortening, and sprinkle with all-purpose flour. Shake pan to distribute flour and tap out excess.

Pour flour, baking soda, baking powder and salt in that order into a triple sifter. Sift onto waxed paper to distribute ingredients; set aside.

Crack egg into a small bowl, and whisk briefly to combine yolk and white.

Combine mashed banana, sour cream and lemon zest in a small bowl; set aside.

Place butter in the bowl of a heavy-duty mixer. With the flat beater, cream butter on medium speed for 30 to 45 seconds, or until smooth and lighter in color. Maintaining same speed, add sugar in a steady stream. Stop mixer and scrape mixture clinging to sides into center of bowl. Continue to cream at same speed until mixture is light in color and fluffy in appearance, 3 to 4 minutes.

With mixer still on medium speed, pour in egg, very cautiously at first, as if you were adding oil when making mayonnaise. Continue to cream for 1 to 2 more minutes, scraping sides at least once. When mixture is quite fluffy and has increased in volume, turn off mixer and detach beater. Tap beater against edge of bowl to free excess.

With a metal spatula, lift half the flour mixture and sprinkle over creamed mixture. Stir in with a rubber spatula. Add mashed banana mixture, stirring to blend. Scrape sides with each addition. Add remaining flour mixture and stir until smooth.

Scoop thick batter onto five different areas over two-thirds of the prepared baking sheet. With a metal spatula, spread and coax batter to cover two-thirds of the sheet. Extend to the rest of sheet in as even a layer as possible. The layer will be very thin.

Bake 8 to 10 minutes, or until cake is light golden brown, the sides are beginning to contract from the metal and cake springs back when lightly touched in center.

Remove pan from oven. Using a thin-bladed knife, gently release any portion sticking to sides. Pull up on the foil overhangs, one at a time, to release from the pan's edges. Finally, loosen foil from bottom by gently lifting up on flaps, and transfer to a large rack to cool.

Place foil over cake and fold in a tent fashion (this holds in moisture, but prevents foil from sticking to cake).

Cool for 30 minutes.

From *The Simple Art of Perfect Baking* © 2004 by Flo Braker. Used with permission.

Marcel Desaulniers

"Try your best not to be intimidated."

At first reference, the name Marcel Desaulniers may invoke the image of a French pastry chef. With his reputation for work in chocolate and his unofficial title as the "Guru of Ganache" it's hard to imagine, but not only is Desaulniers as American as apple pie, he served with the U.S. Marine Corps.

The Woonsocket, Rhode Island native worked in food service in high school and knew that he wanted to cook, so he enrolled at the Culinary Institute of America, when it was still located in New Haven, Connecticut. After graduating in 1965, he went to work in New York City and after a few months, he was drafted for the war in Vietnam. After serving a stint in the Marines, Desaulniers went back to New York and back to work. After jobs at several clubs and the Hotel Pierre, he moved to Virginia in 1970, to work for Colonial Williamsburg.

Ten years later he opened his acclaimed restaurant, The Trellis, where he served as executive chef for twenty-nine years, until 2009, when he and his longtime business partner sold it. The *Trellis Cookbook*, released in 1988, was his first writing venture. But it was Desaulniers' foray into desserts, specifically chocolate, that earned him a national reputation. His 1992 masterpiece *Death by Chocolate, the Last Word on a Consuming Passion*, won a James Beard Award and solidified his reputation as the country's chief chocoholic. When touring for the book that year, Desaulniers visited the Zona Spray Cooking School to teach about his favorite dessert medium. "I love chocolate. I have had a life-long love of chocolate and wanted to feature chocolate desserts (at Trellis). We definitely hit a home run with that," he said.

Death by Chocolate spawned a television show by the same name, and was followed by eight other books, including *Desserts to Die For, Death by Chocolate Cookies, Death by Chocolate Cakes* and *I'm Dreaming of a Chocolate Christmas*. In his career, Desaulniers has earned a total of four James Beard Awards, including best chef and best pastry chef for the Mid-Atlantic Region. Over the years, Desaulniers had to get used to the fact that many chocolate fanatics were buying his books out of chocolate lust. They would tell him how they would read them at night before bed, instead of a novel, in order to satisfy their chocolate desires. When teaching, Desaulniers discovered that while many of the students wanted to learn something, it did not mean they intended to put the knowledge to use. "There is definitely an intimidation factor with desserts," he noted.

His advice to novice bakers is to try not to be afraid and, elementary as it may sound, to read the recipe carefully and thoroughly before attempting it. Desaulniers said a big stumbling block for home bakers is getting halfway through a recipe and discovering they don't have all of the needed ingredients to complete it. When it comes to chocolate, he said it is easier to work with than most novice bakers would believe, but it does require one's full attention because it can be ruined by even the slightest inattention.

"Invest the time in reading and give it a little bit of concentration. Buy the chocolate and sit down with a glass of port and you can always eat the chocolate," he said.

Chocolate Honey Almond Crunch

4 cups sliced almonds

6 ounces unsalted butter

1½ cups granulated sugar

½ cup water

¼ cup Myers's Dark Rum

¼ cup honey

8 ounces semisweet chocolate, chopped into ¼-inch pieces

4 ounces unsweetened chocolate, chopped into ¼-inch pieces

Preheat oven to 325 degrees. Toast 2 cups almonds on a baking sheet in preheated oven until golden brown, 12 to 14 minutes. Remove almonds from oven and cool to room temperature. Transfer almonds to a large dish or other suitable container and set aside until needed.

Melt butter in a 2½-quart saucepan over low heat, stirring constantly, so it does not simmer or boil. As soon as butter is completely melted, add sugar, water, rum and honey. Increase heat to medium-high. Heat mixture to 220 degrees, stirring constantly. Add untoasted almonds and continue to heat and stir until mixture reaches 225 degrees.

Evenly divide honey-almond mixture between two 9 by 13-inch baking sheets with sides. Place baking sheets on the top and middle oven shelves and bake until mixture is evenly caramelized, 24 to 26 minutes. Rotate baking sheets from top to bottom about halfway through the baking time. Remove from oven and cool for 5 minutes.

Combine semi-sweet and unsweetened chocolate pieces and evenly divide and sprinkle over caramelized honey-almond mixture. Let stand for 5 minutes. Use a spatula to spread chocolate throughout mixture. Evenly divide and sprinkle toasted almonds over chocolate. Place both baking sheets in freezer for 20 minutes.

Remove from freezer and break into irregular pieces. Store in a sealed plastic container in freezer or refrigerator.

Makes about 2¾ pounds.

Adapted from *Death by Chocolate* (Rizzoli International Publications, 1993).

Lucy's Chocolate Diamonds

For the Chocolate Cake:

½ pound unsalted butter
  (2 tablespoons melted)

6½ ounces semisweet chocolate,
  broken into ½ ounce pieces

9 egg yolks

1 cup granulated sugar

4 egg whites

For the Chocolate Ganache:

1 cup hazelnuts

3½ cups heavy cream

4 tablespoons unsalted butter

¼ cup granulated sugar

2 pounds semisweet chocolate,
  broken into ½-ounce pieces

For the Raspberry Filling:

½ pint red raspberries

2 tablespoons granulated sugar

Lightly coat bottom and sides of two 10 by 15-inch baking sheets with melted butter. Line each sheet with parchment paper and lightly coat parchment paper with more melted butter. Set aside.

Preheat oven to 325 degrees. Heat 1 inch water in bottom half of a double boiler over medium heat. Place remaining half pound butter and 6½ ounces semisweet chocolate in top half of double boiler. Tightly cover top with film wrap. Heat for 10 to 12 minutes. Remove from heat, stir until smooth and hold at room temperature.

Place egg yolks and 1 cup sugar in the bowl of an electric mixer fitted with a paddle. Beat on high until lemon-colored and slightly thickened, about 4 minutes. Scrape down the sides and beat on high for 2 more minutes.

While egg yolks are beating, whisk egg whites in a large stainless steel bowl until stiff but not dry, 3 to 4 minutes.

Using a rubber spatula, fold melted chocolate mixture into beaten egg yolk mixture. Add a quarter of the beaten egg whites and stir to incorporate. Gently fold in remaining egg whites.

Divide between prepared baking sheets, spreading evenly and bake on the top and middle shelves in preheated oven, until a toothpick inserted in center comes out clean, 20 to 22 minutes. Rotate cakes from top to bottom about halfway through baking time. Remove cakes from oven and cool in baking sheets for 30 minutes.

While cakes are cooling, toast hazelnuts for ganache. Skin toasted hazelnuts, and allow nuts to cool to room temperature. In a food processor fitted with a metal blade, chop nuts into ⅛-inch pieces.

Invert a cake onto a large cutting board (or use corrugated cardboard cut to slightly overlap a 10 by 15-inch baking sheet), and refrigerate for 30 minutes. Hold remaining sheet cake at room temperature until needed.

To prepare ganache, heat heavy cream, 4 tablespoons butter and ¼ cup sugar in a 2½-quart saucepan over medium-high heat, stirring to dissolve sugar. Bring mixture to a boil. Place 2 pounds semisweet chocolate in a stainless steel bowl. Pour boiling cream over chocolate and let stand for 6 to 7 minutes. Stir until smooth.

Combine 3 cups ganache with chopped hazelnuts. Hold this mixture at room temperature to use for filling. Remove 1 more cup ganache and refrigerate for 1 hour (this will be used to decorate the diamonds). Keep remaining ganache at room temperature until needed.

Now make raspberry filling by puréeing raspberries and 2 tablespoons sugar in a food processor, fitted with a metal blade, for 12 to 15 seconds. Strain purée directly into a stainless steel bowl. Cover with film wrap and refrigerate until needed.

To assemble and decorate diamonds, remove cake from refrigerator. Using a cake spatula, spread raspberry purée over the chilled, inverted cake layer. Spread evenly to the edges. Spread ganache and hazelnut mixture over raspberry purée, evenly to the edges of cake. Invert the other cake layer on top of ganache-covered cake. Remove parchment paper and gently press the cakes together. Place entire cake in freezer for 1 hour.

Remove cake from freezer. Using a very sharp, serrated knife, cut away uneven edges so that it measures 9 by 13½-inches. Use a serrated slicer to cut cake widthwise into 9 1½-inch wide strips. Trim a 1-inch diagonally-cut piece from each end of each strip and cut the strip diagonally 3 times to form 4 uniformly-sized diamonds per strip.

Place a cooling rack on a baking sheet with sides. Put 9 to 12 diamonds onto cooling rack. Spoon 2 tablespoons room-temperature ganache over each diamond, allowing flowing ganache to coat top and sides. Using a fork, remove ganache-covered diamonds from cooling rack and place them on a baking sheet covered with parchment paper and refrigerate. Scrape ganache from first baking sheet and return to bowl of room-temperature ganache. Warm ganache to proper consistency over hot water. Continue this procedure until all diamonds are covered with ganache and have been refrigerated for at least 20 minutes.

Transfer refrigerated ganache to a pastry bag fitted with a medium-sized star tip. Decorate each diamond with a ganache star. Refrigerate diamonds for at least 1 hour before serving. Allow diamonds to come to room temperature 15 to 20 minutes before serving.

Makes 36 diamonds.

Adapted from *Death by Chocolate* (Rizzoli International Publications, 1993).

The Essential Chocolate Mousses

Dark Chocolate Mousse

3 ounces unsweetened chocolate,
    broken into ½-ounce pieces

2 cups heavy cream

¾ cup granulated sugar

White Chocolate Mousse

10 ounces white chocolate,
    broken into ½-ounce pieces

4 tablespoons water

2 cups heavy cream

To make Dark Chocolate Mousse, heat 1 inch water in bottom half of a double boiler over medium heat. Place unsweetened chocolate in top half of double boiler. Tightly cover top with film wrap and heat for 4 to 5 minutes. Remove from heat and stir until smooth. Transfer melted chocolate to a stainless steel bowl, using a rubber spatula to remove all chocolate from double boiler.

Place heavy cream and sugar in the well-chilled bowl of an electric mixer fitted with a well-chilled balloon whip. Mix on medium until soft peaks form, 4 to 5 minutes.

Using a hand-held whisk, vigorously whisk 1½ cups whipped cream into melted chocolate, scrape down the bowl with a rubber spatula and continue to whisk until cream and chocolate are smooth and completely incorporated. Add combined whipped cream and chocolate to remaining whipped cream and use the rubber spatula to fold together until smooth.

Transfer Dark Chocolate Mousse to a plastic container and refrigerate for 2 to 3 hours before serving.

For White Chocolate Mousse, heat 1 inch water in bottom half of a double boiler over low heat. When water is hot (do not allow to simmer), place white chocolate and 4 tablespoons water in top half of double boiler. Using a rubber spatula, constantly stir white chocolate and water until melted, 4 to 5 minutes. Remove from heat and keep at room temperature until needed.

Place heavy cream in the well-chilled bowl of an electric mixer fitted with a well-chilled balloon whip. Mix on high until stiff, about 1 minute. Remove bowl from mixer. Using a hand-held whisk, vigorously whisk one-third of the whipped cream into melted white chocolate. Scrape down bowl with a rubber spatula, and continue to whisk until smooth and thoroughly combined. Add combined whipped cream and white chocolate to remaining whipped cream and use a rubber spatula to fold together until smooth.

Transfer White Chocolate Mousse to a plastic container and refrigerate for 2 to 3 hours before serving.

Yields 1 quart of each mousse.

Adapted from *Death by Chocolate* (Rizzoli International Publications, 1993).

Jim Dodge

"Make sure you are using quality ingredients."

The way Jim Dodge sees it, people have to eat to live, so most of them will learn to cook something, if only for survival's sake. They don't have to learn to bake. That is where Dodge enters the picture. A nationally-renowned pastry chef and baking instructor, Dodge understands that even the best cooks don't always know what they are doing when it comes to baking. "People are intimidated about baking and my objective is to give them confidence," he said.

What most students don't realize is how the quality of the ingredients plays a major role in the success or failure of their baking. Baking involves chemistry. The amount of water in butter, for instance, will determine how soft pie dough will be and how difficult it will be to work with. Dense European butters, which have been churned to have less water, are preferred for making pastry because they will stay solid longer and will produce more pliable dough for rolling. It is these specifics of pastry making that are the hallmark of Dodge's teaching.

Want your eggs to beat up higher and lighter? Get ones from a hen that wasn't stressed—Dodge prefers eggs from free-range chickens. "What I've always done is stress the importance of the ingredients—what to look for when buying eggs, what kind of butter to buy, how to inspect the butter—I talk about ingredients a lot," he says. Better ingredients will produce a better product, but also will make the baking process easier and help to guarantee success.

Dodge grew up in New Hampshire, born into the seventh generation of a family-run hotel. He started working in the hospitality field at age ten, shoveling snow, tending the flower beds, weeding the vegetable garden, or doing whatever else needed to be done at the resort. But it was in the kitchen where he felt most at home, and when the opportunity came about in his early twenties to apprentice with Swiss Pastry Chef Fritz Albicken, his family encouraged him to go. He learned from bakers whose craft was so finely honed they could tell how much a scoop of flour or sugar weighed just by looking at it. They baked by sight, touch and intuition that came from years of practice.

While he left his family's resort, Dodge didn't leave hotel work. He found jobs as a hotel pastry chef in Florida and the Grand Hotel on Michigan's Mackinac Island, before becoming executive pastry chef for the Stamford Court Hotel in San Francisco, where he became nationally-known. While in San Francisco, Dodge met Mary Risley, owner of the Tante Marie Cooking School, who encouraged him to teach, and who Dodge says, taught him how to be a teacher. After his acclaimed book, *The American Baker*, was released in 1985, he began to teach at schools across the country, including the Zona Spray Cooking School. For traveling cooking teachers, Dodge said the Zona Spray stood out. The students were enthusiastic and the staff was exceptionally prepared.

Over the years Dodge co-owned a restaurant, American Pie, in Japan and was a frequent teacher of American baking techniques in that country. He later joined the staff of the New England Culinary Institute, where he taught for many years and served as vice president. He is currently based in San Francisco where he serves as director of the specialty culinary programs for Bon Appétit Management Company and still teaches at Tante Marie.

Warm Pear Tart

For the tart dough:

8 tablespoons cold, unsalted butter

2 teaspoons sugar

¼ teaspoon salt

1½ cups all-purpose flour

⅓ cup heavy whipping cream

For the poached pears:

4 pears

2 cups sugar

3 cups water

1 vanilla bean

2 teaspoons all-purpose flour

1 teaspoon orange zest

To prepare dough, cut butter into inch cubes. Combine with sugar, salt and flour. Mix to a coarse meal. Add cream and mix until dough comes together. Wrap and chill dough until needed.

To prepare pears, peel, core and cut pears in half. Bring to a boil sugar, water and vanilla bean. Add pears and continue cooking at a low simmer, only until pears are tender. Remove from heat and cool. Preheat oven to 400 degrees. Roll out dough into a 9-inch circle. Line bottom of an 8-inch pie plate and trim edges so they are even. Sprinkle bottom with flour and orange zest. Arrange pear halves over pastry shell.

Bake for 20 to 25 minutes, until crust is cooked. Cool in pan on a rack. Serve with Brandied Chocolate Sauce (recipe follows).

Makes 8 servings.

Brandied Chocolate Sauce

8 ounces semi-sweet chocolate

½ cup heavy cream

¼ cup brandy

Melt the chocolate in a double boiler over simmering water. Stir in the cream and then the brandy. Spoon the sauce over the top of the fruit in each slice.

Chocolate and Coconut Cream Cake

For the cake:

6 tablespoons unsalted butter, soft

1 cup sugar

1 large egg, beaten

1 cup all-purpose flour

1 teaspoon baking powder

⅓ cup unsweetened cocoa powder

½ cup milk

For the coconut cream:

1 small coconut

2½ cups whipping cream

4 tablespoons sugar

4 ounces white chocolate

Preheat oven to 350 degrees and adjust oven rack to middle lower level. Butter an 8 by 2-inch cake pan. Line bottom with parchment paper and dust insides with flour.

Using a corkscrew, screw out three eyes of coconut and drain juice into a bowl. Strain juice through a sieve and chill, covered, until needed. Place coconut on a heavy brown paper bag and working outside or on a hard surface, hit coconut with a hammer, breaking into large pieces. Use an oyster knife to remove coconut meat from shell. Leave thin brown skin on the meat, it will add color and flavor.

On a cutting board, cut meat into 1-inch pieces. Chop by hand into ¼-inch chunks or use a food processor, using pulse action. Measure 1 cup coconut for use. Freeze remaining coconut in a sealed plastic container for another recipe.

In a heavy 1-quart saucepan, combine 1 cup cream, 1 cup chopped coconut meat and 2 tablespoons sugar and heat to a boil over a moderately-high flame. Reduce to a simmer and cook for 20 minutes. Set aside to cool or cool over a bowl of ice water, stirring occasionally.

Grate chocolate through a large-hole grater. Set aside until needed. Whip 1½ cups cream and 2 tablespoons sugar to soft peaks. Fold 1 cup whipped cream into the cooled coconut cream.

To assemble cake: Moisten layers with reserved coconut juice. Spread coconut cream evenly over 1 layer. Center second layer on top of cream. Spread remaining cream over top and sides. Gently cup grated chocolate in your hand. Press chocolate against the side, opening your hand to conform to the round edge. Sprinkle remaining chocolate on top. Cover and chill until ready to serve.

Elinor Klivans

"Have a good time."

There's just something about a cake. It's sweet, but not too sweet, just sweet enough, really. A cake has enough sugar to enhance the flavors of the other ingredients in its mix, but not enough to overpower them. And all of these reasons are why it is Elinor Klivans' favorite dessert to bake.

"It's not super sweet. It has just enough sweetness to bring out the other flavors," Klivans said. "I don't like to bury things in sugar. You want to taste the flavor of it. Sugar brings out of the flavor of it to a point," she says.

As you might expect, she has given this some thought. She's had plenty of experience with all of the baked goods—cookies, pies, brownies, cakes. She has done all of the comparisons. Klivans prefers cakes to pies because she can't see why one wouldn't want to eat ripe delicious fruits right out of hand. "I don't like to cook fruit. If I'm going to eat a peach, I want to eat a peach. I love fruit in the raw. When it's summer and fruit is in season, I just want to eat it as simply as possible. If I'm buying peaches, I'm not going to make a pie. I'm going to eat one every morning for breakfast." So when she chooses cake as her favorite, you know it's because it has a purity of flavor that appeals to her.

And now you understand why Klivans' name is synonymous with baker. She has more than a dozen cookbooks to her name, including ones she penned for Williams-Sonoma, and she is a name that home bakers rely on for her successful recipes. She has studied, practiced, written about or taught baking for more than thirty years.

Klivans' obsession with all things that come out of the oven started at a young age, when she would bake with her mother growing up in Lakeland, Florida. "My mom was a home baker, and we would bake together and I always thought it was fun," she said.

After marrying, Klivans moved around a bit, from San Francisco and later back to Miami, and wherever she landed, she would take cooking classes from whatever experts happened to be visiting her current city. In 1981, after moving to Camden, Maine, Klivans began putting her class work to use when she started baking for a local restaurant, Peter Ott's. For twelve years, she was pastry chef at the restaurant, where she had the freedom to experiment, try out new recipes and construct menu after menu of desserts and baked goods. She also went to France, where she studied pastry at LaVarenne and Lenôtre cooking schools. Later she took lessons from Swiss-born Pastry Chef and Master Chocolatier Albert Kumin, who was the original pastry chef at Manhattan's Four Seasons restaurant when it opened in 1959, and who later served as White House pastry chef.

After her years in the pastry kitchen, Klivans decided she wanted to work on a book. In 1994, her first book, *Bake and Freeze Desserts*, was released to critical acclaim.

Klivans taught at the Zona Spray Cooking School in 1997. She recalls that the class was made up of a mix of young and old, all of whom had a keen interest in baking. "They were really nice Midwestern people," she said.

When she teaches, Klivans said she encourages her students to just "have a good time." "What's the worst that can happen? You throw away $2, $4, or $5 worth of ingredients, and you can do it again," she said. But the best that can happen, Klivans said, is a dessert that comes out perfectly. "It's so fabulous when it comes out successfully."

Mocha Confetti Chiffon Cake

For the Chiffon Cake:

1⅓ cups cake flour

1 teaspoon baking powder

1½ cups sugar

1½ cups (9 ounces) miniature
   semisweet chocolate chips

10 large egg whites,
   at room temperature

¾ teaspoon cream of tartar

¼ teaspoon salt

3 large egg yolks

2 tablespoons instant decaffeinated
   coffee granules, dissolved in ¼ cup
   warm water

2 teaspoons vanilla extract

For the Coffee Glaze:

1 cup powdered sugar

1 teaspoon instant decaffeinated coffee
   granules, dissolved in 2 tablespoons
   plus 1 teaspoon warm water

To prepare cake, position an oven rack in middle of oven. Preheat oven to 350 degrees. Line bottom of a 9½ or 10-inch tube pan with at least 3¾-inch-high sides with parchment or wax paper. Do not grease pan.

Sift flour and baking powder into a medium bowl. Whisk in ¾ cup sugar. Set aside.

Put chocolate chips in the work bowl of a food processor fitted with the steel knife and process, about 30 seconds. Some of the chocolate chips will be finely grated and some will form small crumbs. Set aside.

Put egg whites, cream of tartar and salt in the clean large bowl of an electric mixer and with clean dry beaters, beat on low speed until egg whites are foamy. Increase speed to medium-high, and beat just until soft peaks form. Slowly add remaining ¾ cup sugar, 1 tablespoon at a time. Put egg yolks in a small bowl. Whisk in dissolved coffee and vanilla. Pour egg yolk mixture over beaten egg whites and use a large rubber spatula to fold yolk mixture into egg whites. Fold chocolate chips into egg mixture. Gently fold flour mixture into egg mixture ¼ cup at a time. Use a ¼ cup measuring cup to measure and sprinkle the flour mixture. Pour batter into prepared pan. Smooth top with a thin metal spatula. Bake about 1 hour and 5 minutes. Insert a toothpick in the center; when toothpick comes out clean, cake is done.

If the tube pan has feet, invert cake onto them. Or invert tube pan over the neck of a bottle. Cool thoroughly, about 2 hours. Use a small sharp knife to loosen the cake carefully from the sides and the center tube. Invert cake onto a cake plate or cardboard cake circle. Carefully remove and discard the paper lining the cake bottom. Turn cake right side up.

Prepare glaze by putting powdered sugar in a small bowl. Stir dissolved coffee into powdered sugar until mixture is smooth. If glaze is too thick to be poured, add 1 teaspoon water. Immediately use a small spoon to drizzle glaze in zigzag lines over top. Let some glaze drip down onto sides; glaze will firm as it sits.

Makes one cake, 12 servings.

Cranberry Hazelnut Pie

For the crust:

1 cup all-purpose flour

⅓ cup cake flour

½ teaspoon salt

1 tablespoon sugar

6 tablespoons (¾ stick) cold unsalted butter, cut in 4 pieces

2 tablespoons plus 2 teaspoons cold vegetable shortening

3½ to 4 tablespoons ice water

sifted cake flour for rolling pie crust

For the filling:

1½ cups peeled, toasted hazelnuts, chopped coarsely

3 large eggs

1 cup packed light brown sugar

¾ cup pure maple syrup

¼ cup (half a stick) unsalted butter, melted and cooled

¼ teaspoon salt

1 teaspoon vanilla extract

1 cup fresh (or previously frozen and defrosted) unsweetened cranberries, coarsely chopped

To prepare crust, lightly grease a 10-inch pie pan with vegetable shortening, or alternatively, spray pie pan with a vegetable oil spray.

Put all-purpose flour, cake flour, salt and sugar in the large bowl of an electric mixer and mix on low speed just to blend ingredients, about 10 seconds. Stop mixer, add butter and shortening and mix just until butter and shortening pieces are the size of small lima beans, about 20 seconds. They will not all be the same size and you will still see loose flour. Slowly add water, one tablespoon at a time. Stop mixing as soon as mixture begins to hold together, about 20 seconds. You may not need all of the water. The dough will form large clumps and pull away from the sides of the bowl, but will not form a ball.

Turn dough mixture out onto a lightly floured rolling surface. With the heel of your hand, push dough down and forward against the rolling surface. Fold dough in half and repeat 6 times. The dough will now look smooth. Form dough into a round disk about 4 inches in diameter. Wrap dough in plastic wrap and chill in refrigerator for at least 20 minutes or as long as overnight.

Remove dough from refrigerator. If dough has become cold and hard, let sit at room temperature for 5 to 10 minutes, until easy to roll. Lightly flour rolling surface and rolling pin. Roll dough from the center out into a circle about 4 inches wider than the bottom of the pie pan. Don't flip dough over while rolling, but lift and turn dough several times as you roll, to prevent it from sticking to rolling surface. Roll dough circle over rolling pin and unroll onto pie pan. Press dough into pie pan. Trim edges evenly to overhang ¾-inch over edge. Press a ½-inch edge of dough under itself to form an even edge. Form a crimped edge around top by pressing dough between your thumb and forefinger.

For filling, position an oven rack in the middle of the oven and preheat oven to 400 degrees. Put eggs in a large bowl and, with a large spoon or an electric mixer on low speed, mix egg yolks and whites together. Add brown sugar and stir until eggs and brown sugar are combined thoroughly. Mix in maple syrup, melted butter, salt and vanilla. Stir in chopped hazelnuts and chopped cranberries. Pour filling into pie crust. Bake 10 minutes. Reduce oven temperature to 350 degrees and continue baking until filling is set, 30 to 35 minutes. Check to see that pie is set by giving it a gentle shake; center should remain firm. Cool thoroughly at room temperature.

Makes a 10-inch pie, which serves 8 to 10.

Wendy Kromer

"Pursue your passions."

Wendy Kromer has followed her passions in life; down a Paris runway, into New York pastry school, onto the pages of *Martha Stewart Living* and along a fondant-covered path all the way back home.

Home is Sandusky, Ohio, where Kromer returned in 2005 after spending more than twenty years living abroad and in New York, where she made her mark as the artist behind many of the elegant wedding cakes that grace the pages of *Martha Stewart's Weddings* magazine. She couldn't bear the thought of her family home being sold, so she pulled up stakes and moved her business from New York to Sandusky. She has been a visiting instructor at the Western Reserve School of Cooking since 2005.

In 2007, Kromer co-authored the book *Martha Stewart's Wedding Cakes,* which is filled with more than a hundred of her cake designs. Her favorites—yes, she will admit to having favorites—include one styled after Wedgewood china, another after eyelet creamware and cakes done in blue and brown damask. Kromer's cakes embody the elegant simplicity that is the hallmark of Martha Stewart style. It was a style that Kromer had already embraced for her designs as she began building her cake portfolio. The irony is that it was a gaudy design—a cake Kromer decorated to look like a Mae West-style corset—that first caught the attention of *Martha Stewart* editors.

Kromer studied fashion design and merchandising at Notre Dame College in Cleveland. She dreamed of becoming a women's fashion buyer, but when she graduated in 1983, she found a scarcity of jobs in fashion beyond retail sales clerk. Her parents were heading to Paris that summer to visit Kromer's aunt and uncle, and since she hadn't found a job, she went along. Her aunt suggested that she look for modeling jobs in Paris, since Europeans at the time were big on "the American look." Her parents returned home in two weeks, but Kromer stayed and after a year was supporting herself as a model. For the next ten years, Kromer worked the runways of France, Italy, Germany and Japan.

By the time she passed thirty, Kromer knew her modeling days were numbered and she started to think about what she might do next. A dessert lover and long-time baker, she began to consider the idea of a career in pastry. She moved to New York and eventually enrolled in the professional pastry and baking program at the Peter Kump School of Culinary Art. Kromer knew on her first day of class that she had found her calling. She followed school with time working for New York cake designer Colette Peters, who she credits with teaching her the business of running a bakery and also with introducing her to rolled fondant icing, gum paste flowers and techniques for sculpting cakes.

In 1995, Kromer entered her corset cake in the Manhattan Culinary Art Show. Drawing on her fashion background, Kromer felt the fitted lines of the corset would be a good way to showcase her piping skills. Her creation of red and black and gold stood alone in a sea of traditional wedding cakes covered in flowers. Kromer was convinced her cake would offend the judges, but she returned several days later to discover that it had delighted instead. The cake caught the attention of *Martha Stewart Living*, and Kromer has been a contributing editor ever since. As her work with Martha Stewart flourished, so did her own cake business. She made Brooke Shields' wedding cake, and was hired by Oprah Winfrey to create a seventieth birthday cake for Maya Angelou. Along with her celebrated clientele, Kromer makes cakes for brides in Ohio and Michigan, sells her decorations wholesale and runs a bakery and café in Sandusky, where her latest passion is redevelopment of the city's historic downtown.

In class, Kromer teaches the essentials of wedding cake baking and decorating, demonstrating techniques in fondant, butter cream, gum paste and chocolate. But her most important lesson is one she learned outside of the classroom: to follow one's passions. "I kept pursuing the things I felt passionate about. This is a 365-day-a-year-thing. There is no taking a day off. So you better enjoy getting up every day and going in. Otherwise you are just going to fail."

White Butter Cake

This versatile cake is best baked the day before it will be served (wrap well and refrigerate). To add moisture and flavor, brush the layers with simple syrup. We like to use 2-inch high pans when baking cakes. With this recipe, we will fill our pans between ½ to ⅔ full. In general, most white cakes made with butter taste best, freshly baked. However, this recipe freezes beautifully, as long as it is very well-wrapped with plastic wrap. I do not recommend freezing for longer than one month.

14 tablespoons (1¾ sticks) unsalted butter, at room temperature, plus more for the pans

3¼ cups sifted cake flour (not self-rising), plus more for the pans

1½ tablespoons baking powder

¼ teaspoon salt

1 cup plus 2 tablespoons milk

1 tablespoon pure vanilla extract

1¾ cups sugar

5 large egg whites, at room temperature

Preheat oven to 350 degrees. Brush cake pans with butter. Line with parchment paper; butter parchment and dust with flour, tapping out any excess. Set aside.

Whisk together flour, baking powder and salt into a medium bowl; set aside. Stir milk and vanilla to combine; set aside. In the bowl of an electric mixer fitted with the paddle attachment, cream butter until pale and fluffy, about 3 minutes. Add sugar in a steady stream; mix until pale and fluffy, about 3 minutes.

Reduce speed to low. Add flour mixture in three additions, alternating with milk mixture and beginning and ending with flour; mix just until combined.

In a clean mixing bowl, whisk egg whites just until stiff peaks form. Fold one-third of the egg whites into batter to lighten. Gently fold in remaining whites in two batches. Divide batter among prepared pans; smooth tops with an offset spatula. Firmly tap pans on a work surface to release any air bubbles.

Bake until a cake tester inserted into centers comes out clean and tops are springy to the touch. Let cool in pans on wire racks for 15 minutes. Invert cakes onto racks. Remove parchment; reinvert and cool completely.

Makes 6 cups batter, enough for two 6-inch round layers with some batter left over, or two 7-inch round layers.

From *Martha Stewart's Wedding Cakes* by Martha Stewart, with Wendy Kromer. Copyright © 2007 by Martha Stewart Living Omnimedia, Inc. Used by permission of Clarkson Potter.

Fresh Raspberry Preserves

This recipe halves nicely.

7½ pounds fresh
  (or frozen) raspberries

10 cups sugar (77½ ounces)

18 ounces apple jelly

Place all ingredients into large, heavy bottomed pot. Set over medium heat and stir to combine. Bring to a simmer, stirring occasionally and cook until preserves thicken, approximately 30 minutes. To see if preserves are finished, take a teaspoon of the hot liquid and place into small bowl. Let cool a few minutes. The preserves will thicken to a gel-like consistency when ready.

Allow mixture to cool and strain through a sieve to remove seeds. Pour into quart containers. Refrigerate.

Yields 4 quarts (128 ounces).

Recipe courtesy of Wendy Kromer Confections.

Vanilla Swiss Meringue Buttercream

This is one of my favorite buttercreams! Don't skimp on ingredients here...good quality butter and vanilla extract are essential. Swiss Meringue Buttercream lends itself beautifully to other flavors. Try these options, (flavor "to taste"): chocolate (white, dark or milk), must be good quality, and chocolate must be melted/cooled; fruit purées (passion fruit, black currant, mango, raspberry, etc.), reduce purée and let cool before stirring into the buttercream; espresso, use fresh, cooled espresso; liqueurs, Grand Marnier, dark rum, crème de cassis, Limoncello, Frangelico, Amaretto, etc.; peanut butter, use smooth varieties; Nutella; spices, cinnamon, nutmeg etc.; and salted caramel.

10 liquid ounces egg whites
(approximately 10 large egg whites)

2½ cups (20 ounces) granulated sugar

2 pounds unsalted butter,
at room temperature

1 tablespoon pure vanilla extract
(if adding vanilla bean, reduce to 2
teaspoons vanilla extract and add the
seeds from one vanilla bean pod)

Place egg whites and sugar in heatproof bowl of an electric mixer, set over a pan of simmering water. Whisk constantly until sugar is dissolved and mixture registers 140 degrees on an instant-read thermometer, 2 to 3 minutes.

Transfer bowl to mixer; fit mixer with whisk attachment. Beat on high until mixture is fluffy and cooled, about 10 minutes.

Reduce speed to medium-low; add butter ¼ cup at a time, mixing well after each addition. Add vanilla/vanilla bean.

Makes about 9 cups.

Note: If buttercream has a curdled appearance it is because the meringue mixture and the butter were not at the same temperature before combining. To correct this problem, use the "heat and beat" method to bring it back together. Simply place mixing bowl over hot water bath and stir with a spatula—mixture will come together.

Recipe courtesy of Wendy Kromer Confections.

Emily Luchetti

"Don't get so worried and nervous about it. Follow your common sense and enjoy it."

Emily Luchetti is an artist who has chosen butter, flour, sugar and chocolate as her medium. Her desserts have graced the tables of some of San Francisco's finest restaurants ever since she slipped out of the main kitchen and into the corner occupied by the pastry chef.

It was 1987 and Luchetti had spent three years in the kitchen of the city's Stars Restaurant, when she abandoned the salty side for the sweet. "My brain works better using the ingredients in a pastry kitchen versus a savory kitchen," Luchetti explains.

In all, it was just eight years after college when Luchetti found her life's work. The Corning, New York, native graduated from Ohio's Dennison University in 1979 with a degree in sociology, but wasn't sure what she wanted to do after graduation. Returning home to New York, she decided on cooking school, but after four years of college, wasn't up for too many more years of study. She eventually enrolled in the New York Restaurant School, and after finishing the program, worked at various New York establishments, including the famed Silver Palate gourmet food shop, before accepting a job to be part of the kitchen staff when Jeremiah Tower opened his celebrated Stars restaurant in 1984.

By this time, Luchetti had met her future husband, who was from the Bay area, so the job meant a move back home for him, while Luchetti got to work in San Francisco, which was emerging as one of the country's most important food cities. After three years in the kitchen, Luchetti was appointed head pastry chef, a job she would hold for the next nine years.

It was during her time at Stars that Luchetti penned her first two books—*Stars Desserts*, which was released in 1991, followed by *Four Star Desserts* in 1995. It was also at this time that she received an invitation to Hudson, Ohio, from Zona Spray. She can still visualize the room, with its small kitchen and the enthusiastic, friendly students.

When she teaches, Luchetti said she tries to take the anxiety out of baking for her students. "I think people, when they think about baking, get nervous. It's not like taking a biology final or a chemistry final," she said. Luchetti tries to tell her students, "Don't get so worried and nervous about it. Follow your common sense and enjoy it. You may make something ten times and the tenth time it will come out perfect, but the other times, it's probably pretty close and really good and close to perfect and surely good enough to eat."

Since the 1990s, Luchetti has moved on to serve as executive pastry chef at Farallon restaurant and the Waterbar restaurant, both in San Francisco. She has written two more books and in 2004, was named Pastry Chef of the Year by the James Beard Foundation.

Luchetti continues to find her inspiration for her dessert creations in classic, old-fashioned desserts, which she presents with her own personal twist. Using the calendar as her guide, she focuses on creating seasonal sweets that are old and familiar and at the same time new and interesting. In the summer, she works with berries and other fresh fruit. In the winter, her tastes lean toward chocolate. Always, she approaches her work by asking, "How do you make it taste better than it really is, but don't mess it up? How do you make it different and interesting?"

Bistro Apple Tart with Cider Caramel Glaze

1 package (17¼ ounces) frozen puff pastry, thawed

4 Granny Smith apples, peeled, cored and thinly sliced

2 tablespoons unsalted butter, melted

⅓ cup sugar

Caramel Cider Sauce (recipe follows)

whipped cream for garnish

Roll out each sheet of puff pastry to a 9 by 12-inch rectangle and cut 3 4-inch circles from each sheet (save scraps for another use or discard them). Place circles on parchment-lined baking sheets.

On each circle, arrange apple slices in overlapping rings to cover pastry. Brush with melted butter and sprinkle with sugar. If not baking tarts right away, store in refrigerator until ready to bake.

Bake tarts 15 to 20 minutes in a preheated 450-degree oven, until puffed and golden. Remove from oven and let cool 2 to 3 minutes. Drizzle with Caramel Cider Sauce and serve warm with a dollop of whipped cream.

Makes 6 tarts.

Caramel Cider Glaze

1½ cups sugar

¾ cup water

1 cup apple cider

In a medium saucepan, stir together sugar and water. Cook over medium heat until sugar dissolves. Increase to high heat and cook mixture until golden amber in color. Do not stir after you increase heat.

Remove saucepan from heat and stir in a few tablespoons of cider. Let caramel bubble and subside; add a few more tablespoons cider. Be careful—caramel will sputter as cider is added. Slowly add remaining cider.

Let sauce cool to room temperature. It can be made in advance and stored in refrigerator. Bring back to room temperature before using.

Adapted from Emily Luchetti, *Stars Desserts* (William Morrow, 1993).

Toasted Almond and Sour Cherry Strudel

2 cups dried sour cherries

1¼ cups granulated sugar

½ cup water

¼ cup honey

2½ cups (10 ounces)
   sliced almonds, toasted

1 teaspoon cinnamon

8 sheets phyllo

6 tablespoons (¾ stick)
   unsalted butter, melted

In a medium saucepan combine cherries, ¾ cup sugar, water and honey. Cook over medium heat until slightly syrupy. Remove from heat and stir in almonds. Set aside to cool.

In a small bowl, mix remaining ½ cup sugar with cinnamon. Stack phyllo and keep covered with plastic wrap and a damp towel. Remove one sheet and place lengthwise on work surface. Brush sheet with some melted butter and sprinkle with 2 teaspoons sugar mixture. Place a second sheet on top. Butter and sugar it. Continue stacking, buttering and sprinkling until there are four layers of phyllo.

Using remaining sheets, make a second stack of layers in the same manner. Preheat oven to 350 degrees.

Spread cherry-almond mixture over one stack of phyllo, leaving a ½-inch edge on all sides. Carefully lift and place second stack of phyllo on top of the cherry-almond mixture. From one of the short ends, roll phyllo into a cylinder. Tuck ends of the roll under the bottom. Brush top with any remaining butter and sprinkle any leftover cinnamon sugar on top. Bake until golden brown, 15 to 20 minutes. Slice and serve warm with whipped cream or ice cream.

Makes 6 to 8 servings.

Adapted from Emily Luchetti, *Four-Star Desserts* (HarperCollins Publishers, 1996).

Nick Malgieri

"Use the finest ingredients."

Nick Malgieri went to culinary school, because, after graduating with a degree in French, he couldn't imagine spending his days teaching high school students how to conjugate verbs. But he didn't escape the classroom. Instead, he spends his days teaching some of America's finest pastry chefs how to be better. Malgieri is one of America's foremost baking and pastry instructors.

He's taught at the Western Reserve School of Cooking so many times school records stopped tracking his visits. The file of his recipes bulges with cakes, pies and cookies. He teaches classes across the country and also is director of the pastry program at the Institute of Culinary Education in New York, where he counts Martha Stewart wedding cake designer Wendy Kromer among his students.

"I have to admit, I didn't know anything about baking until I started teaching. You get a completely different perspective on what you do when you see it through the eyes of other people," he says.

Over the course of his career, Malgieri has kept one foot in the world of professional baking and one in the world of home baking, a dual presence which has served him well in places like Hudson, Ohio, where the classes are typically a combination of home bakers and local professionals.

It's not surprising that Malgieri became a chef. Growing up in an Italian-American family in Newark, New Jersey, Malgieri said the kitchen was always the hub of his home. It was the place where his mother could be found cooking or ironing, and the place where he would sit and do his homework. His grandmother lived with his family and he was exposed to her love of baking from the time he was a young child.

After college, culinary school was always in the back of his mind, but even he could not have predicted his celebrated career. "I knew I always liked it, but you really don't know whether that is exactly what you are going to wind up doing for the rest of your life until you have some experience with it," he recalled.

He graduated from the Culinary Institute of America, apprenticed in Switzerland and worked in France before returning to New York. Formerly the executive pastry chef at the acclaimed Windows on the World restaurant, Malgieri has written nine books, which have received a list of accolades, including James Beard Foundation Cookbook Awards and the Julia Child Award from the International Association of Culinary Professionals.

When it comes to baking, Malgieri is a purist. He insists on the highest quality ingredients: butter, butter, always butter. (Don't even think of using vegetable shortening in one of his recipes.) The variables in baking are so great that introducing more variables with poor quality ingredients can turn the whole venture into a crap shoot, he contends. But the finest ingredients can turn even the most humble baked good into art. Malgieri prefers more basic items, a pie, a tart, or a pound cake, particularly if he is the one doing the entertaining. "I really like very simple things," he says. The following recipes are adapted from Nick Malgieri, author of *BAKE!* and *The Modern Baker.*

Cherry and Almond Tartlettes

The combination of cherries and almonds works well because the slight bitter almond flavor of the filling is perfect with the tartness of the cherries.

For the cookie dough:
1 stick unsalted butter
¼ cup sugar
1 teaspoon vanilla extract
1 egg yolk
1¼ cups cake flour

For the almond filling:
¼ pound almond paste
¼ cup sugar

1 egg yolk
1 teaspoon grated lemon zest
½ stick soft butter
1 egg
3 tablespoons flour
6 dozen canned or
    frozen sour cherries, drained
½ cup sliced almonds
confectioners' sugar for finishing

For dough, beat butter and sugar with the paddle on medium speed until very soft and light. Beat in vanilla and egg yolk and continue beating until smooth and shiny, about 3 more minutes. Stop mixer, sift cake flour and add to butter mixture. Pulse mixer on and off to incorporate flour. Scrape dough onto a piece of plastic wrap and chill until firm.

For almond filling, combine almond paste, sugar, egg yolk and lemon zest and beat by machine until smooth. Beat in butter, scrape bowl and beaters and beat in egg. Continue beating until light. Stir in flour.

Roll chilled cookie dough ⅛-inch thick on a floured surface. With a floured fluted cutter, cut dough into 24 disks. Line 24 tartlette pans with disks. Arrange 3 cherries in each dough-lined pan and pipe on almond filling to cover. Cover almond filling evenly with sliced almonds.

Bake tartlettes at 350 degrees for about 25 minutes, until dough is baked through and filling is set. Cool in pans, unmold and dust with confectioners' sugar.

Makes 24 tartlettes.

Lemon Cream Meringue Pie

I have never liked the idea of water as the main ingredient in a lemon meringue pie filling, so in this recipe milk replaces the water. It makes for a richer and more delicate flavor, but is still sharp enough to please the most dedicated lemon lovers. The Swiss meringue I use here is probably different from meringue pie toppings you have already encountered. Heating the egg whites and sugar together before whipping the meringue makes it more stable and less likely to weep after it is baked.

For the filling:

2 cups milk

⅔ cup sugar

3 to 4 medium lemons

¼ cup cornstarch

4 egg yolks

2 tablespoons unsalted butter, softened

For the meringue:

4 egg whites

⅔ cup sugar

pinch of salt

Flaky Pie Dough for a single-crust pie
(recipe follows)

To make filling, combine milk and sugar in a nonreactive saucepan, preferably enameled iron. Strip zest from lemons with a sharp vegetable peeler, making sure you remove yellow zest, but none of the white pith beneath. If you do remove some of the white pith, scrape it off strips of zest with the point of a paring knife and discard. Add zest to milk and sugar and bring to a simmer over low heat. Remove from heat and steep for 5 minutes. Remove strips of zest with a slotted spoon or skimmer and discard them.

Squeeze lemons to make ½ cup strained juice. Place juice in a mixing bowl and whisk in cornstarch and egg yolks.

Return milk and sugar mixture to a boil over low heat and whisk about a third of the boiling milk into lemon juice mixture. Return remaining milk and sugar mixture to a boil once more and whisk lemon juice and yolk mixture back into it, whisking constantly until filling comes to a boil and thickens. Boil, whisking constantly, for about 30 seconds. Remove from heat, whisk in butter and pour into a nonreactive bowl. Press plastic wrap against surface of filling and chill until it is approximately 75 degrees. (If you prepare filling in advance, let it come to room temperature before proceeding.)

Set an oven rack at the middle level and preheat to 350 degrees. Roll out dough to make a bottom crust and arrange in pan. Chill crust until firm.

To bake crust, pierce all over with the tines of a fork at ½-inch intervals. Line with a disk of parchment or wax paper and fill with cherry stones or dried beans. Bake

Famous Chefs & Fabulous Recipes

about 20 minutes, until lightly colored. Remove paper and beans and continue baking until crust is a deep golden brown. Cool crust on a rack.

Spread cooled filling evenly in cooled crust.

Set a rack at the middle level of the oven and preheat to 400 degrees.

To make meringue, bring a small pan of water to a boil. Lower heat so that water simmers. Combine egg whites, sugar and salt in the bowl of the mixer or, if you are using a hand whisk, another heat-proof bowl. Place bowl over pan of simmering water and whisk gently for about 2 minutes, until egg whites are hot (about 140 degrees) and sugar has dissolved. Whip meringue on medium speed until cooled and able to hold a shape; it should not be dry. Distribute spoonfuls of meringue all over the top and use the back of a spoon or a small offset metal spatula to spread meringue evenly. It should cover the top of the pie and touch the edges of the crust all around. Here and there, bring up the surface of meringue so that it is swirled. Place pie on a cookie sheet and bake for 5 to 10 minutes, until meringue is colored evenly. Cool on a rack.

Makes 1 pie, 6 to 8 servings.

Flaky Pie Dough

Of all the pie doughs I have ever worked with, this is the best and easiest to prepare and roll out. Though it is not much effort to mix the dough by hand, I find that using a food processor makes it almost instant.

For a one-crust pie, about 10 ounces

1¼ cups all-purpose bleached flour

¼ teaspoon salt

⅛ teaspoon baking powder

8 tablespoons (1 stick) cold unsalted butter

2 to 3 tablespoons cold water

For a two-crust pie, about 1¼ pounds

2½ cups (about 11 ounces) all-purpose bleached flour

½ teaspoon salt

¼ teaspoon baking powder

16 tablespoons (2 sticks) cold unsalted butter

4 to 6 tablespoons cold water

To mix dough by hand, combine flour, salt and baking powder in a medium-sized mixing bowl and stir well to mix. Cut butter into 1-tablespoon pieces and add to dry ingredients. Toss once or twice to coat butter. Using your hands or a pastry blender, break butter into tiny pieces and pinch and squeeze into dry ingredients. Keep mixture uniform by occasionally reaching down to the bottom of the bowl and mixing all ingredients evenly together. Continue rubbing butter into dry ingredients until mixture resembles a coarse-ground cornmeal and no large pieces of butter remain visible.

Sprinkle the minimum amount of water over butter and flour mixture and stir gently with a fork. The dough should begin holding together. If mixture still appears dry and crumbly, add remaining water, 1 teaspoon at a time for the smaller quantity of dough, a tablespoon at a time for the larger quantity, until dough holds together easily.

Notes: The baking powder encourages the dough to puff slightly during baking so that it presses into the hot pan bottom and bakes through evenly. This helps prevent an underdone bottom crust.

The amount of water added to the dough is always variable. When the flour and butter are rubbed together to create a fine mixture and they have warmed slightly, the dough will absorb less water; when it is dry and cool, and a little under mixed, it will absorb more. Too little water makes a flaky crust that will crack when it is rolled out; too much water makes an elastic, bread-like crust that lacks flakiness. To avoid erring in either direction, use this simple test. After you have added the minimum amount of water, pick up several tablespoons of the dough and squeeze gently; if the dough holds together easily without cracks and dry areas, it has absorbed enough water. If it does not hold together, add remaining liquid about a teaspoon at a time, testing again after each addition.

This dough may be baked blind (without a filling) and used for one-crust pies with creamy fillings that are added after the crust is baked. It may also be used for 2-crust pies with fairly dry fillings, such as apple or mincemeat.

Adapted from *How to Bake* by Nick Malgieri (William Morrow, 1995).

Vermont Farmhouse Devil's Food Cake

This recipe was recently shared by Copeland Marks, the famous teacher of Asian and South American cooking. He suggests substituting canned Thai coconut milk, diluted with an equal quantity of water, for the sour cream and boiling water.

For the batter:

2½ cups cake flour

2 teaspoons baking soda

½ teaspoon salt

1 stick unsalted butter, softened

2½ cups dark brown sugar

3½ ounces unsweetened chocolate, melted and cooled

3 large eggs

½ cup sour cream

2 teaspoons vanilla extract

1 cup boiling water

Preheat oven to 350 degrees. Butter a 10-inch round cake pan and line bottom with a disk of parchment or wax paper.

Mix flour, baking soda and salt, sift once and set aside. With an electric mixer set at medium speed, beat butter until soft and light. Add sugar and continue beating until very light, about 5 minutes. Beat in chocolate, then eggs, one at a time, continuing to beat until light and smooth.

Beat in half the sour cream and half the flour mixture, scraping bowl and beater(s). Repeat with remaining sour cream and flour mixture, scraping again. Combine vanilla and boiling water and gently beat into batter. Pour batter into prepared pan and bake for about 45 minutes, until firm and well-risen. Cool in pan on rack for 5 minutes. Unmold and cool on a rack.

To finish, cover top with frosting, swirling from the center outward. To serve, cut with a moist knife, wiping the blade with a cloth between each slice.

Makes one 10-inch cake, serves 8 to 10.

Adapted from *How to Bake* by Nick Malgieri (William Morrow, 1995).

Old-Fashioned Boiled Frosting

3 egg whites	pinch of salt
⅔ cup sugar	2 tablespoons orange liqueur
⅓ cup light corn syrup	1 finely grated orange zest

For frosting, combine all ingredients, except zest, in bowl of mixer. Whisk to combine and place over a pan of simmering water, gently whisking until mixture is hot and sugar is dissolved. Whip on medium speed until cooled, but not dry. Beat in orange zest.

Makes enough frosting for one 10-inch cake.

Alice Medrich

"The details do make a difference."

T he next time you eat a chocolate truffle from your favorite confectionary, thank Alice Medrich. America's queen of chocolate introduced the country to truffles at her groundbreaking Berkley, California, store Cocolat. Not a bad feat for someone who grew up in a Hershey Bar-eating family.

Medrich moved to Paris in 1973 for her husband's job and began to discover food on a new level. As she explored, took classes and sampled from the finest pastry shops, her chocolate receptors came alive. The chocolate was dark and rich and not overly sweet. Chocolate was about the chocolate, not about the sugar. True revelation came when her landlady made her a batch of homemade truffles for her birthday. Tiny, bittersweet and dusted in cocoa, they were like nothing Medrich had ever experienced. Madame Estelle presented Medrich with the recipe as a going-away present.

Not sure what she wanted to do after her year in France, Medrich began taking business classes in California and started making truffles, experimenting with Madame Estelle's hand-written recipe. "I worked the recipe over until it tasted like how I remembered hers," she recalls.

Eventually she offered them for sale at Victoria Wise's Pig-by-the-Tail charcuterie shop in Berkley, across the street from Alice Waters' famed Chez Panisse restaurant. The truffles were new and different and well-received by the Berkley community. Medrich began experimenting with more complex desserts, taking limited orders from Wise's customers for a special weekly creation. As her dessert work became more sought after, Medrich knew that she wanted to open her own store, but also knew that more training was in order. She returned to Paris to study at Ecole Lenôtre, the school run by Gaston Lenôtre, who founded the country's chain of famous pastry shops.

Medrich opened Cocolat in 1976, in the same block as Chez Panisse and Pig-by-the-Tail, helping to create Berkley's famous "gourmet ghetto." She offered her signature truffles and a wide array of chocolate desserts, as well as some relief from chocolate—a linzertorte and a lemon mousse were among customer favorites. Her first book, inspired by her store, *Cocolat: Extraordinary Chocolate Desserts*, appeared in 1990 and won the James Beard Award for Best Cookbook of the Year. Seven other books and many more awards have followed.

In 1995, she came to the Zona Spray Cooking School to teach her chocolate techniques and is now surprised at the complexity of the recipes she taught at the time. She still teaches several times a year, mostly in California, but now doesn't worry about finding one recipe that will show off four or five pastry techniques. Rather, she has simplified formulas, and given intense attention to detail. She painstakingly tests and retests recipes, to determine the best methods for each step in the process, including selecting the best ingredients. Medrich values the elegance of simplicity in her foods and believes in using the highest-quality ingredients and then essentially creating formulas that won't upstage them. In the end, she achieves recipes that will ensure success for the home baker.

"The details do make a difference. Every different thing you do will make a difference. The details are the ingredients and the technique. Increasingly, I like people to understand that if all those details are in place, then simplicity is almost always the best approach to anything," Medrich said. "I believe even more than ever if you have a stunning ingredient, an ingredient that you want to honor, keeping everything simple is the best way to appreciate that ingredient," she said.

Hot Chocolate Soufflés

8 ounces semisweet or bittersweet chocolate (not to exceed 62% cacao), very finely chopped

1 tablespoon unsalted butter

1 tablespoon flour

½ cup milk

3 egg yolks

1 teaspoon vanilla extract

4 egg whites

⅛ teaspoon cream of tartar

⅓ cup sugar

2 to 3 tablespoons powdered sugar, to dust top (optional)

1 cup heavy cream

1 teaspoon vanilla extract

2 to 3 teaspoons sugar, or to taste

Preheat oven to 375 degrees. Butter 8 soufflé cups (4½ ounces each) and sprinkle with granulated sugar.

In a small saucepan, melt butter. Add flour, stir and cook for a minute or two. Add milk, whisking briskly over medium heat until mixture forms a smooth sauce. Continue cooking and whisking, until mixture thickens (1 to 2 minutes). Take off heat and whisk in egg yolks and vanilla. Add chocolate and whisk until chocolate is melted and mixture is completely smooth. Transfer mixture to a medium-large bowl. Set aside.

Beat egg whites with cream of tartar in a clean, dry bowl at medium speed until soft peaks form. Gradually sprinkle in sugar and continue to beat, at high speed, until whites are stiff but not dry. Fold a fourth of the whites into chocolate mixture to lighten and fold in remaining whites.

Divide mixture among prepared cups, filling them about ¾ full. If desired, soufflés may be prepared to this point, covered and refrigerated, to be baked the next day.

Bake on a cookie sheet in preheated oven until a wooden skewer plunged into the center tests still moist but not completely gooey or runny, 15 to 17 minutes. Soufflés will puff and crack before they are done. Remove soufflés from oven, sift powdered sugar over them, if desired, and serve immediately with slightly sweetened whipped cream.

Makes 8 servings.

Note: These soufflés seem to be indestructible. They always rise, and they can even be prepared a day ahead. If soufflés normally scare you, I urge you to throw caution to the wind and try these.

Hot Chocolate Soufflés adapted and reprinted from *Chocolate Holidays*, copyright © 2001 by Alice Medrich, used by permission of Artisan, a division of Workman Publishing, Inc. All rights reserved.

Black Bottom Banana Napoleons

5 tablespoons sugar

4 teaspoons flour

4 teaspoons cornstarch

1 egg

1 egg yolk

1 cup 1% milk

1 teaspoon vanilla

1½ ounces semisweet or bittersweet chocolate (not to exceed 62% cacao), finely chopped

4 phyllo sheets, defrosted according to package instructions

4 teaspoons melted clarified butter

2 tablespoons caramel powder (recipe follows)

2 small or 1 large banana

2 to 3 tablespoons powdered sugar

Make chocolate and vanilla custard: combine 3 tablespoons sugar with flour and cornstarch in a small bowl. Add whole egg and yolk and beat with a handheld electric mixer until mixture is pale and thick, 1 to 2 minutes. Set aside.

Scald milk in a medium nonreactive saucepan. Pour hot milk gradually over egg mixture, beating until half the milk is added. Scrape egg mixture back in saucepan with remaining milk. Cook on medium heat, stirring constantly with a wire whisk, reaching all over the bottom and sides, until custard thickens and the first simmer bubble is seen at the edge. Continue to cook and whisk vigorously for an additional 30 to 45 seconds. Scrape custard into a clean bowl. Whisk in vanilla.

Measure a slightly rounded ½ cup hot custard and transfer to a small bowl with the chopped chocolate. Stir until chocolate is completely melted. Cover both mixtures so that plastic wrap comes in direct contact with custard to prevent a skin from forming. Refrigerate (up to 2 days) until needed.

Position oven rack in the center of the oven and preheat to 375 degrees. Line a heavy baking sheet with parchment paper.

Pile defrosted phyllo sheets on a tray. Cover with plastic wrap and a damp towel; keep well covered until each sheet is needed. Remelt clarified butter, if necessary.

Place one sheet on the counter in front of you. Brush with 1 teaspoon melted clarified butter, making sure to cover sheet completely. Sprinkle sheet with 1 teaspoon sugar. Place a second phyllo sheet on top. Brush with melted butter and sprinkle with sugar as before. Measure and cut the 2-layer phyllo in thirds the long way. Stack pieces on top of each other and neaten edges. You now have a 6-layer phyllo strip about 4 inches wide and 17 to 18 inches long. Cut strip into 9 rectangles about 4 inches wide and nearly 2 inches long.

Slide a long metal spatula or knife under the rectangles and transfer them to heavyweight baking sheet lined with parchment (okay if rectangles are right next to each other). Cover pastry rectangles with parchment. Place a lightweight baking sheet directly on top of parchment to weight the pastry.

Bake 5 minutes. Remove weight and parchment. Rotate baking sheet from front to back for even baking. Bake, uncovered, for an additional 3 to 5 minutes, watching very carefully, until pastry is dark golden brown. Cool pastry on a rack.

Repeat steps 6 and 7 with remaining 2 sheets. Bake for 5 minutes with parchment and weight. Remove baking sheet from oven. Remove weight and parchment. Turn six rectangles upside down and separate them from one another and from the rest of the pastry pieces. Sprinkle six pieces evenly with ¾ to 1 teaspoon caramel powder. Return to oven and bake 3 to 5 more minutes until dark golden brown and caramel has melted. Cool on a rack. Store all pastry pieces in an airtight container. Do not stack or layer caramel-topped pieces; other pieces may be layered between waxed paper. Layers may be stored for 2 days before using.

To assemble napoleons, scrape cold chocolate custard (without stirring or beating) into a pastry bag fitted with a No. 3 star tip. Pipe two neat lines chocolate custard down the length of one plain pastry piece, equidistant from each other and the edges of the pastry. Repeat with 5 more plain pastry pieces. Slice banana(s) into 30 rounds, each ¼-inch thick. Embed 5 overlapping banana slices in chocolate custard. Pipe two more lines chocolate custard next to each other on top of bananas. Top each with a plain pastry piece pushed gently into chocolate custard. Rinse and dry pastry bag; refit with tip. Scrape vanilla custard into bag. Pipe three lines custard right next to each other, down the center of each napoleon, leaving about ⅜ inch bare pastry along the edges. Pipe another two lines custard on top between the first three lines. Napoleons may be assembled to this point, covered and refrigerated for up to 2 ½ hours before serving. Keep caramelized pieces stored airtight until ready to serve.

To serve: Top each napoleon with a caramel-coated pastry piece pushed gently into custard. Serve immediately.

Makes 6 servings.

From *Chocolate and The Art of Lowfat Desserts* (Warner Books, 1994) by Alice Medrich.

Caramel Powder

½ cup sugar

Line a baking sheet with foil or parchment. Have a white saucer and long handled heat-proof silicone spatula or wooden spoon at hand. Pour ¼ cup water into a 1 quart saucepan. Pour sugar in center to form a mound. Don't stir. Use your fingers to pat sugar down just until entirely moistened. There should be water all around sugar to edges of pot. Cover pot and cook on medium-high heat for a 2 to 3 minutes (without stirring) until syrup looks clear. Uncover pot and continue to cook, never stirring until syrup begins to color slightly. Turn heat to medium. If syrup colors unevenly, swirl pot gently, rather than stirring, to even color. To judge the color of the caramel, use the tip of the heat-proof silicone spatula to drop a bead of caramel on the white plate. Watch carefully and test often; caramel will go from pale gold to amber to reddish amber very quickly. As soon as caramel is reddish-amber, pour caramel onto lined pan and let set until cool. When caramel has cooled and hardened, break into pieces and pulverize in a dry food processor. Store in an airtight container.

Mexican Chocolate Cookies

1 cup all-purpose flour

½ cup plus 1 tablespoon unsweetened natural or Dutch process cocoa powder

¼ teaspoon baking soda

¼ teaspoon salt

½ cup plus 1 tablespoon brown sugar

½ cup plus 1 tablespoon granulated sugar

3 tablespoons unsalted butter, slightly softened

3 tablespoons stick margarine (or unsalted butter)

½ teaspoon ground cinnamon

generous pinch of ground black pepper

generous pinch of cayenne

1 teaspoon vanilla

1 egg white

Combine flour, cocoa, soda and salt in a medium bowl. Mix thoroughly with a whisk. Set aside. Combine sugars in a small bowl and mix well with fingers, pressing out any lumps. (Process in food processor if lumps are stubborn.)

In a medium mixing bowl, beat butter and margarine until creamy. Add sugar mixture, cinnamon, peppers and vanilla. Beat on high speed for about 1 minute. Beat in egg white. On low speed, add flour mixture just until incorporated. Gather dough together with your hands and form into a neat 9 to 10 inch log. Wrap in waxed paper. Fold or twist ends of paper without pinching or flattening log. Chill at least 45 minutes, or until needed.

Place oven racks in the upper and lower third of the oven and preheat to 350 degrees. Line cookie sheet with parchment paper or aluminum foil.

Use a sharp knife to slice off rounds of dough a scant ¼-inch thick. Place 1 inch apart on prepared baking sheets. Bake 12 to 14 minutes. Rotate baking sheets from top to bottom and front to back about halfway through. Cookies will puff and crackle on top, and begin to settle down slightly when done. Use a metal spatula to transfer cookies to a wire rack to cool. Allow cookies to cool completely before storing or stacking. Store in an airtight container up to two weeks, or freeze up to 2 months.

Makes 40 to 45 cookies.

From *Chocolate and The Art of Lowfat Desserts* (Warner Books, 1994) by Alice Medrich.

Roland Mesnier

"Work with room temperature ingredients."

When Chef Roland Mesnier comes to the Western Reserve School of Cooking, it's hard to tell whether his classes sell out due to the decadent recipes he teaches or the delicious stories he has to tell about his twenty-five years as executive pastry chef at the White House. Mesnier has come to Western Reserve to teach nearly every year since his retirement from the White House in 2004.

A classically-trained pastry chef, Mesnier began his career at age fourteen, when his mother arranged an apprenticeship for him at a pastry shop in Besancon, France, not far from where he was raised in the village of Bonnay. The seventh of nine children, Mesnier likes to boast that he was raised in post-war France with no electricity and hand-me-down clothes and from there made it all the way to the White House.

It was First Lady Rosalynn Carter who lured Mesnier to Washington in 1979, hiring him away from the Homestead Resort in Hot Springs, Virginia. From that moment, Mesnier began a twenty-five-year mission to create the most spectacular desserts in the world to help showcase the first families and the nation's home.

From elaborate spun sugar creations to his annual Christmas gingerbread houses, Mesnier created and tasted every dessert that was served during his tenure, from the simplest cookie to the most complicated cake.

He served five administrations and his desserts were regularly enjoyed by kings and queens, celebrities and heads of state. Mesnier says he liked all of the first families that he served, but it's clear he has a soft spot for First Daughter Chelsea Clinton, for whom he began a tradition of serving freshly-made warm doughnuts on silver platters on the mornings after her frequent slumber parties.

Since retiring at age sixty, he has written five books on pastry and the White House and regularly teaches throughout the country. When he teaches, his lessons are simple. He stresses using quality ingredients, and making sure that all of them are at room temperature before beginning. Eggs, butter, milk—all of it he leaves sitting on the counter for hours before beginning to bake, a technique that shocks some of his students.

Mesnier keeps coming back to Western Reserve because he likes the intimate setting that allows him to interact closely with students. "They ask questions about their favorite presidents. I don't need to make anything up because I have ample material," he says. His material includes an infamous story about First Lady Nancy Reagan, who Mesnier praised for the keen interest she took in all aspects of White House entertaining, from the food to the flowers. On one occasion, however, Mrs. Reagan waited until two days before a dinner to request that Mesnier make 16 spun-sugar baskets filled with spun-sugar tulips for each of the tables. When Mesnier delicately tried to explain to her that the centerpieces would be a difficult undertaking since he had just two days to complete them, Mrs. Regan replied: "Yes, but you also have two nights." Mesnier finished the baskets on time.

Fresh Carrot Cupcakes with Pineapple, Apricot, Carrot and Ginger Topping

This recipe was created with spelt flour to accommodate President Bill Clinton's dietary needs. President Clinton was allergic to wheat, chocolate and dairy. When Clinton would indulge in those foods, Mesnier always knew because the president would have a red and puffy appearance in photos. Traditional all-purpose flour can be substituted for the spelt in this recipe.

For the cupcakes:

1½ cups spelt flour or all-purpose flour

½ cup cornstarch

2 teaspoons baking soda

1 teaspoon salt

1 teaspoon ground cinnamon

4 large eggs, at room temperature

1½ cups canola oil

1½ teaspoons pure vanilla extract

2 cups sugar

3 cups shredded carrots

1 cup coarsely chopped pecans

For the topping:

1 jar (12 ounces) apricot jam, strained

1½ cups canned pineapple chunks, drained and patted dry

1 carrot, peeled and finely shredded with a lemon zester or Microplane grater

2 tablespoons finely chopped crystallized ginger, dusted with sugar to keep it from sticking together

Preheat oven to 350 degrees. Line two 12-cup muffin tins with paper liners.

Combine spelt flour, cornstarch, baking soda, salt and cinnamon in a medium bowl.

Place eggs, oil, vanilla and sugar in the bowl of an electric mixer fitted with the whisk attachment. Whisk on high speed until mixture resembles a runny mayonnaise, about 5 minutes. Stir in flour mixture until just combined. Stir in carrots and pecans.

Divide batter among muffin cups and bake until a toothpick inserted into the center comes out clean, 19 to 20 minutes. Cool cupcakes in their pans for about 5 minutes. Invert cupcakes onto a wire rack and reinvert them onto another rack so they are right-side up. Let cool completely.

Combine jam and pineapple in a medium bowl and toss until pineapple is completely coated. Spoon some pineapple mixture on top of each cupcake.

Combine shredded carrots and crystallized ginger in a small bowl. Place a pinch of the mixture on top of each cupcake.

Makes 2 dozen cupcakes.

Blueberry Upside-Down Cake with Yogurt Sauce

Wholesome healthy ingredients like blueberries and yogurt make this cake a good choice for breakfast or brunch. I found myself making it more often when I discovered delicious Greek yogurt, which makes absolutely the best garnish. In place of plain yogurt, you can serve fruit-flavored yogurts in contrasting colors. Little dollops of peach, raspberry and lemon yogurt placed alongside slices of cake make a pretty presentation.

3 cups fresh blueberries	pinch of salt
4 large eggs	1 teaspoon pure vanilla extract
½ cup sugar	¼ cup red currant or grape jelly
¾ cup plus 1½ tablespoons all-purpose flour	2 cups plain yogurt, mixed with ¼ cup honey or ½ cup fruit preserves of your choice; or 2 cups fruit yogurt, stirred

Preheat oven to 375 degrees. Rinse blueberries under cold water and transfer them to a plate lined with paper towels to air-dry. Pick through them and remove any stems.

Grease a 9 by 2-inch deep round cake pan. Line bottom of pan with parchment paper and grease paper. Dust pan with flour and tap out any excess. Arrange blueberries in an even layer on bottom.

Pour 2 inches water into a medium saucepan and bring to a bare simmer. Combine eggs and sugar in the bowl of an electric mixer fitted with the whisk attachment.

Place bowl over simmering water and whisk constantly, by hand or with a hand-held mixer, until egg mixture is just lukewarm to the touch, 86 to 90 degrees on an instant-read thermometer.

Return bowl to the mixer and whisk on high speed for 5 minutes. Reduce speed to medium and whisk until mixture is completely cool, thick and shiny, another 12 minutes.

Using a rubber spatula, fold in flour, salt and vanilla. Pour batter over blueberries. Tap cake pan on counter four or five times to eliminate any large air bubbles. Bake until a toothpick inserted into the center comes out clean, about 40 minutes.

Remove pan from oven and let cake cool in pan for 5 to 10 minutes. Turn cake out onto a cardboard cake round, berry side up. Carefully peel away parchment. Place round on a wire rack and allow cake to cool completely.

Heat jelly in a small pot until loose and just warm. Pour jelly through a fine-mesh strainer into a small bowl. Using a pastry brush, brush warm jelly over blueberries to glaze them. Slice and serve with yogurt sauce on the side.

Blueberry Upside-Down Cake is best served on the day it is baked. Alternatively, leave parchment paper on top of cake as it cools. When completely cooled, wrap in plastic wrap and freeze for up to 2 weeks. Remove paper, glaze berries and slice while still lightly frozen, for beautiful, clean slices.

Chocolate Cupcakes with Chocolate Ganache

1¼ cups flour, sifted

½ teaspoon baking soda, sifted

¼ teaspoon salt

8 tablespoons unsalted butter, at room temperature

1¼ cups sugar

2 large eggs, at room temperature

1¼ teaspoons vanilla extract

1 cup whole milk, at room temperature

½ cup cocoa powder, sifted

Chocolate Ganache (recipe follows)

Preheat oven to 350 degrees. Line a standard cupcake pan with baking cups and a second pan with 6 cups.

Sift together flour, baking soda and salt.

Place butter in the bowl of a stand mixer or, using a hand mixer, beat on medium speed until fluffy. Stop to add sugar; beat on medium speed until well incorporated.

Add eggs, one at a time, mixing slowly after each addition.

Combine vanilla and milk in a large liquid measuring cup.

Reduce speed to low. Add one-third of the flour mixture to butter mixture. Gradually add one-third of the milk mixture, beating until well incorporated. Add another one-third of the flour mixture, followed by one-third of the milk mixture. Stop to scrape down the bowl as needed. Add remaining flour mixture, followed by remaining milk mixture and beat until just combined.

Add cocoa powder, beating on low speed until just incorporated.

Bake at 350 degrees for about 15 minutes, or until cupcakes spring back when touched lightly in the center. Cool, frost with Chocolate Ganache.

Makes 18 cupcakes.

Chocolate Ganache

1 cup semi-sweet chocolate chips   ½ cup heavy cream

Place chocolate in a heat-proof bowl.

In a saucepan over medium heat, bring cream to a near boil. Pour hot cream over chocolate and whisk until smooth. Cool to room temperature.

Use ganache immediately or refrigerate for up to 2 weeks. Before using, warm in microwave until softened.

Ganache also can be whipped to resemble a light-chocolate buttercream. Transfer cooled mixture to the bowl of an electric mixer and, with the whisk attachment, whip until light and fluffy.

Makes about 1 cup.

Lemon Parisian Macaroons

These cookies are a challenge to make but well worth the effort. Baking conditions have to be just right or they will spread and crack on top. Baking the cookies on doubled baking sheets, one stacked on top of the other, ensures that the cookies will be crisp on the outside but soft on the inside. Make sure that you use rimmed baking sheets, so that the water poured under the parchment paper doesn't spill out onto the counter and the floor! If you'd like to, omit the Lemon Cream and sandwich the macaroons together while their bottoms are still wet. Or omit the food coloring and sandwich the cookies together with ganache or the jam of your choice.

1 cup plus 2 tablespoons almond flour

1½ cups confectioners' sugar

3 large egg whites, at room temperature

6 tablespoons granulated sugar

1 teaspoon grated lemon zest

1 drop yellow food coloring

¼ cup Lemon Cream (recipe follows)

Preheat oven to 375 degrees. Line two rimmed baking sheets with parchment paper. Place each baking sheet on top of another unlined baking sheet.

Sift almond flour and confectioners' sugar together in a medium bowl and set aside.

Place egg whites in the bowl of an electric mixer fitted with the whisk attachment, and whip on high speed until just about to hold soft peaks. With mixer still on high, pour in granulated sugar in a slow, steady stream. Whip until meringue holds stiff peaks. Stir in lemon zest and food coloring. Fold almond flour mixture into egg whites, making sure everything is well combined but being careful not to deflate mixture.

Spoon batter into a pastry bag fitted with a plain No. 6 tip and pipe quarter-size portions on prepared baking sheets, leaving half an inch between cookies. You should have about 90 cookies. Bake until cookies are risen and lightly colored, 10 to 12 minutes.

As baking sheets come out of oven, place them on wire racks, lift one end of the parchment and carefully pour about ½ cup water between the parchment paper and the baking sheet to moisten the paper. Let stand for 2 minutes and transfer cookies to a dry baking sheet, flat side up, and cool completely.

Sandwich cookies together, using ¼ teaspoon Lemon Cream as the glue between two flat sides. Lemon Parisian Macaroons will keep in an airtight container at room temperature for 2 days, or in freezer for up to 1 week.

Makes 45 cookies.

Lemon Cream

5 large lemons	4 large eggs
1½ cups sugar	1 cup (2 sticks) unsalted butter, cut into cubes

Remove zest from lemons with a grater and set aside. Cut each lemon in half and squeeze juice into a small bowl.

Combine zest, juice, sugar, eggs and butter in a heavy-bottomed saucepan and bring to a boil over medium-high heat. Boil for 30 seconds, whisking constantly and making sure that mixture is not sticking to the bottom.

Remove pan from heat and pour mixture through a fine-mesh strainer into a non-reactive bowl. Cool to room temperature. Refrigerate Lemon Cream in an airtight container for up to 1 week or freeze for up to 2 months.

Makes about 2 cups.

Reprinted with the permission of Simon & Schuster, Inc., from *Dessert University: More Than 300 Spectacular Recipes and Essential Lessons from White House Pastry Chef Roland Mesnier* by Roland Mesnier and Lauren Chattman. Copyright © 2004 by Roland Mesnier and Lauren Chattman. All rights reserved.

Colette Peters

"Keep your sense of humor."

It should come as no surprise that Colette Peters' philosophy on life is to always keep your sense of humor. This is, after all, the woman who invented the crooked cake. Its topsy-turvy layers have been copied the world over and it is the one item that students who take her classes at the Western Reserve School of Cooking are most anxious to learn how to make.

Peters invented the cake on a lark. It was 1984, and Peters was working as a designer at Tiffany & Co. in New York City. A life-long baker, Peters often would make cakes for her friends and co-workers to help supplement her income. Her boss at the time, Tiffany design director John Loring, was having a photo shoot of a Tiffany table setting done at his home for a magazine and asked Peters to make him a cake to accent the table. "Something whimsical," he said. That weekend after experimenting with various shapes, the crooked cake was born. Part fine art and part Dr. Seuss, the cake is Peters' signature. Make that one of her signatures—there have been many others. The Tiffany wedding cake, for instance, with its stack of blue Tiffany gift boxes topped with that signature white ribbon, was another cake that Peters created for Loring, for the book *The Tiffany Wedding*.

In Peters' case, the baker preceded the artist. But the bakery came much later. She grew up outside Chicago in Brookfield, Illinois, in a family where baking was the norm. Cakes, pies, Christmas cookies—Peters made them all. "I like to bake because I like to eat," she says. But she longed to be an artist and, from the time she first visited in the sixth grade, knew she wanted to make her home in New York City. After college at the University of Northern Illinois and art school at the Rhode Island School of Design, Peters headed to New York to attend the Pratt Institute. She took a job at Tiffany's designing china patterns, stationery, jewelry and silver items.

But it was the cakes she made for Loring that brought her real fame. The cakes caught the attention of a book agent who asked Peters if she was interested in doing a book. With a promise of a $25,000 advance (more than she was making in a year at Tiffany's) Peters found herself in an unusual situation—a designer with a contract for a book on cakes, but no bakery.

She quit her job, finished the book and then got around to opening that bakery in 1991, after the book was released. There's been no looking back for Peters, who operates Colette's Cakes in New York. Peters is, quite simply, the queen of cakes. Her designs, fueled by her background in painting and sculpture, feature brightly colored fondants and gum paste decorations. They are instantly recognizable and unmistakably Peters'.

She has made cakes for European royalty and American celebrities, including Yoko Ono, Presidents Bill Clinton and George W. Bush, Bette Midler and Britney Spears. Her 1995 cake for duty-free heiress Marie-Chantal Miller's wedding to Crown Prince Pavlos of Greece received a full-page photo in Vanity Fair magazine. (Barbra Streisand had a copycat version of the cake for her 1998 wedding, but Peters didn't make it.)

Peters helped to start the annual cake design competitions, which have found an enthusiastic audience on television's Food Network. She discovered Duff Goldman and his show on Food Network, Ace of Cakes, was her idea. Peters still bristles a bit at the fact that she pitched the idea for a show in a bakery, but Food Network didn't pick her bakery for the show. But she clearly enjoys her role as the fairy godmother of the cake world. "You have to love what you do and I think you have to have a sense of humor. That's what kind of sets me apart," she says, explaining that most of her creations contain a hidden joke, a pun, or some humorous aspect. "I try not to take myself too seriously."

Crooked Cake Tips

- Only use a fondant-covered cake.

- Use a sturdy cake—not a mix.

- Use foam under the tiers—NOT cardboard.

- Stack the tiers with royal icing, not buttercream.

- Sharpen the long dowels in a pencil sharpener and push the sharp end through the cake.

- To cut foam, use a serrated knife and then use small-grained foam to shape it.

- Always attach a piece of foamcore to the bottoms of the foam wedges—these will be sitting on the dowels. Use hot glue or royal icing to attach the foamcore to the foam. Elmer's Glue won't work.

- If possible, assemble the top tiers on site.

- Tell the person in charge at the site about the dowels and how to disassemble the cake.

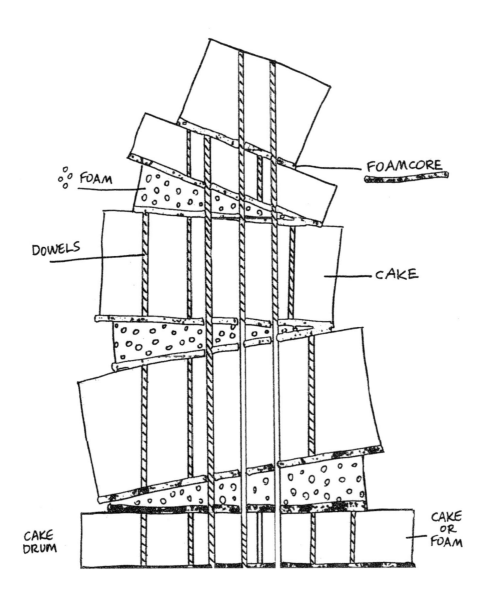

FOAMCORE

FOAM

DOWELS

CAKE

CAKE
DRUM

CAKE
OR
FOAM

The Recipes

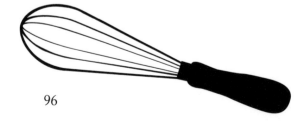

Chapter 4

By Bread Alone

Lora Brody

"We can learn from each other."

With eighteen cookbooks to her credit, Lora Brody has written and taught it all—chocolate, broccoli, slow cookers, baking and kitchen survival. But it was her venture into bread machine cookbooks that brought her to what was then the Zona Spray Cooking School in the 1990s.

Brody remembers well her visits and meeting Spray. "I remember hearing that she was very tough. People said that she was formidable. I went in thinking, 'Oh, this could be very scary,' because her reputation was that she was very exacting and very demanding. But she was extremely nice to me," Brody recalled.

The Cookery was selling one of Brody's bread machine baking enhancer products and the stop was part of her promotion for two books—*Bread Machine Baking, Perfect Every Time* and *Pizza, Focaccia, Flat and Filled Breads From Your Bread Machine: Perfect Every Time.*

It was a friend who ran a bookstore who suggested that Brody write a book on bread machines. He noticed the trend of people buying bread machines or getting them as gifts, but then not really knowing what to do with them.

Brody sold the book idea to a publisher, but found that she had taken on a lot more than she expected. At the time, every bread machine operated differently so she needed to write a different recipe for every machine that was on the market. The process required endless testing and retesting and Brody eventually enlisted the help of her mother to work on recipes. Their effort proved worthwhile. "It sold half a million copies and I got to laugh all the way to the bank," Brody said.

Brody didn't start out to be a cooking teacher or cookbook author and she is emphatic that she's not a chef (she reserves that honor for her son Max, who is a graduate of the Culinary Institute of America). Of course, her son was not without inspiration at home. As children, he and his brother once donned chef's hats, aprons, Groucho Marx-style glasses with mustaches and presented the family's dinner guest—Julia Child—with a rubber chicken on a platter. Without missing a beat, Child looked at the bird and proclaimed in her signature voice, "Oh, pollo al dente."

A native of Hartford, Connecticut, Brody attended New York University, married and spent much of the late 1960s and early 1970s living in New York. At the time, New Yorkers were beginning to discover Europe and all of its foods. With two small boys, Brody said she began hosting a lot of dinner parties to socialize. She had a copy of Maida Heatter's *Book of Great Desserts* and her recipe for Mushroom Meringues became Brody's signature. Giving the meringues away as gifts, Brody's friends began asking her to bake for them, which turned into catering parties.

After relocating to Massachusetts and having a third son, Brody began writing and teaching, focusing on chocolate, the subject of several of her books. She has taught classes in church basements and French chateaus. Regardless of the setting, her classes tend to be filled with the same two types of students: those who are terrified to do anything but follow a recipe to the letter and those who think recipes are unnecessary. "My job is to bring the two ends toward the middle, so the creative people get to be creative and people who think they can just wing it, have more respect for the chemistry. Students have a whole range of abilities and we can learn from each other."

Hazelnut Lavosh

This is a cross between a cookie and a cracker. If you love the rich buttery taste of hazelnuts, but aren't crazy about super sweet cookies, then this should please you. The trick is to get the dough as thin as possible and remove from the oven as soon as the lavosh is browned but not burned. This recipe calls for rolling out the dough on the bottom of an upside-down oiled jelly roll or sheet pan. Since you cook these at a very high temperature, make sure that there are no burned-on foods stuck to the bottom of your oven—they will smoke and make the lavosh taste unpleasant. Toasted filbert butter is available in health food stores (look in the peanut butter section), as is raw or turbinado sugar. If you cannot find it, substitute a like amount of dark brown sugar.

1 cup whole wheat flour

2 cups all-purpose unbleached white flour

1½ teaspoons salt

½ cup raw sugar, or ½ cup dark brown sugar, firmly packed

2 tablespoons sweet butter, very soft

1 cup water

1 jar (8 ounces) toasted filbert butter, including the oil at the top

Preheat oven to 500 degrees, with rack in center position. Turn 2 jelly roll or sheet pans upside down and spray the back with nonstick vegetable spray. Place all ingredients in bread machine, program for dough or manual and press start. When dough is well-mixed and has formed a soft, smooth ball, remove from machine and divide into 4 pieces.

Roll one section of dough directly onto the bottom pan. Roll carefully away from the center where dough is thickest, out to the edges, trying to achieve as even a layer as possible. The dough should be paper thin. You don't have to rush this job— it's better to take your time; the thinner the dough is in the center, the crispier all the pieces will be. If you find that the pan is sliding around on the counter, try placing a wet dish towel or couple of damp sponges underneath to keep in place.

Use a knife or pizza cutter to cut dough into 4 strips lengthwise and into 5 to 6 strips crosswise. Place pan in oven (still upside-down) and bake for 8 to 10 minutes or until pieces on the edges are browned. During this time roll out another section of dough on the second pan. Remove pan from oven and use a metal spatula to lift off the browned pieces. Return pan to oven and continue baking until all pieces are brown.

Allow lavosh to cool on racks and cool pans before proceeding with remaining dough. It isn't necessary to respray pans.

Makes about 80 pieces.

Apple Quitza

....

The divine inspiration for quitza came from my determination to combine two of my favorite dishes: pizza and quiche. This dessert sports a rich, creamy, rum-enhanced custard studded with bits of dried apples and marron glacé (candied chestnuts) in a brioche crust. Warm from the oven or at room temperature, it makes a fabulously indulgent ending to a meal, or the high point of a dessert buffet table. This dessert is best made in a springform pan.

....

For the crust/brioche dough:

1 tablespoon active dry yeast

½ cup sugar

3 tablespoons non-fat dry milk

1½ teaspoons salt

3¼ cups unbleached all-purpose flour

1½ sticks (6 ounces) sweet butter, melted and slightly cooled

3 extra large eggs

For the filling:

6 extra large egg yolks

2 cups heavy cream

⅔ cup brown sugar

⅓ cup dark rum

1 cup dried apple rings (or pieces)

1 jar (10 ounces) candied chestnuts in syrup, broken into pieces, syrup reserved

Place all brioche ingredients in bread machine, program for dough or manual and press start. The dough will be extremely sticky at first, slightly less so as kneading progresses. Some will continue to stick to the bottom of pan. Don't be tempted to add more flour—this is quite a loose dough. It will firm up when chilled.

At the end of the final knead, place dough in a well-oiled 2-quart bowl, cover with plastic wrap and refrigerate for at least 24 hours or as long as 36 hours. Generously butter a 12 or 13-inch springform pan with 2-inch high sides.

On a lightly oiled work surface, roll chilled dough into a 16-inch circle. Fit dough into pan, pushing excess up sides to top. Form a fluted crust by pinching edge between your fingers. Allow crust to rise, uncovered, in a warm place until puffed.

Preheat oven to 425 degrees, with the rack in the center position.

Make filling by whisking together yolks, cream, sugar and rum. Prick bottom of crust all over with a fork. Pour in filling, sprinkle on apples, chestnuts and drizzle syrup over surface. Bake for 15 minutes; reduce oven temperature to 375 degrees and bake for another 30 minutes.

Allow quitza to cool for 15 minutes before removing springform pan's ring. Cut into wedges and serve warm or at room temperature.

Makes 12 servings.

Ciril Hitz

"Get yourself a scale."

There is a reason why a Swiss watchmaker is used as the finest example of precision. But Ciril Hitz will have you putting Swiss bakers in the same category. His respect for precision in all things baking has helped him rise to the top of the ranks among the country's best artisan bread bakers. In Hitz's case, the emphasis is on the art in artisan. When you see his creations, breads that have been sculpted, twisted, shaped and molded into intricate designs and elaborate decorations, it will come as no surprise that this baker has a degree in industrial design.

Hitz came to the United States at age eleven, when his stepfather's job as a foreign exchange trader with a Swiss bank transferred the family to New York. He graduated from the Rhode Island School of Design with a degree in industrial design and a concentration in ceramics. But as Hitz was finishing design school, he had a notion that he would like to be a pastry chef. To this day, Hitz isn't sure where the idea came from. "Something happened in art school, I'm not quite sure what," he said. As part of his work in ceramics, Hitz was designing dinnerware. He realized that what he really longed for was something nice to put on the plates he was creating.

Hitz remembers how decorative and fun the pastry was in his childhood, and decided to return home to Switzerland to study. After a three-year pastry and chocolate apprenticeship and further studies in France, Hitz returned to the U.S. and began working in Rhode Island, first as a pastry chef in Newport News, and later in product development for Hauser Chocolates. In 1996, Johnson & Wales University in Providence, advertised for a Swiss-trained pastry chef and it seemed as if the job had been created just for Hitz.

In 2002, he earned a spot on Team USA for the Bread Bakers Guild competition in Paris and the team won the silver medal. Two years later, he competed in the National Bread and Pastry Team Championship in Atlantic City, where his team took first place and Hitz won all of the individual bread awards.

After the competitions, Hitz became a sought-after teacher at schools across the country. With many offers, but little time to teach, Hitz created two DVD series that teach baking techniques and bread art. In 2008 and 2009, he released back-to-back baking books, *Baking Artisan Bread* and *Baking Artisan Pastries & Bread*. He has managed to find time to teach at the Western Reserve School of Cooking and enjoys the intimate setting, which he likened to a family setting.

When he teaches, Hitz stresses the need for precision in baking. His best advice is for students to invest in a scale to weigh all ingredients. He refuses to work in cups and teaspoons, which can vary widely depending on how they were manufactured. An extra half an ounce of salt can be the difference between success and failure in baking, Hitz says. All of his recipes are written by weight. "Get yourself a scale. The accuracy in our industry is of such a great importance to obtain a consistent product," he said. "The scale is the single most important tool in the pastry chef/baker's profession."

Despite its exacting nature, Hitz said bread baking satisfies his artistic yearnings due to the close relationship between working with clay and working with dough. "This is where my love of art landed me. One you can eat out of and one you can eat," he said.

Because Hitz believes bakers should measure by weight, his recipes require a scale to prepare accurately and are written in ounces as measured on a scale.

Buttermilk Scones

11¾ ounces all-purpose flour	3 ounces dried fruit
1½ ounces granulated sugar	sanding sugar for dusting tops
pinch of salt	*or*
½ ounce baking powder	1 ounce crumbled blue cheese
4 ounces (1 stick) unsalted butter	2 ounces toasted walnuts
2 ounces whole egg	¾ ounces caramelized onions
6¼ ounces buttermilk	½ ounce crumbled blue cheese for topping

Sift dry ingredients together. By hand, work butter into dry ingredients until butter pieces are the size of a pea.

Whisk together liquid ingredients. Make a well in the center of the dry ingredients and fill with all of the liquid ingredients. Work two ingredients together, folding dry into wet. When batter is still a little lumpy add dried fruits or blue cheese, walnuts and onions.

Place batter on flour-dusted table and fold together until workable. Cut dough into 2 pieces and gently work each piece into a round disc. Roll each disc into a circle about 6 or 7 inches across. Cut each circle into 6 or 8 triangular wedges. Place scones on parchment lined baking sheet pan and let rest for half an hour.

Brush top with wash of 1 egg, loosely beaten with 2 tablespoons of water. Sprinkle with sanding sugar or top with blue cheese crumbles. Bake in a preheated 350-degree oven for 15 minutes.

Makes 12 to 16 scones.

Whole Wheat Bread

1 pound, 7 ounces whole wheat flour

16 ounces water (at 75 degrees)

1¾ ounces honey

0.1 ounce instant yeast (about ⅞ teaspoon)

10¼ ounces biga (preferment) (recipe follows)

½ ounce salt

1¾ ounces sunflower seeds (shelled)

1¾ ounces pumpkins seeds (shelled)

1¾ ounces sesame seeds

rolled oats (optional for topping)

Mix everything except seeds on low speed of an electric stand mixer for 4 minutes. Mix 2 minutes on medium speed. Reduce mixer to low speed and add seeds, mixing until completely incorporated.

Cover dough with a cloth, let rest for 1 hour. Give one stretch and fold. Cover and let dough rest an additional hour.

Cut dough in two. Shape each half into a loaf. Mist tops of loaves with water and sprinkle with rolled oats, if desired. Place in pans sprayed with a nonstick cooking spray.

Cover and allow dough to proof an additional 1½ to 2 hours.

Bake in preheated 425-degree oven for 20 minutes. Drop temperature to 350 degrees and bake an additional 20 to 30 minutes.

Makes 2 large loaves.

Biga

6½ ounces unbleached, unbromated flour, such as King Arthur All-Purpose

3¾ ounces water (70 degrees)

scant half teaspoon of instant yeast

With an electric stand mixer, mix all ingredients on low speed for 3 minutes.

The biga will be dry and feel tight and somewhat rubbery after mixing. Do not add any additional water.

Place biga in an oiled container that will allow it to grow approximately two times its initial size. Cover with plastic wrap or a lid.

Allow biga to stay out at room temperature for 1 to 2 hours. Punch down and refrigerate if you are not going to use it until the following morning.

Joe Ortiz

"You have to observe what is going on."

For a house painter, Joe Ortiz learned how to bake a fine loaf of bread. Make that for a would-be journalist-turned-would-be lawyer-turned-part-time musician/part-time-house painter. Ortiz's path into baking certainly wasn't a direct route; it was more of a default decision.

He was born in Queens, New York, to an Italian mother and Puerto Rican father, so food was a big part of his life. When he was seven years old, his family relocated to southern California. After high school, Ortiz went to junior college and later San Jose State University, where he studied journalism and considered law school. He ended up working as a house painter to make ends meet and dabbling in music on the side.

In 1978, his wife, Gayle, decided that she wanted to open a bakery. Gayle had worked at Alice Waters' legendary Chez Panisse restaurant in Berkley, subbing one summer for Pastry Chef Lindsey Shere. She learned to bake and cooked up a dream of opening her own bakery. The original concept for Gayle's Bakery was pastries and cakes, but her father insisted that she sell bread as well, telling her that "Joe could probably figure out how to make bread."

Ortiz thought the bakery was a good idea and figured that working for himself would be more inspiring than painting. In the beginning, it was Gayle, Joe and a sales clerk. More than thirty years later, Gayle's Bakery in Capitola, California, is going strong, with one hundred and fifty employees and about a thousand customers each day.

While Gayle's is still known for its bakery, the market includes rotisserie-cooked meats and a full menu of foods for dining in or carrying out. "It turned out to be very artistically satisfying and a good living for us," Ortiz said.

After the first five years, the bakery began to show real growth and along with the business, Ortiz's interest in bread grew. He and Gayle traveled to Europe to study bread-making techniques and bread became a true passion for Ortiz. His book, *The Village Baker, Classic Regional Breads from Europe and America*, was released in 1993, which sent Ortiz on a national promotional tour. One of his stops was at the Zona Spray Cooking School.

Ortiz said he can remember some bad experiences as he visited cooking schools across the country, but not in Hudson. "She was one of the good ones," he recalled, noting how Spray had even arranged for Ortiz to get local news coverage during his visit.

Ortiz said he always tried to give his students a little bit of himself along with their baking lesson. Students, he discovered, liked to be entertained as much as informed.

His book focused on why bread behaves the way it does. "We're putting something in motion, in process, and we have to see how it is behaving and respond to its behavior. If it is going slow, we have to go slow. If it's going fast, we have to go fast. Once it's in motion, you have to observe what is going on. That's how you make a loaf of bread," he said.

Challah

This is a very simple recipe for a light and flavorful bread.

2 packages (1 tablespoon plus 2 teaspoons; 1½ ounces) active dry yeast

2 cups warm water

2 whole eggs or 4 egg yolks, beaten

3 tablespoons corn or soy oil

3 tablespoons sugar

1 tablespoon salt

6 cups organic unbleached white or all-purpose flour

1 egg beaten with 1 tablespoon cold milk for glaze

poppy seeds or sesame seeds for topping

Proof yeast in a little of the warm water and when creamy, about 10 minutes, add to the rest of the water, eggs, oil and sugar. Mix salt in with flour and start adding dry mixture to liquid mixture by handfuls while mixing with a spoon. Continue adding flour until you have only a few handfuls left and dough has come together somewhat; this will take 10 minutes.

Empty dough out onto a work table, clean off your hands and the bowl with a plastic dough scraper and knead dough for another 5 to 8 minutes while incorporating the rest of the flour.

When dough is soft and satiny, round into a ball and let rise in a large container or bowl, covered with a damp towel, until it doubles in size, 1 to 1¼ hours.

Punch dough back and flatten out. Fold piece of dough in half, over onto itself and away from you. Square outer edges and push dough in on either side about 1 inch towards the center. Roll loaf up into a tight log, sealing dough with the heel of the hand at each turn. Let this loaf, covered with a moist towel, rest on flour-dusted work table for 10 to 15 minutes.

To shape challah, cut loaf in half and cut each half into three equal parts. Shape each of these pieces into small skinny strands in the same way as the first loaf was shaped, each measuring about 2 by 4-inches. Roll out each log until it is 8 inches long.

Use 3 strands for each loaf; connect them at the top and start braiding by putting the left strand over the middle one, the right strand over the middle one, and so forth until the strands are all braided. Seal the end with the heel of the hand. Repeat procedure with remaining 3 strands to shape the second loaf.

Place loaves either on a cookie sheet lined with parchment paper or in a well-greased bread pan that measures 9 by 5 by 2½-inches.

Let loaves rise, covered with a moist towel, for 35 to 40 minutes until indentation of a finger made in dough fails to spring back.

Glaze each loaf with egg glaze and sprinkle with poppy seeds or sesame seeds. Bake in a preheated, 400-degree oven for between 25 and 30 minutes or until loaves sound hollow when thumped on the bottom.

Makes 2 braided 1¼-pound loaves.

Adapted from *The Village Baker*, by Joe Ortiz (Ten Speed Press, 1993).

Pain Ordinaire

All serious bakers, students and cooks should have this basic recipe for regular classic yeasted French bread in their repertoire. By making the bread three or four times and by committing the recipe to memory, anyone should be able to produce an individual, subtle version of this classic daily bread. The simple recipe can be done in three different ways: by hand, with a food processor or with a stand mixer.

2 packages (2 scant tablespoons;
  ½ ounce) active dry yeast

2½ cups water

6 cups organic unbleached white
  or all-purpose flour

1 tablespoon salt

1 egg white whisked into
  ½ cup cold water for glaze

Proof yeast by stirring into 1 cup warm water (115 degrees). When mixture is creamy, after about 10 minutes, pour into a large mixing bowl and add 1½ cups lukewarm water.

Start adding flour, handful by handful, stirring after each addition, first gently and then vigorously, with a wooden spoon. As batter becomes thicker it will also become more elastic. You are actually trying to create strands of dough, much like taffy, that extends from the spoon to the dough in the bowl each time it is whipped in wide, slow, sweeping motions.

After all but 1 cup flour has been added (this will take about 10 minutes), turn dough out onto a work table, sprinkle salt over dough and knead for about 5 or 6 minutes while adding the rest of the flour. Because dough has been whipped up vigorously in the batter stage, it will not have to be kneaded as much in dough stage. The dough should be moist and satiny.

Place dough in a bowl large enough to accommodate its doubling in volume. The bowl can be greased or ungreased as you prefer. Cover bowl with a moistened dish towel and let dough rise in a warm spot, out of the way of drafts, for 1½ to 2 hours, or until doubled in volume. Punch back and let rise again for another 30 to 45 minutes.

Divide dough into 2 pieces and divide one of the halves in two again. Round each of the 3 pieces of dough into tight balls and allow them to rest on the table for 15 minutes, covered with a cloth so that the outside does not crust over.

Shape the two small balls of dough into baguettes by flattening each piece into a rectangular shape that measures approximately 6 by 3-inches. With the 6-inch side toward you, fold over a third of the dough down from the top and seal the edge with the heel of the hand. Do this 2 or 3 times until the piece is in the shape of a log of about 8 inches long. Stretch each log out by rolling on the table under the palms of your hands until it is between 12 and 14 inches long. Place each in an oiled baguette tray or on a cookie sheet that has been greased or lined with parchment paper.

Shape the larger piece of dough into a tight, round loaf by first flattening it and folding the outer edges over into the middle. Repeat process of folding dough 4 or 5 times and sealing each fold by pressing down on dough with the heel of the hand. With folds underneath, drag round ball of dough across work table with some pressure on top to make a tight loaf without any air bubbles. Place on a baking sheet lined with parchment paper.

Let loaves rise, covered, for 45 minutes to an hour, until they have doubled in volume. If you are using a baking stone, place in a cold oven and preheat oven to 450 degrees for at least 1 hour. Otherwise, simply preheat oven to 450 degrees.

With a razor blade, slash each baguette 4 or 5 times diagonally on top and brush them with glaze. Slash round loaf with a razor blade in a tick-tack-toe pattern, and brush with glaze as well.

Place loaves in oven. Bake baguettes for 20 to 25 minutes and round loaf for 40 to 45 minutes. When they are done, loaves will look golden brown in color and sound hollow if they are thumped on the bottom. Place loaves on a wire rack to cool.

Makes 2 10-ounce baguettes and 1 1¼-pound round loaf.

Adapted from *The Village Baker*, by Joe Ortiz (Ten Speed Press, 1993).

Peter Reinhart

"The lesson comes from the bread itself."

The phrase "bread of life" is probably more aptly applied to Peter Reinhart than any other baker. Bread baking is a process of transformation and baking bread has helped Reinhart transform his life in ways deep and spiritual.

Reinhart calls himself "an accidental baker." Through years of spiritual study he found his path in life dusted with flour and the journey transformed him into one of the most celebrated bread bakers in the country.

It began in 1970 when Reinhart, a native of Philadelphia, was fresh out of Boston University with a degree in film. He didn't feel ready to start making movies and, like many of his generation, was attempting to find himself. He connected with a group of people at what he describes as "a hippie veggie café" outside of Boston. There he learned to cook and began to explore his spirituality. He eventually joined the Holy Order of Mans, a non-denominational esoteric Christian order of men and women who were, like him, searching for the meaning of life. After experimenting with yoga, meditation and eastern mysticism, Christianity was the last place Reinhart, who was raised Jewish, expected to end up. But he moved to California to join the group's headquarters.

Living in the Christian commune, Reinhart once again found himself in the kitchen. For fun, he decided to experiment with baking bread. He credits Julia Child's recipe for classic French baguette as one of his first inspirations. The six-page recipe helped him to understand the process of making bread, including the second punching down of the dough, which he believes gives the bread a better flavor than other baguettes.

Through his studies, Reinhart learned of a Celtic tradition of baking multi-grain bread called struan, which the Irish made to celebrate the feast of St. Michael the Archangel on September 29. The women gathered a variety of grains and baked bread that would be taken to morning Mass to be blessed and then given to the poor. Reinhart found beauty in the ritual and began making struan, developing a recipe of high-gluten bread flour, cornmeal, rolled oats, wheat bran, brown rice, honey and brown sugar.

As he excelled at baking, Reinhart and his wife, Susan, who was also a member of the order and an accomplished cook, decided to open a small café as a community outreach project and as a means to develop their many food interests. Reinhart baked baguette and struan, Susan cooked and their bakery/café was a success. They named the place Brother Juniper's, after the comic-strip monk character. Struan bread was one of the best sellers at Brother Juniper's. Years later, when he and Susan visited Scotland, they found bakers still make struan and discovered the word means, "convergence of streams," a meaning which delights Reinhart for the personal connection he found to the bread. "I am the result of the convergence of many streams and it is still my favorite bread," he said.

Brother Juniper's Café was getting noticed. In 1986, it became one of the first restaurants in America to serve mesclun salad and the bread caught the attention of Chef John Ash, whose own restaurant was located nearby in Northern California. Ash asked Brother Juniper's to supply the bread for his restaurant— a move that elevated the bakery's profile to new heights. Reinhart went from baking twenty loaves of bread a day to forty, from forty to two hundred and from two hundred to two thousand. So successful was the bakery that Reinhart and his wife closed the restaurant to focus on baking. Brother Juniper's Bakery moved to a larger location and Reinhart, in 1991, was able to write his first bread book, *Brother Juniper's Bread Book: Slow Rise as Method and Metaphor.*

At the same time their bakery was succeeding, the Holy Order of Mans was changing. The members' years of study of Christianity brought them to the conclusion that their beliefs already existed in the traditional Christian church, in the form of Greek Orthodoxy. Orthodoxy satisfied members who joined the order seeking a monastic way of life, but also worked for members who were married with families and who sought life outside a cloister. Their order was accepted into the Greek Orthodox Church and Reinhart remains a practicing Greek Orthodox to this day.

Reinhart and his wife, who purchased the bakery from the order, sold it when the business grew so rapidly they almost couldn't control it. "The business had grown to the point where it wasn't, for us, what we wanted to do anymore," Reinhart recalls. By the 1990s, Reinhart began studying in earnest with bread masters around the world, writing and then teaching. "Every time I'd learn something, I'd write about it." A string of acclaimed books followed. In 1998, *Crust and Crumb* earned him his first James Beard Award. *The Bread Baker's Apprentice, Mastering the Art of Extraordinary Bread,* in 2001, was his second Beard Award and also was named Cookbook of the Year by the International Association of Culinary Professionals. Another Beard Award followed for *Peter Reinhart's Whole Grain Breads,* released in 2007. In all, Reinhart has written eight books, mostly on bread.

In 1999, he and Susan left California and he began teaching at Johnson & Wales University in Providence, Rhode Island, transferring to the school's Charlotte, North Carolina, campus when it opened in 2003. Reinhart teaches bread baking full-time at the school, but also travels the country speaking and teaching about bread. In recent years, his schedule has included stops at the Western Reserve School of Cooking, where his gentle style and extensive knowledge make his classes highly sought-after.

Reinhart says he tries to teach what his life journey has taught him. Bread has emerged as the guiding metaphor for his transformation as a Christian. "The lesson comes from the bread itself. Bread is transformational food. What makes bread is a series of transformations that change wheat into dough and dough into bread. At each stage, something emerges from each due to natural processes and the actions of the baker," he explains.

The bread baker's apprentice said the ultimate lesson he has learned is how to engage with others through food. "If I had to summarize what I write about, what I teach about, it all boils down to connectedness. The actual root word of religion, *religio*, means 'to be connected to.' Imbedded in the cooking and baking lessons is an increasing hunger for connectedness. That's what coming to the table is."

Focaccia Dough

Focaccia Dough

4½ cups (20½ ounces by weight) unbleached bread flour

1¾ teaspoons (.33 ounces) salt

1¼ teaspoons (.15 ounce) instant yeast

2 cups (16 ounces) cold water

2 tablespoons (1 ounce) olive oil

about ¼ cup extra olive oil, for oiling the storage bowl and the baking pan

Herbed Oil Topping

8 tablespoons (4 ounces) olive oil

1 tablespoon granulated garlic powder

1 teaspoon dried basil

1 teaspoon dried oregano

1 teaspoon fresh or dried rosemary

1 teaspoon paprika or hot paprika

¼ teaspoon black pepper, coarse

1 teaspoon kosher or sea salt, or to taste

Day One: Make focaccia dough by mixing all dough ingredients, except olive oil, in a mixing bowl or bowl of an electric mixer. (Instant yeast can be added directly to flour—it does not have to be hydrated first as active dry yeast does. See notes below.) Use paddle attachment if using an electric mixer. Mix or knead for about two to three minutes, until all flour is hydrated. Add 2 tablespoons olive oil and mix an additional 15 seconds to coat dough.

Set bowl aside, cover and let rest for 15 minutes. Resume mixing for approximately 30 seconds. It will be very soft and sticky (see notes below for additional mixing tips), but gluten will be developed and dough will be stretchy. Place dough in an oiled bowl (or directly on an oiled sheet pan), cover and refrigerate immediately, overnight.

Day Two: Remove dough from refrigerator 3 hours before you plan to bake (it will have nearly doubled overnight). Cover bottom of a baking pan with either baking parchment or a silicone pad. Drizzle 2 tablespoons olive oil over the surface and rub around to coat the entire surface area. If using, make herbed oil by whisking together all topping ingredients in a mixing bowl.

Transfer dough from bowl to baking pan with a bowl scraper or rubber spatula that has been dipped in water. Drizzle 1 tablespoon herbed oil (or plain, unseasoned olive oil) over top and use your fingertips to press and spread dough into pan (begin from the center and work out towards the edges of pan). It will only cover about ⅔ of the pan before starting to spring back. Stop pressing and let dough rest for 20 minutes to relax gluten.

Drizzle half the remaining herbed oil over surface and evenly press out dough as in previous step. This time dough will cover nearly the entire surface but will probably spring back a little at the end. Let rest another 20 minutes.

Drizzle on remaining herbed oil and press out dough one final time. It will be nicely dimpled and should be evenly spread. Do not flatten with the palms of your hands but only with fingertips, making dimpled pockets in which the oil will settle. Lay plastic wrap or a food-grade trash bag over top of pan and let dough rise for two hours at room temperature. It will fill pan.

While dough is rising, preheat oven to 450 degrees (400 degrees, if convection). When dough has risen, remove plastic and bake on middle shelf for 10 minutes. Rotate pan 180 degrees and bake an additional 10 to 15 minutes. Monitor dough and bake until top is golden brown. Check under dough to be sure that the bottom is also golden (caramelized). If the top is baking faster than the bottom, move to a lower shelf. If the bottom is done before the top, move to a higher shelf. (Note: when making cake pan focaccia, increase oven temperature to 550 degrees or as high as oven will allow.)

Remove pan from oven and break the focaccia's contact with the walls of the pan by loosening with a pastry blade or knife. Place on a cooling rack. With a metal spatula, carefully position it between focaccia and parchment and loosen. Slide focaccia from pan onto cooling rack. If parchment is still attached to bread, simply lift focaccia and slide parchment out from under it after you've removed it from pan. If there is any extra oil in baking pan, drizzle over top of focaccia. Cool for at least 30 minutes before slicing with a bread knife (not a pizza roller) and serving. The focaccia pieces should be about ½ to ¾-inches in thickness, perfect for topping with tapenades and spreads.

Makes 1 sheet pan or up to 4 cake pan versions.

Notes: When mixing wet, sticky dough by hand, dip your own hands or the mixing tools in cold water; sticky dough won't stick to wet hands or tools. If you only have dry active yeast, increase the amount to 2½ teaspoons and hydrate it first for three or four minutes in 4 ounces of lukewarm water. Try not to press out all the air pockets when dimpling the dough in the pan; these pockets become the basis for the nice large, irregular holes in the finished product.

The herbs in the herbed oil can be varied according to taste. You can make it milder or spicier or use other herbs, including fresh herbs. The topping variations can be as varied as your imagination. Typical savory toppings can include tomato slices or thinly sliced potatoes marinated in the herb oil and then baked on top, or caramelized onions, blue cheese and walnuts, various pestos, or cheese and sauce combos.

Napoletana Dough

Prepare this dough a day in advance.

5 cups (22½ ounces) unbleached
all-purpose flour

1¾ teaspoons (0.4 ounce) salt or
3¼ teaspoons kosher salt

1 teaspoon (.11 ounce) instant yeast

15 ounces cool water
(approximately 65 degrees)

With a large metal spoon stir all ingredients together in a 4-quart bowl (or the bowl of an electric mixer) until all flour is absorbed. If using an electric mixer use dough hook and mix on medium-low speed for approximately 4 minutes. Let dough rest for 5 minutes. Mix again on medium-low speed for an additional 2 to 3 minutes. The dough should clear the sides of the bowl and just stick a little to the bottom of the bowl.

If you are mixing by hand, repeatedly dip one of your hands or the spoon in cold water and use it, much like a dough hook, to work dough vigorously into a smooth mass while rotating the bowl in a circular motion with the other hand. As dough begins to firm up and strengthen, continue this wet hand mixing for about 6 minutes. The dough should be slightly sticky and feel soft and supple. If it is too sticky to hold its shape, add more flour. If dough seems too stiff or dry, add more water a tablespoon at a time. It should pass the windowpane test. (For the windowpane test, pinch off a small amount of dough. Stretch it with your fingers so that the center is so thin you can see through it like a window. If you can do this successfully, dough has been kneaded enough. If dough tears or splits, it needs additional kneading.)

Transfer dough to a floured counter, dust top of dough with flour to absorb surface moisture and fold dough from the four corners into a ball. Place dough into a bowl that has been brushed with olive oil, roll dough in the bowl to coat entire surface and cover bowl with plastic wrap. Let dough sit at room temperature for 30 minutes. Place in refrigerator overnight. If making the pizzas on the same day, give dough 90 minutes to rise before refrigerating and refrigerate for at least 3 hours.

The next day (or later the same day), remove bowl of dough from refrigerator three hours before you plan to make pizza. The dough will have expanded somewhat and the gluten will be very relaxed. Using a plastic bowl scraper dipped in water, or with wet hands, gently transfer dough to a floured counter, trying to retain as much of the gas as possible. Divide into 6 equal pieces (approximately 6 ounces each) with a pastry blade that has been dipped in water. Gently round each piece into a ball and brush or rub pieces with olive oil. Line a sheet pan with either baking parchment or a silicone pad. Brush parchment or pad with olive oil. Place each dough ball on pan and loosely cover pan with either plastic wrap or a food-grade plastic bag. (If you do not plan to use all the pieces, place extra ones in individually-zippered food storage bags, sandwich size is sufficient, and either refrigerate or freeze.) Allow dough balls to sit at room temperature for three hours before making pizzas. They will be usable for two days in refrigerator or for up to three months in freezer.

Note: I always have one or two extra dough balls ready, in case of mishaps such as dropping or tearing. If you don't use them, they can still be chilled for later use, preferably within 24 hours.

The Recipes

Chapter 5

Travel the World from Hudson, Ohio

Giuliano Bugialli

"My goal is for them to learn about Italy."

Giuliano Bugialli has been one of the most popular Italian cooking teachers in America for more than thirty years and while it is cooking that he teaches, it is Italy that he is hoping his students will come to learn.

A native of Florence, Bugialli arrived in New York in the early 1970s to work as a teacher of Italian language, not food. He struggled when he first arrived, trying to find the kind of food he was accustomed to in Italy. Bugialli's father was director of a large winery and he was used to a home filled with the classic dishes of Tuscany. What he found was a shocking lack of authentic ingredients and an ignorance about Italian food and cooking.

Bugialli attributes the American version of Italian cooking to the waves of destitute immigrants who came here in the early years of the twentieth century. "The first immigrants left Italy because they were starving. They didn't know Italian food. Food was what they had," he explains. Immigrants found a land where they were able to buy meat, fish or chicken on a daily basis and they embraced their prosperity, creating a type of cuisine that was never classically Italian, even for the wealthy there, Bugialli maintains.

For his first few years, Bugialli traveled back and forth to Florence, where he began a cooking program in 1972, while still teaching Italian language in New York. When Bugialli finally had to decide between his two careers, food won out and he embarked on a career as a traveling cooking teacher that has spanned more than four decades. At the time, the country had a large network of small cooking schools and he was able to teach at thirty or forty schools each year in the U.S. and abroad.

He wrote his first book in 1976 drawing on his own Tuscan background and titled it *The Food of Tuscany*. When his publisher released it in 1977, Bugialli likes to note that the only thing changed was the title. Believing that no one would know where Tuscany was, the publisher changed the title to the *Fine Art of Italian Cooking*, a move that chagrins Bugialli to this day. Nine more books have followed since his first, each involving meticulous research about a specific region and its food. He searches out historical manuscripts and information from ancient families who helped to form their societies.

Bugialli respects all cuisines as long as they are authentic and true to the country's history. In the great cultures of the world it is considered criminal to forget about the country's heritage and history and it is a lesson that Bugialli stresses repeatedly to his students.

He first arrived in Hudson, Ohio, on an invitation from Zona Spray. Despite Spray's classical French training, Bugialli found a welcoming host and eager students. He strives for his students to understand the philosophy behind Italian food and how food must be understood mentally before it can be enjoyed physically. He spends time explaining the subtleties like how the delicate balance of ingredients can make or break a dish. "You don't touch something perfect," he says.

At his school in Florence, students come for a submersion in the Tuscan culture, where they prepare ten or twelve dishes each day and learn about the subtle significance of each ingredient, like when to use fresh pasta versus dried and how the sauce will determine which is best. "You cannot use the same sauce with fresh and dried pasta. The idea is the sauce is not going to overpower the pasta and vice versa. It's more difficult to understand, but in Italian cooking, it's normal."

Bugialli doesn't teach recipes, he teaches food history. "My goal is for them to learn about Italy, not only about food, food as it is part of Italy. Food is not only the cooking of the dish, it is understanding the gastronomy of the dish. I don't like to teach a recipe for the recipe itself—that is not enough. You have to give more," he explains. "Food is a history, it isn't just an attitude. You cannot just have food as a fight, as a competition, as a gimmick. That's not food."

Scaloppine Agli Asparagi

Veal Cutlets with Asparagus Sauce

6 veal cutlets

1 pound asparagus

1½ cups beef or chicken broth

8 tablespoons butter

¼ cup olive oil

1 cup flour, approximately

15 sprigs Italian parsley

salt and freshly ground black pepper,
  to taste

1 lemon cut into wedges

coarse-grained salt

Pound veal cutlets and set aside.

To prepare sauce, boil asparagus. Remove asparagus from stockpot and let rest for a few minutes. Cut off and discard the tough white bottom part. Set half aside. Pass the other half through a food mill into a small bowl.

Transfer passed asparagus to a saucepan and add broth. Place pan over medium heat until it reaches a boil. Put a second saucepan on medium heat with 4 tablespoons butter. When butter is completely melted, add 1½ tablespoons flour and stir with a wooden spoon until flour turns a very light brown color. Add the boiling broth-asparagus mixture all at once, mix very well and let simmer for about 10 minutes. Taste for salt and pepper.

Cut remaining asparagus into 1-inch pieces. Place a large skillet on medium heat with remaining butter and oil. Lightly flour veal cutlets. When butter is melted, add cutlets and sauté them for 2 minutes on each side, sprinkling each side with salt and pepper. Transfer cutlets to a warmed serving dish and cover with aluminum foil. Add sauce and asparagus pieces to skillet, taste for salt and pepper and let simmer for 5 minutes more.

Coarsely chop parsley.

When sauce is reduced, pour over cutlets, sprinkle with parsley and serve immediately with lemon wedges.

Makes 6 servings.

Risotto All'Amatriciana

From Amatrice in Lazio

4 ounces pancetta or prosciutto, in one piece

4 tablespoons olive oil

1 large red onion, cleaned

1½ pounds ripe fresh tomatoes or 1½ pounds canned tomatoes, preferably imported Italian, drained

salt and freshly ground black pepper

½ to ¾ teaspoon hot red pepper flakes, according to taste

2 cups Italian rice, preferably arborio

4 cups chicken or beef broth

6 tablespoons freshly grated Pecorino Romano cheese

Cut pancetta into tiny cubes. Place a heavy, medium-sized casserole, preferably terra-cotta (or a Dutch oven or large saucepan), over medium heat. Add oil. When oil is warm, add pancetta and let sauté for 10 minutes, stirring every so often.

Coarsely chop onion and pass tomatoes through a food mill, using the disc with smallest holes, into a small bowl.

When pancetta is crisp, use a slotted spoon to transfer pieces to a plate. Add onion to casserole and let sauté for 5 minutes more. When onion is ready, add tomatoes, salt and pepper to taste and red pepper flakes. Let simmer for 15 minutes, stirring every so often with a wooden spoon. Remove half the tomato sauce and let stand in a small bowl until seeded.

Heat broth in a small saucepan. Add rice to casserole, stir very well and let sauté for 4 minutes. Start adding hot broth, ½ a cup at a time, constantly mixing with a wooden spoon and do not add extra broth until previously-added broth is completely absorbed by rice. Before adding the last ½ cup broth, add tomato sauce from the small bowl. Taste for salt and pepper. Put in the last half cup broth and let rice incorporate it. By that time rice should be cooked but still retain a bite.

Add pancetta, mix very well and transfer to a large warmed serving platter. Serve immediately with the Pecorino cheese sprinkled over.

Makes 6 servings.

Famous Chefs & Fabulous Recipes

Broccoli Alla Trasteverina

From Rome

2 bunches broccoli	salt and freshly ground black pepper
coarse-grained salt	½ teaspoon hot red pepper flakes
2 large cloves garlic, peeled	4 tablespoons red wine vinegar
½ cup olive oil	¼ cup cold water

Soak broccoli in a large bowl of cold water for a half hour.

Bring a large pot of cold water to a boil over medium heat.

Remove and discard the woody ends of broccoli. Cut flowerets from large stems and keep them separated. Cut stems into strips about 2-inches long and ½-inch thick. Add coarse-grained salt to boiling water, then stems and let boil for 3 minutes. Add flowerets and let cook for 4 minutes more. By that time, stems and flowerets should both be cooked but still al dente.

Drain broccoli, cool under cold running water and transfer to a serving dish, being sure to drain all water from the dish. Coarsely chop garlic. Heat oil in a small saucepan over medium heat and when oil is warm, add garlic and let sauté for 5 minutes or until lightly golden. Add salt and pepper to taste and red pepper flakes. Put in vinegar and let reduce for 3 to 5 minutes. Add water and let cook for 5 minutes more. Remove pan from heat, mix well with a wooden spoon and pour sauce all over broccoli. You may serve immediately or let cool completely first.

Makes 6 to 8 servings.

John Desmond

"Keep it simple."

Although he is a native of County Cork, Ireland, Chef John Desmond is definitely part of the French connection that filled the teaching spots at the Zona Spray Cooking School for many years.

Desmond met Spray at LaVarenne Cooking School in Burgundy in the mid-1970s, where he was teaching classic French techniques. The pair kept in contact after she returned home and Spray gave Desmond an open invitation to come to teach in Hudson, Ohio.

Between 1978 to 1988, Desmond taught at the school about eight times, teaching French techniques to receptive students. The role of cooking teacher wasn't something that Desmond ever envisioned himself doing. "I never knew I was going to take this course in life. This just happened and I just went along with it," he recalled.

After finishing his schooling in Ireland, Desmond signed up for a three-year course to study hotel management. He moved to Germany, where he worked as a food and beverage manger at a Berlin hotel and then moved to the Ritz in Paris, where he started an internship or *stagiaire* in the kitchen. In France, where trainees in the kitchen can be as young as fourteen or fifteen, Desmond was considered old at twenty-three. "In the cheffing world, I did things in the opposite," he said. But after working in the front of the house, Desmond realized that he was more suited for the back. "I preferred dealing with food more than the people," he said. After working at several restaurants in France, he eventually ended up on the staff at LaVarenne.

Desmond has fond memories of coming to Ohio, and said Spray was always a gracious host, even though his lessons sometimes weren't good for her cookware sales at The Cookery. Desmond would encourage his students to not spend their money on too much cookware and gadgets. Desmond said Spray seemed to take it all in stride. "She was probably in total despair that I would use a fork to squeeze a lemon. But it is the most efficient may to squeeze a lemon and she seemed to accept that," he said.

Desmond no longer travels to teach. He and his wife, Ellmary Fenton, run a cooking school and small restaurant, the Island Cottage, on Heir/Hare Island, in Skibbereen, West Cork, Ireland. For eight months of the year, they host pairs of cooking enthusiasts who are interested in upgrading their skills during two-day short courses. Desmond provides private lessons and the setting off the southwest coast of Ireland provides a relaxing retreat. In the winter months, Desmond paints and displays his work at his Island Cottage Gallery.

"Keep it simple," is his best lesson and advice on cooking today. "Don't use too many ingredients, don't mess the food up. Fish should taste like fish, and not like something else. It's the quality of the ingredients that is the most important. They always have to be of superior quality."

Here are recipes for a few of the classic French dishes Desmond taught in Hudson, including the important French foundation ingredient, fish stock.

Fish Stock

This is the easiest of all stocks to make, which is one of the reasons it is made every day in good restaurants.

½ pound onions, finely sliced	4¼ cups cold water
2 tablespoons butter	1 teaspoon coarse salt
2½ pounds fish bones	1 teaspoon peppercorns
½ cup dry white wine	large bouquet garni

In a large saucepan melt butter, add onions and cook until soft but not brown.

Break fish bones into pieces and wash thoroughly under cold running water until no blood remains. Add bones to saucepan, stir and cook very briefly with onions. Add wine and boil until nearly all the moisture has evaporated.

Add water, salt, peppercorns and bouquet garni. Bring to a boil and simmer 20 minutes, skimming foam off top often. Strain.

Makes about 4¼ cups.

Note: Do not add fish skin as it darkens the stock.

Fish Soup Flavored with Fresh Thyme

This is a good soup! Colorful, tasty and not too thick.

4¼ cups fish stock	1 teaspoon saffron threads
3½ tablespoons olive oil	4½ pounds mussels
1 cup carrots, peeled and diced	1 cup white wine
1 cup onions, diced	1 cup heavy cream
½ cup leeks, washed and sliced	salt and freshly ground white pepper
1 pound tomatoes	chopped fresh thyme
2½ cups water	chopped fresh parsley
1½ tablespoons minced garlic	

In a large frying pan set over medium heat, add oil and heat. Add carrots, onions and leeks and sauté gently without browning.

In a medium-size saucepan, bring water to a boil. Add tomatoes and when skins begin to break, remove and put in bowl of cold water. Drain. Remove skin and seed. Chop into small pieces and add to frying pan. Add garlic and saffron.

Clean and wash mussels. Discard any that are open or broken. Put white wine into a very large saucepan and bring to boil. Add mussels. Cover pan and cook until mussels open. Remove mussels from heat and shell them, reserving juice and mussels separately. Strain juice and discard any sand.

To assemble soup in large saucepan, add fish stock, juice of mussels and vegetables. Bring to boil and simmer for 30 minutes. Skim any foam that comes to top.

When ready to serve, put cream in a saucepan and bring to boil. Add to soup. Season to taste with salt and pepper. Divide mussels evenly between eight heated soup bowls. Sprinkle fresh thyme and chopped parsley in each. Ladle in hot soup and serve.

Makes 8 servings.

Beef Fillets with Marchand de Vin Sauce

Serving meat with its marrow gives the meat an incredible flavor and helps to balance the acid of a wine sauce.

8 beef fillets, 6 ounces each

2 tablespoons oil

2 tablespoons unsalted butter

salt and freshly ground white pepper

½ cup shallots, finely chopped

1 cup red wine

2½ tablespoons brown stock glace (glace de viande)

3½ tablespoons cream

1 stick plus 6 tablespoons unsalted butter, cut into small pieces

1 pound bone marrow

2½ cups water

2 teaspoons coarse salt

salt and freshly ground white pepper

Tie 8 fillets neatly with string. Place large frying pan over high heat. Put oil and butter into pan and when hot, season meat and add to pan. When cooked to desired doneness, remove from pan and place on a rack and keep warm. The meat should never sit in its own juice.

Wipe pan clean with a paper towel. Add shallots to frying pan. When cooked, but not browned, add red wine. Reduce over high heat. When there is no liquid left, add glace de viande and cream and bring to boil. Add butter pieces to pan, but do not boil. Keep sauce warm.

Slice marrow into approximately 40 small slices. Bring 2½ cups water to boil. Add salt and remove from stove. Add marrow to water and let sit in pan until ready to serve.

To serve, place a beef fillet on each of 8 large heated plates. Dress with sauce. Remove marrow from water, drain and set pieces on top of sauce on each plate.

Makes 8 servings.

Naomi Duguid

"I want people to be transported."

Naomi Duguid has traveled to some of the remotest parts of the world, meeting the people and chronicling their lives through the foods that they eat. She speaks with equal excitement about the time she spent in Hudson, Ohio in 1995.

Duguid and her then-husband, Jeffrey Alford, had just published their first book, *Flatbreads & Flavors, A Baker's Atlas*, to great acclaim in the food world. The book was named Cookbook of the Year by the James Beard Foundation and won the Julia Child First Cookbook Award from the International Association of Culinary Professionals. Zona Spray contacted Duguid about teaching a class on flatbreads at her school and Duguid recalls their visit vividly for the time she spent getting to know Spray, as well as the students.

"With Zona, food isn't produced, it's not the end. It's a medium, which is a ground for sharing a lot of ideas. There is the how to, which interests a lot of people, but Zona has a much larger view. Food is a medium for an exchange of ideas, for excitement, curiosity," she said.

Her words aptly explain her own view of the food world as well. A native of Ottawa, Canada, Duguid was a lawyer, but decided that she wanted to live "in a larger world" and began traveling. She met Alford in Tibet in 1985, and married shortly after. They decided to try to make a living by traveling and writing, but they wanted to write about something meaningful. Duguid decided she would take photos to document daily life in Nepal for a year. They wrote articles on travel for magazines and along the way began to develop the concept of the *Flatbreads* book. They spent six years researching and writing it, and Duguid discovered that food became a way for her to understand other cultures. "For me, food is understanding. It's not product, it's not the best foie gras I ever ate."

With flatbreads, Duguid noted how the breads came about as a necessity. In nomad cultures the people rarely have the opportunity to bake and when they do, must have a food that will survive being dried out, she explained. What cultures eat is as much about what they have available to them, as it is what they don't have, like cooking fuel. Limited resources help to define a culture's food habits. Likewise, the culture of well-developed countries, where the food is highly-processed, speaks volumes as well. "What are we doing with all this processed stuff? Food is not an arbitrary thing, but deeply connected to our culture and our humanity and it's a link between cultures," she said.

Duguid tries to get her readers and students turned on to what food means in other cultures, "To see the food as a cultural artifact and to see the food as deeply connected to the human condition." The pair's second book on rice offered similar insights. Together, Duguid and Alford wrote six books before divorcing personally and splitting up professionally. Both continue to work independently on new projects.

When she teaches or writes, Duguid said she tries to convey a sense of excitement about other cultures. "I want people to be transported in a way, in a sense, to travel in their kitchens," she said. When it comes to understanding other cultures, Duguid puts it simply: "Food is the bridge."

Armenian Tomato and Eggplant Salsa

The eggplant almost disappears in this eggplant and tomato salsa, yet it gives body and texture to the salsa, as well as a delicious slightly smoky flavor. If you would like a hotter salsa—this version is quite mild—simply increase the amount of chiles used.

½ pound (2 small) eggplant

3 large cloves garlic

1 pound ripe fresh tomatoes, or canned plum tomatoes, coarsely chopped

½ cup cilantro leaves

¼ teaspoon salt

1 jalapeño or ½ red cayenne

3 scallions, finely chopped

You will need a baking sheet or a heavy skillet with a lid and a food processor.

Preheat oven to 425 degrees.

Prick eggplants all over with a fork, place on a baking sheet and roast in oven for 30 minutes or until skin has changed color and eggplant is soft all over. Add garlic to baking sheet for last 5 minutes or so. (Alternatively, place in a cast iron frying pan with a lid and grill, covered, over medium heat, turning every ten minutes for ½ hour; add garlic in the last 5 minutes and turn once.) Set aside to cool.

Halve eggplants and scrape out flesh; discard skin. Place eggplant flesh in a food processor together with roasted garlic and remaining ingredients. Process until puréed and blended. Taste for salt and chile heat, and adjust seasonings as necessary. Turn out into a serving bowl and serve at room temperature.

Serve with flatbreads for dipping, or as a sauce to accompany grilled lamb.

Makes approximately 3 cups.

Adapted from *Flatbreads & Flavors: A Baker's Atlas*, by Jeffrey Alford and Naomi Duguid (William Morrow, 1995).

Classic Pita

Pita, commonly referred to in Arabic as Khubz (or "bread"), is without question the most widely available bread throughout the Eastern Mediterranean. Unfortunately, in these days of mass production, even here the khubz that makes its way to restaurant tables is often the same ubiquitous too-quick-to-go-stale white pita served in restaurants in North America. As for homemade pita, cast away any thought of those white cardboard—like breads. Fresh homemade pita—made with half white, half whole wheat flour are easy to make and delicious. They are most easily made on quarry tiles or baking sheets in a hot oven, but they can also be baked on a griddle or in a cast iron skillet on the stove.

2 teaspoons dry yeast

2½ cups lukewarm water
   (approximately 100 degrees)

3 cups whole wheat flour

about 3 cups unbleached
   all-purpose flour

1 tablespoon salt

1 tablespoon olive oil

You will need a large bread bowl, a rolling pin and unglazed quarry tiles or several baking sheets, or alternatively, a cast iron or other heavy skillet or griddle at least 9 inches in diameter.

Sprinkle yeast over warm water in a large bread bowl. Stir to dissolve. Add whole wheat flour, one cup at a time. Stir 100 times (one minute) in the same direction to activate the gluten in the flour. Let this sponge rest for at least 10 minutes or as long as 2 hours.

Sprinkle salt over the sponge and stir in olive oil. Mix well. Add white flour, one cup at a time. When dough is too hard to stir, turn out onto a lightly floured breadboard and knead for 8 minutes, until dough is smooth and elastic. Return dough to a lightly oiled bread bowl and cover with plastic wrap. Let rise until at least double in size, approximately 1½ hours. Gently punch down.

Dough can be made ahead to this point and stored, covered, in refrigerator for 7 days or less. If at this time you want to save dough in refrigerator for baking later, simply wrap in a plastic bag that is at least three times the size of the dough, pull bag together and secure just at the opening of bag. This will give the dough a chance to expand when it is in the refrigerator (which it will do). From day to day, simply cut off the amount of dough you need and keep the rest in the refrigerator. Dough should be brought to room temperature before baking.

This amount will make approximately 16 pitas if rolled out into circles approximately 8 to 9 inches in diameter and less than ¼-inch thick. You can also make smaller breads. Size and shape all depend on you, but for breads of this dimension the following baking tips apply:

You can bake bread in the oven or on top of the stove. If baking in the oven, place unglazed quarry tiles, or two baking sheets, on the bottom rack of your oven, leaving a one inch gap all around to allow air to circulate. Preheat oven to 450 degrees. Divide dough in half. Set half aside, covered, while you work with the rest. Divide dough into eight equal pieces and flatten each piece with lightly floured hands. Roll out each piece to a circle 8 to 9 inches in diameter. You may wish to roll out all eight before starting to bake. Cover rolled out breads, but do not stack, Bake 2 at a time (or more if your oven is larger) directly on quarry tiles or baking sheets. Bake each bread for 2 to 3 minutes, or until bread has gone into a full "balloon." If there are seams or dry bits of dough—or for a variety of other reasons—your bread may not go into a full "balloon," don't worry, it will still taste great.

The more you bake pitas, the more you will become familiar with all the little tricks and pitfalls, and your breads will more consistently "balloon." But even then, if you're like me, it won't always "balloon" fully and you won't mind because the taste will still be wonderful.

When baked, remove and wrap together with other warm breads in a large kitchen towel (this will keep the breads soft). When first half has been rolled out and baked, repeat for rest of dough, or store in refrigerator for later use, as described above. You can also divide the dough into more, smaller pieces if you wish, to give you smaller breads.

To cook on top of the stove, preheat your griddle or cast iron skillet over medium-high heat. When hot, rub on a little oil to clean and grease surface of griddle (as if making pancakes.) Divide dough in half and divide the first half into eight pieces, as set out above. Flatten each with well-floured hands. Roll out breads one at a time until they are less than ¼-inch thick and 8 inches in diameter. Gently put one bread onto griddle. Cook this first side for 15 to 20 seconds and gently turn to its second side. Cook second side for approximately one minute, until big bubbles begin to appear. Turn bread again to first side, and cook until bread "balloons" fully. To help this process along, you can press gently with a towel on those areas where bubbles have already formed, trying to push the bubble into areas that are still flat. (This is a technique that will quickly improve with practice.) Breads shouldn't take more than 2 minutes to cook, and likewise, they shouldn't cook so fast that they begin to burn. Adjust heat until you find a workable temperature. Roll out and cook the rest in the same way. There is no need to oil griddle between breads, but after four or five breads you might want to rub the same lightly oiled paper towel over surface. When breads are done, wrap in a towel and serve.

Makes 16 pitas, about 8 inches in diameter.

Adapted from *Flatbreads & Flavors: A Baker's Atlas*, by Jeffrey Alford and Naomi Duguid (William Morrow, 1995).

Yogurt and Pomegranate Dip

This Yemenite sauce, Akeel, is a refreshing snack on a hot day and a delicious dip for bread or sauce for grilled meat at any time. Akeel takes only minutes to prepare; preparation is simply a matter of stirring cilantro leaf, pomegranate seeds and chopped scallion into chilled yogurt. Akeel is beautiful served in glass bowls.

1 ripe pomegranate

2 cups plain yogurt, chilled

2 scallions, finely chopped
  (white and tender green)

¼ cup chopped fresh cilantro leaves

sprigs of fresh mint,
  for garnish (optional)

Cut pomegranate in half across its equator. Gently lift out seeds, section by section and set aside in a bowl, discarding any discolored parts. You don't want seeds to "bleed" their juice into yogurt, so try not to bruise or break them.

Place yogurt in a glass or other decorative serving bowl, stir in scallions, cilantro and all but a small handful of pomegranate seeds. Garnish with mint sprigs and sprinkle remaining pomegranate seeds on top. Serve slightly chilled.

Serve akeel to guests on a warm autumn afternoon (when pomegranates are in season) as a refreshing snack on its own or with flatbreads. Alternatively, include in meals as a dip or sauce for bread, grilled meats, or steamed vegetables.

Makes about 2½ cups.

Adapted from *Flatbreads & Flavors: A Baker's Atlas*, by Jeffrey Alford and Naomi Duguid (William Morrow, 1995).

Aglaia Kremezi

"Use seasonal produce and use it frugally."

Aglaia Kremezi is a writer, not a chef, and her lessons are akin to what an immigrant grandmother would have taught you: don't waste food, respect the earth's resources and use what the earth gives you at that particular moment.

It is the basis of Mediterranean culture and the region's celebrated cuisine. From her home on the Island of Kea, Cyclades, Greece, these are the lessons Kremezi continues to teach the many annual visitors to the cooking school she operates with her husband.

Like most Greek women, Kremezi grew up cooking. From the time she was a young girl, she was helping her mother and grandmothers in the kitchen. She always enjoyed preparing food and reading about foods from around the world. "I always liked to experiment, even when I was working more than twelve hours a day," she recalls.

The Athens native studied art, graphic design and photography in London, and never envisioned a career in food. She was working as a freelance photographer when the captions she was sending along with her photos began to catch the attention of editors, who encouraged her to write stories to go along with her photos. She eventually became a full-time journalist, writing about fashion, life-style issues, theater and art, as well rising up the ranks in magazine editing positions. "Even when I was editor-in-chief, I was always, in my free time, making dinner and lunch and thinking about what I was going to write while I was cooking. It helped me focus," she said.

Writing about food, however, was never part of her plan. In the late 1980s, she started to notice a glut of books on Italian cooking and wondered why there were none on Greek food and cuisine. To rectify the situation, she began working on a book, *The Foods of Greece*, which was released in 1992. She thought it would be a one-time project, but the more she traveled to promote the book, the more she came to be regarded internationally as a Greek food expert. A second book in 2000, *The Foods of the Greek Islands*, only solidified her position. She began traveling both to teach and promote her books, and in March 1995, came to teach at the Zona Spray Cooking School, where she taught a selection of spring and Easter foods. What else would she teach at that time of year?

Mediterranean cooking is peasant cuisine, and the poor can't afford to waste a single ingredient, nor can they afford to use foods that aren't in season. "We use seasonal produce and we use it frugally. We are not wasting anything at all. This is the way I was brought up. We cultivate seasonal produce in our garden on the island. There's not a lot of water here and it is expensive to produce what we produce, so we try to use up every bit of it. This is the gist of Mediterranean cooking, all over the Mediterranean."

Kremezi would never consider making stuffed tomatoes in the winter, when tomatoes aren't in season. "There are other things that you can cook with in the winter. Each season has its produce and if you learn to use them properly, you can create quite a lot of very interesting dishes that are flavorful and also not expensive," she said.

In 2000, Kremezi and her husband moved to Kea, where they operate a school for cooking vacations, teaching their guests about the Mediterranean way. "The people who come here go home and rave about the simplicity, and the flavor of the ingredients," she said.

Tunisian Carrot Salad

1 pound carrots

2 garlic cloves, minced

2 to 3 tablespoons sherry or red wine
   vinegar

½ to 1 teaspoon harissa or Tabasco
   or cayenne

1 teaspoon ground caraway

1 teaspoon salted fresh cilantro

3 to 4 tablespoons virgin olive oil

salt, to taste

a few sprigs of parsley

3 to 4 slices of preserved lemons

a few black kalamata olives, for garnish

Wash, peel and cut carrots in half lengthwise. Chop coarsely and transfer to a saucepan. Cover carrots with cold water and bring water to a boil. Reduce heat and simmer until tender, 20 to 30 minutes.

Drain, then mash with a fork in a large bowl. Mix in 2 tablespoons vinegar, ½ teaspoon harissa, garlic, caraway, salted cilantro and olive oil. Stir well and taste. Season with a little salt or more vinegar and harissa if needed. Let cool completely and refrigerate for at least 3 hours or overnight before serving.

Decorate with parsley, chopped preserved lemon and olives just before serving.

Makes 4 servings.

Easter Soup with Chicken

3 pounds chicken parts (necks, backs, wings, legs, thighs)

2 large onions, halved

½ pound chicken livers

sea salt

½ cup olive oil

2 cups finely chopped scallions

1 small chili pepper, minced, or freshly ground pepper, to taste

1½ cups chopped fresh dill

2 eggs

juice of 1½ or 2 lemons

Wash chicken pieces thoroughly and place in a pot with onions. Cover with cold water, season with salt and simmer for about 1 hour, skimming the surface several times.

Remove chicken from pot. Remove chicken meat from bones and cut into small pieces. Strain stock and discard onions. Let stock cool and remove fat. (Up to this point, the preparations can be made a day ahead. You can refrigerate chicken pieces and stock, making it easier to skim off fat.)

To finish soup, wash livers well and cut into small pieces. In a skillet, heat olive oil and sauté livers with scallions and chili pepper, if using. Add chicken with 1 cup dill, and turn a few times with a wooden spoon. Transfer mixture to a pot and add stock plus an equal amount water, and bring to a boil. Reduce heat and simmer for 12 to 15 minutes. Taste and add more pepper and salt if needed.

Beat eggs in a large bowl with about 2 spoonfuls water and the juice of 1 lemon. Slowly add cupfuls of hot soup to bowl, beating continuously with whisk. When egg mixture is very hot, pour slowly into pot, stirring well, over very low heat, to prevent curdling. Taste and add more lemon juice if needed. Sprinkle with remaining dill and serve immediately.

Makes 6 to 8 servings.

Note: Some people add ½ to 1 cup short grain rice to the soup.

Eggplant, Pepper and Walnut Spread

2 large eggplants (about 2 pounds)

3 tablespoons olive oil

½ to 1 teaspoon Near Eastern or Aleppo crushed peppers or red pepper flakes

3 green bell peppers, seeded, halved and cut into ½-inch pieces

1 large clove garlic

1 cup walnuts

2 teaspoons sherry vinegar, or to taste

2 tablespoons extra-virgin olive oil, plus extra for topping the jars

½ teaspoon sea salt, or to taste

Wash and dry eggplants. Preheat broiler. To develop a smoky flavor, broil whole eggplants, turning occasionally, until skins blacken on all sides, about 40 minutes total. (Alternatively, place 3 layers aluminum foil on an electric burner, place eggplants on foil and sear, letting skin blacken on one side before turning to blacken on another side, about 35 minutes total.)

When they are cool enough to handle, peel eggplants and discard any seeds. Let pulp drain in a colander for at least 30 minutes.

Warm 3 tablespoons olive oil in a skillet. Add crushed red pepper and bell peppers and sauté until peppers are soft, 6 to 10 minutes. Let cool.

Cut garlic clove lengthwise and discard green sprout. Place drained eggplant pulp, fried peppers with their oil, walnuts, vinegar, extra-virgin olive oil and salt in the bowl of a food processor. Process, pulsing the motor on and off, until mixture becomes a smooth spread. Taste and add more salt or vinegar if needed.

Place spread in jars, pressing down to eliminate all air pockets. Top each jar with a little olive oil and refrigerate. Serve this spread as an appetizer, with crudities or toast. It is also good on baked or steamed potatoes.

Eggplant, Pepper and Walnut Spread will keep for 3 to 4 weeks in refrigerator.

Makes about 3½ cups.

Beatrice Ojakangas

"I simplify everything."

She's as American as apple pie, but her name and her writings fool many into thinking she's fresh from Scandinavia. Beatrice Ojakangas is, after all, known as the Scandinavian Chef. But this native of Duluth, Minnesota, and author of more than two dozen cookbooks even got her start as part of an iconic American tradition—the Pillsbury Bake-Off.

Ojakangas graduated from the University of Minnesota in Duluth with a degree in home economics on a Friday, got married two days later, and was immediately off to England, where her husband was stationed in the Air Force.

It was 1957 and on a whim, Ojakangas saw an entry form for the bake-off at the officers' wives club. She decided to create a recipe for a yeast bread with cheese in it, but her first experiment was far from successful. The cheese all fell to the bottom and the loaf turned into one giant cheese sandwich. She noticed that smaller pieces of the cheese seemed to stay suspended in the bread, so she changed her recipe and Chunk O' Cheese Bread was born.

By the time she found out she was a finalist in the bake-off, Ojakangas was pregnant with her first child, due October 14, 1957, the same day as the bake-off. Back home in Minnesota by then, Ojakangas delivered her daughter early, on October 1, and was able to compete in the bake-off, while her mother cared for the baby at home. The bread won second place and Ojakangas walked away with a $5,000 prize. While the money helped pay for her husband's graduate school, the honor helped to spark her fifty-year writing career, which includes twenty-eight cookbooks covering a myriad of topics.

Ojakangas is probably best known for her work in Scandinavian cooking, which came about partly due to her Finnish heritage and partly, again, because she was trying to find something to do while a stranger in a foreign land. Her husband was serving a Fulbright Scholarship in Finland, and with her bake-off experience behind her, Ojakangas contacted the U.S. Information Service and asked if she could talk to local women's groups. With the few words of Finnish that her grandmother had taught her, she would visit a different village every weekend, explaining to the group what an American woman's life was like and in turn, learning about their days in Finland. Her mother was anxious to know about the homeland of her parents, and told Ojakangas to pretend that she was a bird on her shoulder, with the request to tell her everything that she would see from her perch. She learned the details of daily life in Finland—their meals, their holidays, their celebrations—and returned to the States with a box of recipes.

The family's next move was to California, where her husband worked on his doctoral degree at Stanford, and Ojakangas got a job at *Sunset Magazine* as a typist in the food department. While she typed other writers' stories by day, at night she was writing her own cookbook of the recipes she had collected in Finland.

In 1964, *The Finnish Cookbook* debuted; it has never been out of print. The same year, Ojakangas' husband completed his PhD and the family returned to Minnesota. Book after book followed, because, as she likes to point out, once you get the first one published, the rest are easier to get into print.

Over the years, Ojakangas has traveled extensively to teach and in 1992, she came to Zona Spray's school to demonstrate how to bake specialty Christmas breads. While she doesn't teach much these days beyond Minnesota, Ojakangas still writes books regularly and said her goal in both is the same, "simplicity."

"I get so frustrated trying to follow someone else's recipes. You can do it so much easier. I simplify everything," she says.

Perhaps because she is rooted in the Midwest, Ojakangas is committed to writing recipes that are accessible to all, regardless of where they live. If she can find the ingredients in her hometown of Duluth, then she's fairly certain the ingredients can be found just about everywhere. "Things have to be totally do-able and totally clear," she said.

While she knows her attitude may never earn her a spot among the world's food elite, she's content to write books on food topics that are ordinary, not trendy. But when it comes to food elite, don't count her out there either. In 1990, her skills earned her a spot as a guest on Julia Child's PBS show, *Baking with Julia*, where the pair baked Danish pastry together, and her 1988 book, *The Great Scandinavian Baking Book*, was inducted into the James Beard Foundation's Cookbook Hall of Fame in 2005.

Wild Rice Three Grain Bread

2 packages active dry yeast

2½ cups warm water
   (105 to 115 degrees)

½ cup honey

1 cup instant nonfat dry milk

4 tablespoons butter or lard,
   melted and cooled

1 tablespoon salt

1 cup rolled oats, regular
   or old-fashioned

1 cup dark rye flour

1 cup whole wheat flour

2 cups cooked wild rice

4 to 4½ cups bread flour
   or unbleached all-purpose flour

for glaze, 1 egg beaten
   with 1 tablespoon water

½ cup hulled sunflower seeds
   salted or plain

In a large bowl, dissolve yeast in warm water; add honey. Let stand a few minutes until yeast begins to bubble. Add milk, butter, salt, oats, rye flour, whole wheat flour, wild rice and 2 cups bread flour. Beat until smooth.

Let dough rest for 15 minutes. Stir in enough bread flour to make a stiff dough. Turn out onto board and knead for 10 minutes until dough feels springy, adding only enough flour to keep dough from sticking.

Turn dough into a clean, oiled bowl. Turn over to oil top. Let rise until doubled, about 2 hours. Punch down and knead briefly on a lightly oiled board.

To shape, divide dough into 3 parts and shape into rope-like strands about 36 inches long. Shape into a braid and place on baking sheet in a wreath; trim about 1 cup dough off ends and pinch ends to seal together into a wreath. Shape reserved dough into a strand and fashion into a bow. Place bow over sealed ends.

Let rise in a warm place until about doubled, about 45 minutes.

Brush with egg-water mixture. Sprinkle with sunflower seeds. Bake in a 375-degree oven, baking 40 to 45 minutes or until bread tests done.

Makes 1 large wreath.

Fruited Christmas Bread

Cardamom is optional here, as are the candied fruits, but in Norway and Denmark, it's not Christmas without this traditional fruited bread.

2 packages active dry yeast

½ cup warm water (105 to 115 degrees)

2 cups milk, scalded and cooled to lukewarm

½ cup sugar

½ cup (1 stick) butter, softened

2 eggs, beaten

2 teaspoons salt

1 teaspoon freshly ground cardamom, optional

7 to 8 cups flour

1 cup golden or dark raisins

1 cup mixed candied fruits, optional

egg wash, made of 1 egg and 2 tablespoons milk

pearl sugar or crushed sugar cubes and chopped almonds

1 cup powdered sugar

2 to 3 tablespoons heavy whipping cream

½ teaspoon almond extract

In a large mixing bowl, dissolve yeast in warm water and let stand for 5 minutes, or until yeast foams. Beat in milk, sugar, butter, eggs, salt and cardamom (if using). Stir in half the flour and beat well. Add enough of the remaining flour to make a soft dough. Cover and let rest for 15 minutes.

Turn dough out onto a lightly floured board. Knead for 10 minutes, or until dough is smooth and satiny. Knead in raisins and candied fruits (if using). Wash bowl, lightly grease it and return dough to it. Turn dough over so that it is greased on all sides. Cover and let rise in a warm place until doubled, 45 minutes to 1 hour. Punch down and let rise again until doubled in bulk, 45 minutes to 1 hour.

Butter three 8 or 9-inch round cake pans. Turn dough out onto a lightly oiled work surface. Divide dough into three equal parts. Shape each portion into a smooth round loaf and place in a baking pan, smooth-side up. Cover and let rise until doubled, 45 minutes to 1 hour.

Preheat oven to 375 degrees. Stir together egg and milk to make egg wash. Brush tops of loaves with egg wash and sprinkle with sugar and/or almonds. Bake for 25 to 30 minutes, until golden and a wooden skewer inserted in the center comes out clean. Cool loaves in their pans on wire racks.

To prepare glaze, stir together powdered sugar, 2 to 3 tablespoons cream and almond extract in a small bowl until smooth. Add remaining tablespoon cream, if necessary.

Remove loaves from pans and spread an equal amount of glaze on each.

Makes 3 loaves.

Marzipan Birthday Kringle

This irresistible birthday cake has a buttery, flaky, yeast-risen pastry which requires twelve hours of refrigeration—and an almond paste filling. It is twisted into a pretzel shape and coated with sliced almonds. Throughout Scandinavia, the symbol of the pretzel marks the bakery section of a supermarket or bakery shop on the street.

For the bread:

1 package active dry yeast

1 tablespoon sugar

½ cup warm milk (105 to 115 degrees)

1 cup heavy whipping cream,
  at room temperature

3½ cups flour

¼ cup sugar

1 teaspoon salt

1 teaspoon freshly ground cardamom

½ cup (1 stick) firm unsalted butter,
  cut into tablespoons

For the almond filling:

1 package (8 ounces) almond paste,
  about 1 cup

½ cup chopped, blanched almonds

½ cup sugar

1 teaspoon cinnamon

1 teaspoon almond extract

For the topping:

½ cup sugar

1 egg white, beaten

¼ cup sliced almonds

In a small bowl, combine yeast, sugar and milk. Let stand until yeast dissolves and begins to foam, about 10 minutes. Gently stir in cream.

In a large bowl, combine flour, sugar, salt and cardamom. Cut in butter until batter resembles coarse meal. Fold in yeast mixture just until all of the dough is moistened. Cover and refrigerate for 12 to 24 hours.

To prepare filling, just before rolling out dough, blend together almond paste, almonds, sugar, cinnamon and almond extract.

Turn chilled dough out onto a lightly floured surface. With a rolling pin, pound dough until flattened to about a 2-inch thickness. Roll dough out to make a 24-inch square. Spread filling to within 1 inch of the edges of the square and roll dough up as tightly as possible.

Sprinkle sugar for topping on the work surface. Roll dough firmly into sugar to coat it well, and, at the same time, stretch to form a log of dough measuring 36 to 40 inches long. Cover a baking sheet with parchment paper. Place roll on the paper in the shape of a pretzel.

Brush surface with egg white and sprinkle with almonds. Cover and let rise for 45 minutes, or until puffy but not doubled. Preheat oven to 375 degrees. Bake for 25 to 30 minutes, until golden. Makes approximately 16 servings.

Steven Raichlen

"I teach the seven methods of live fire cooking."

I t's hard to imagine from the image of Steven Raichlen on the cover of his popular barbecue books—sunglasses, denim shirt, tongs in hand—that he is actually trained in classical French cuisine.

But it was France where he trained, France where he met Zona Spray and French cuisine that he taught, when he came to Spray's cooking school throughout the 1980s and 90s.

Raichlen, who majored in French literature at Reed College, was on a fellowship in France in 1975 to study medieval cooking, when he asked Anne Willan, founder of the LaVarenne Cooking School, if he could interview her for his studies. He walked out as one of her employees. With his knowledge of French and English, Willan tapped Raichlen to be a translator at the school, and he began to study cooking there.

Raichlen recalls that in the 1970s, anyone who was interested in food came to LaVarenne and the school helped to fuel the American awakening to food and the country's awe and wonderment of French cuisine. "LaVarenne was the manifestation of that period. Every major food writer, every major editor of food magazines, came through LaVarenne at that point."

Raichlen met Spray at the school and the two became friends. When LaVarenne chefs toured in the U.S., they typically would come to Hudson, Ohio, to teach classes at Spray's school and Raichlen first arrived there in the capacity of a translator. He later returned numerous times, teaching French cuisine and technique in dishes like bouillabaisse, lobster thermidor, pâté and quiche. "My recollection was that it was exceedingly well-run and surprisingly sophisticated for a school of its kind. One doesn't think of Hudson, Ohio, as a hot bed of culinary innovation." Raichlen said in some small cooking schools at the time, chefs could not even be assured that someone would have purchased their ingredients, but that wasn't the case at Zona's school.

"I do always remember Zona with enormous fondness. So many big names from around the world came to this tiny town, Hudson, Ohio."

Over the years, Raichlen's cooking and teaching evolved until he eventually cultivated a specialty in barbecuing, which he describes the perfect prism through which to study the world. "It's the world's oldest cooking method and the world's most universal cooking method. It enabled me to embrace all of my interests—history, anthropology, evolution, culture and travel."

With twenty-eight books to his credit, five James Beard Awards and three awards from the International Association of Culinary Professionals, Raichlen now confines his teaching to his own school, Barbecue University, held yearly at the Broadmoor Resort in Colorado Springs, Colorado. Raichlen said he approaches each class with a deliberate method of teaching. "I have a body of knowledge I am trying to impart—the seven methods of live fire cooking. I teach iconic dishes of barbecue in North American and beyond. I have a very deliberate approach."

Bouillabaisse a la Bostonaise

2 onions, diced

2 leeks, diced

1 small bulb fennel, diced (optional)

4 cloves garlic, smashed

4 tablespoons olive oil for sautéing

4 to 5 tomatoes, seeded and finely chopped

½ cup fresh chopped parsley

rind and juice of ½ orange

pinches of bay leaf, thyme, oregano, basil, savory

generous pinch of saffron

4 pounds firm-fleshed fish, such as monkfish, halibut, hake, sea bass or striped bass, turbot, grey mullet, Pollack or red snapper

1 or 2 small lobsters, cut up and shells cracked

3 pounds shellfish, mussels, clams, shrimp, scallops

1 pound flimsy fish, such as whiting, flounder, sole, scrod

salt and fresh black pepper

12 cups fish stock or water

2 tablespoons Pernod

juice of the other ½ orange

Sauté onion, leeks, fennel and garlic in 4 tablespoons olive oil until soft. Add tomatoes and flavorings and cook to evaporate excess liquid.

Layer firm-fleshed fish and shellfish on top of vegetables, salting and peppering each layer. Add fish stock to cover and boil for 6 minutes. Add flimsy fish next and fish stock to cover. Return to a boil and boil until fish is cooked (another 3 minutes).

Transfer fish to a warm platter, keeping kinds together. Reduce fish broth by boiling until it's really well flavored. Force through a vegetable mill or strainer. Correct seasoning and add a splash Pernod and orange juice. Serve broth and fish separately.

Makes 10 to 12 servings.

Lobster Thermidor

This dish was invented, so legend holds, on January 24, 1894, at the restaurant Maire (since disappeared) at the corner of the Boulevardes Strassbourg and Saint Denis. On that evening, a play by Sardou called Thermidor was due to play at the Comedie Francaise; and Monsieur Maire created lobster Thermidor in its honor. The play flopped, but the critics devoured the lobster dish with gusto. Originally, Thermidor was the name given to the month of July by the zealots of the French Revolution. The 9th of Thermidor (July 27, 1794) is a red letter day in French history: On this day, Robespierre was arrested and sentenced to the guillotine, thereby ending the bloodiest phase of the French Revolution. There is no easy way to kill a lobster, but steaming it, as described below, seems much less cruel than cutting it up alive, as the traditional recipes call for. Court bouillon means "short bouillon," referring to an aromatic poaching liquid that can be made much more quickly than stock.

2 live 1½ pound lobsters

For the court bouillon:

1½ cups water

½ cup dry white wine

1 carrot, finely chopped

1 stalk celery, finely chopped

1 onion, diced

1 bouquet garni

10 black peppercorns

To finish the sauce:

4 tablespoons butter,
	plus 2 tablespoons for baking

2 tablespoons very finely chopped
	shallots

4 tablespoons flour

¼ cup dry white vermouth

1 cup heavy or whipping cream

2 tablespoons cognac

1 to 2 teaspoons good Dijon-style
	mustard or 1 teaspoon dry mustard

2 teaspoons tarragon, finely chopped

4 tablespoons breadcrumbs

Combine ingredients for court bouillon and bring to a boil in a large pot. Add lobsters, cover pot tightly and steam lobsters for 12 minutes. Remove lobsters and let cool. Strain court bouillon into a saucepan and boil until only ¾ cup liquid remains.

To prepare sauce, melt butter in a saucepan and sauté shallots over medium heat for 2 minutes, or until lightly browned. Stir in flour and cook for 2 minutes. Combine reduced court bouillon, vermouth, cream and cognac and whisk them into roux (butter-flour mixture) off heat. Return pan to heat, bring sauce to a boil, whisking constantly, reduce heat and simmer sauce for 5 minutes, or until well flavored and thickened.

Remove large claws from lobsters and carefully cut bodies in half lengthwise (it is important not to damage shells, as these will be used for serving). Remove tail meat from each shell, discard vein and cut meat into ½-inch dice. Scoop tomalley (the greenish paste) from lobster heads and reserve for sauce. Discard paper-like sack on the forward most part of lobster shell. Crack claws, extract meat and cut into ½-inch dice. You are now ready to finish sauce and bake the lobster Thermidor.

Remove sauce from heat and whisk in reserved tomalley, mustard and tarragon. Season with pepper—it is unlikely you will need salt, because court bouillon is salty. Stir in lobster meat. Spoon this mixture into empty half lobster shells. Sprinkle stuffed lobsters with breadcrumbs and dot tops with remaining butter. The lobster Thermidor can be prepared up to 12 hours ahead of time to this stage and kept in refrigerator.

Preheat oven to 400 degrees. Bake lobsters for 20 minutes, or until filling is hot and top is browned.

Makes 4 servings.

Note: You may wish to run the lobster under the broiler to brown the top. Serve the lobsters on folded white napkins.

Alsacian Onion Tart

For the dough:

1 envelope dry yeast

1 cup warm milk

1 teaspoon sugar

pinch of salt

¾ cup warm milk

7 tablespoons butter, softened

1 whole egg

1 egg yolk

2 teaspoons salt

3½ cups flour, sifted

For the filling:

4 ounces bacon, diced

3 tablespoons butter

2½ pounds onions, thinly sliced

¼ cup sour cream

2 eggs, lightly beaten

1 teaspoon caraway seed

1 teaspoon salt

3 tablespoons minced parsley

For dough: Proof yeast in ¼ cup warm milk with sugar and pinch of salt. In a large bowl, combine yeast mixture with remaining ingredients.

Knead dough on a floured surface until smooth and elastic, adding tablespoons of flour as needed if dough is sticky.

If using a food processor, proof yeast. Place flour, salt and butter in work bowl and process 5 seconds. Add eggs and process with 2 or 3 on-off turns. Add yeast mixture, process just to blend and with machine running, add remaining milk through the feed tube and process until dough forms a soft smooth ball.

Transfer dough to a lightly buttered bowl or baka bowl and let rise, covered with a towel (or baka lid), until doubled, about 45 minutes to an hour.

For filling: Cook bacon in butter until translucent; add onions and cook until they are very soft and golden in color. This will take 20 to 30 minutes or more over low heat. Let cool slightly.

Stir sour cream, eggs, caraway and salt into onions.

To assemble: Punch down dough and roll into a rectangle 13 by 19-inches. Transfer to a baking sheet lined with parchment and push up a one-inch rim around the edge.

Spread filling over dough and bake tart at 400 degrees for 40 to 45 minutes, or until edges are brown and filling is set. Sprinkle tart with parsley, cut into squares or strips and serve warm.

Makes 20 to 24 squares.

Sauce Rouille (Red Pepper Sauce)

2 red peppers, cored and seeded

2 cloves garlic, peeled

2 to 3 slices white bread, crusts removed, soaked in water and squeezed dry

pinch of saffron

pinch of cayenne

salt

5 tablespoons olive oil

Broil peppers until skin blisters and place in a paper bag for 5 minutes. Peel off skin. Purée peppers with garlic, bread and spices in a mortar and pestle or a food processor. Gradually beat in olive oil.

Serve sauce rouille spread on slices of toasted or fried French bread rubbed with a cut clove of garlic.

Makes about 1 cup.

Michele Scicolone

"Feel comfortable in the kitchen"

If you're looking for Michele Scicolone, check the airport. It's likely that she's on her way to Italy or on her way back. Scicolone has spent the past forty years traveling to Italy, transporting so much of its cuisine back to the United States that you can almost imagine her stuffing it into her suitcase on every trip.

She first opened that suitcase for us in the early 1980s, when Scicolone wrote a magazine article for *Food and Wine*, detailing the various kinds of gnocchi made in Italy. It was an education for American palates, which, at the time weren't familiar with gnocchi that didn't involve potatoes. But Scicolone was anxious to share all that she had learned in her travels to the land of her grandparents and husband, wine expert Charles Scicolone, which began on their honeymoon to Rome in 1970.

With sixteen books and countless classes behind her, Scicolone is one of the country's leading experts on Italian food and she has far exceeded her life's goal of wanting to one day write about food.

Scicolone grew up in Brooklyn, New York, in a typical Italian-American family. Food was central to her family life. "Everybody cooked. It wasn't a big deal, it wasn't a chore," she recalls. "It was a big part of our life and it was a very enjoyable thing for us." Scicolone's first adventure in the kitchen was making espresso. "I loved coffee. I don't like milk to this day. When I was a child, I couldn't drink milk unless there was some coffee in it. If no one else was making coffee, I'd make sure I made it. Coffee and wine weren't forbidden to us."

After high school, she worked in secretarial and other office jobs, but later returned to school attending New York University and Hunter College were she studied journalism, food science and nutrition with the hopes of one day being able to write about food.

She started out working at a public relations agency, but less than a year later, landed a job on the editorial staff of *Ladies Home Journal*, working in the magazine's test kitchen developing recipes and stories. After a few years at the magazine, she took off to travel in Europe and her adventures in Italy began in earnest.

In the early 1980s, she started teaching at the New School Culinary Center in New York, and it didn't take the owner long to limit her teaching to only Italian classes. A steady string of cookbooks followed, and by the 1990s she was traveling the country teaching Italian cooking techniques and promoting her books.

Zona Spray brought her to her cooking school in December 1995, where she taught about Italian appetizers and holiday entertaining and again in March 1997, when she taught from one of her most popular books, *Fresh Taste of Italy*.

It was her own background that she drew on when HBO approached her about creating recipes for a cookbook to accompany its acclaimed series *The Sopranos*. Scicolone had never watched the show, but when meeting with its creators, she talked about what Carmella would cook for Tony and what Tony would like to eat. "I named things I grew up with," Scicolone said. "That's how I got the job." *The Sopranos Family Cookbook* came out in 2002, followed in 2006 by *Entertaining with the Sopranos*.

When she teaches, Scicolone said her hope is that she will make her students feel comfortable in the kitchen, and to not feel that cooking is a chore. Students often approach cooking as difficult and messy and a lot of work. "It doesn't have to be that way," she said. "I want them to enjoy being there preparing their food and have a good time."

Scicolone's teaching trips to places like Ohio are few these days, preferring to spend her travel time going back to Italy, where she and Charles take culinary tour groups or conduct research for future writing. "I always find a reason to go back," she says.

Roman Pizza di Ricotta

For the crust:

1½ cups all-purpose flour

⅓ cup sugar

½ teaspoon salt

½ teaspoon baking powder

8 tablespoons (1 stick) unsalted butter, softened

1 large egg, lightly beaten

For the filling:

1 package (3 ounces) cream cheese, softened

¼ cup sugar

1 tablespoon dark rum

1 large egg yolk

1 cup (8 ounces) whole milk ricotta cheese

To make crust: In a large bowl, combine flour, sugar, salt and baking powder. With a pastry blender or a fork, cut in butter until mixture resembles coarse meal. Stir in egg until a soft dough forms. Pat dough into the bottom and up the sides of a 9-inch fluted tart pan with a removable bottom. Refrigerate for 30 minutes.

To make filling: Preheat oven to 350 degrees. In a large bowl, beat together cream cheese, sugar and rum. Beat in egg yolk until well blended. Add ricotta and beat until smooth.

Pour cheese mixture into prepared tart shell. Bake for 45 minutes, or until puffed and golden brown. Cool for 10 minutes on a wire rack. Remove pan rim and let tart cool completely. Serve at room temperature or lightly chilled. Store in refrigerator.

Serves 8.

Adapted from *La Dolce Vita* by Michele Scicolone (William Morrow, 1993).

Polenta and Olive Focaccia

(Focaccia di Granoturco)

1 package active dry yeast
  (or 2½ teaspoons)

¼ cup warm water (105 to 110 degrees)

1¼ cups warm milk

2 tablespoons olive oil

3 to 3½ cups unbleached
  all-purpose flour

1 cup fine yellow cornmeal

1 teaspoon salt

1 cup green olives, pitted
  and coarsely chopped

In a large bowl, sprinkle yeast over warm water. Let stand 5 minutes to soften.

Stir in milk and olive oil. Add 3 cups flour, cornmeal and salt. Stir well until a dough forms. Turn dough out onto a lightly floured board.

Knead dough until smooth and elastic, adding additional flour as needed to prevent dough from sticking.

Oil a large bowl. Place dough in the bowl, turning over to oil top. Cover with a towel and let rise in a warm place until doubled in bulk, about 1 hour.

Flatten dough to eliminate air bubbles. Knead in olives.

Oil a 15 by 10 by 1-inch jelly roll pan. Add dough, patting with your hands to fit the pan evenly. Cover with a towel and let rise until puffy, about 45 minutes.

Preheat oven to 450 degrees. Bake dough until browned and crusty, about 30 minutes. Slide bread onto a rack to cool slightly. Cut into 3 by 2-inch rectangles and serve.

Makes 8 servings.

Adapted from *A Fresh Taste of Italy* by Michele Scicolone (Broadway Books, 1997).

Onion and Tomato Frittata

¼ cup extra-virgin olive oil

2 medium onions, peeled
and thinly sliced

1 large tomato, cored and thinly sliced

6 large eggs

2 ounces prosciutto,
coarsely chopped (about ½ cup)

¼ cup freshly grated
Parmigiano-Reggiano

2 tablespoons chopped fresh basil

salt and freshly ground black pepper

In a 10-inch ovenproof skillet, heat 2 tablespoons of oil over medium-low heat. Add onions and cook, stirring occasionally, until very tender but not browned, about 10 minutes. Stir in tomato and cook for 10 minutes more. Transfer to a bowl and let cool slightly. Do not clean pan.

In a bowl, beat eggs until well blended. Stir in prosciutto, cheese, basil and salt and pepper to taste. Stir in onion mixture.

In the same skillet, heat remaining 2 tablespoons oil over medium-low heat. Add egg mixture. Cook, lifting edges two or three times to allow uncooked egg to slide under cooked portion, until frittata is set around edges but still moist in center, about 10 minutes.

Transfer skillet to broiler. Cook just until top of frittata is set, about 1 minute. Watch carefully so that it does not brown.

Invert frittata onto a serving dish. Serve warm or at room temperature, cut into wedges.

Makes 6 servings.

Adapted from *The Antipasto Table* by Michele Scicolone (William Morrow, 1991).

The Recipes

Chapter 6

Cuisine American

Pam Anderson

"The one principle I like to talk through is how to cook without a book."

Pam Anderson sees herself as the "every cook" and her book topics seem to speak to every cook, no matter where they are in their culinary development. They track Anderson's own evolution, too, from working wife and mother to an award-winning cookbook author and national food columnist for *USA Weekend Magazine.* "All of my books are very different and deal with different aspects of the cooking life. I've come to see myself as the every cook. My books really follow my life," she says.

She's written books about finding the perfect recipe, how to get dinner on the table every night and how to have people over without stressing, all topics born out of her own life. Her struggle with weight issues was chronicled in her 2008 book, *The Perfect Recipe for Losing Weight and Eating Great.* She is in many ways the embodiment of the American home cook.

Anderson (yes, she is used to being questioned about *Baywatch*, and no, different Pam Anderson) grew up in Panama City, Florida, and her southern roots are deep in fried chicken and biscuits. After college, she worked in an office job and spent her evenings cooking. Eventually, she started working as a caterer, trying to earn some money from all of that cooking. In 1986, she and her husband moved to Connecticut, and she discovered that she was just thirty minutes away from the offices of *Cook's* magazine, which had long been one of her favorites. The following year she accepted a job in the magazine's test kitchen. Although the pay was low, it did save her cooking school tuition and she was the publication's food editor by the time it folded. In 1992, when it was reincarnated as *Cook's Illustrated*, Anderson began researching and writing articles for the magazine, but by 1996, decided to venture into books. She is currently at work on her seventh book.

Anderson first came to the Western Reserve School of Cooking in 1999, when Carole Ferguson owned the school. Anderson was touring for her first book, *The Perfect Recipe.* She has returned several times since, often to promote one of her latest books. The irony is that Anderson's message is that one doesn't need a recipe to cook. It was, in fact, the title of her second book, *How to Cook Without a Book*.

When she teaches, regardless of the subject, Anderson's goal is to help students feel comfortable cooking without a recipe. "The one principle I like to talk through is how to cook without a book. If people can see certain recipes as techniques and formulas, as opposed to individual isolated recipes, once you start cooking in that way, it frees you up to create. You are cooking in your own way and you aren't so recipe dependent."

Anderson believes that getting a meal on the table is much easier if you can rely on yourself, rather than a recipe. She likes helping cooks realize that they don't need twenty different recipes for sautéed chicken with a pan sauce. They just need to learn the technique once and then follow their creativity based on what they have, not run to the store for special ingredients. "Recipes are rigid. When people open the refrigerator and can't see dinner, that's when people should have the knowledge to be able to cook based on what they've got, what's in season," she said.

The newest evolution in Anderson's life is sharing her writing with her grown daughters, Maggy and Sharon. The trio writes a blog together, Three Many Cooks, and in 2011, began sharing the writing duties of Anderson's *USA Weekly* column as well.

The Best Macaroni and Cheese

If you are in a hurry, or prefer to sprinkle the dish with crumbled common crackers or saltines, skip the bread crumb step. You can make fresh bread crumbs by grating bread on the large holes of a box grater, but the easiest method, by far, is processing it to coarse crumbs in a food processor fitted with the steel blade.

For the toasted bread crumbs:

1 cup fresh bread crumbs from French or Italian bread

pinch of salt

1½ tablespoons melted butter

For the macaroni and cheese:

salt

½ pound elbow macaroni

4 tablespoons butter

2 large eggs

1 can (12 ounces) evaporated milk, heated to warm

¼ teaspoon hot red pepper sauce

ground black pepper

1 teaspoon dry mustard, dissolved in 1 teaspoon water

10 to 12 ounces (3 cups) shredded mild Cheddar, American or Monterey Jack cheese

Heat oven to 350 degrees and set a 1½ quart heat-proof dish, such as a soufflé pan, in oven to warm. Prepare bread crumbs by mixing bread crumb ingredients together in a small baking pan; set aside.

Bring 2 quarts water to a boil in a large soup kettle. Add 1½ teaspoons salt and macaroni; cook until almost tender, but still a little firm to the bite. Drain and transfer to preheated dish and stir in butter to melt.

Meanwhile, mix eggs, 1 cup evaporated milk, pepper sauce, ½ teaspoon salt (or ¼ teaspoon if using highly processed cheese like American or even Velveeta), ¼ teaspoon pepper and mustard mixture in a small bowl. Pour egg mixture over noodles along with three-fourths of the cheese; stir until thoroughly combined and cheese starts to melt.

Toast bread crumbs in oven until golden brown, 10 to 15 minutes. Remove from oven and set aside. Bake macaroni and cheese for 5 minutes. Remove pan from oven, thoroughly stir macaroni mixture, adding a little remaining milk and cheese. Return to oven and cook 5 minutes longer. Remove from oven and stir thoroughly so that macaroni and cheese cooks evenly; adding additional cheese and milk if mixture does not look moist and creamy. Return to oven for a total of 20 minutes, removing pan from oven once more to stir in remaining milk and cheese. Serve immediately, sprinkle with bread crumbs.

Makes 4 main dish servings, 6 to 8 side dish servings.

Bacon-Wrapped Meat Loaf with Brown Sugar-Ketchup Glaze

If you like, you can double the glaze and omit the bacon wrapping from the loaf. Brush on half the glaze before baking and the other half during the last 15 minutes of baking time.

For brown sugar ketchup glaze:

¼ cup ketchup or chili sauce

2 tablespoons light or dark brown sugar

2 teaspoons cider or white vinegar

For meat loaf:

2 teaspoons vegetable oil

1 medium onion, chopped

2 garlic cloves, minced

2 large eggs

1 teaspoon dried thyme leaves

1 teaspoon salt

½ teaspoon ground black pepper

2 teaspoons Dijon mustard

2 teaspoons Worcestershire sauce

¼ teaspoon hot red pepper sauce

½ cup milk, buttermilk
  or low-fat plain yogurt

2 pounds meatloaf mix
  (50 percent ground chuck, 25 percent
  ground veal, 25 percent ground pork)

⅔ cup crushed saltine crackers (about
  16) or quick oatmeal
  or 1⅓ cups fresh bread crumbs

⅓ cup minced fresh parsley leaves

6 ounces thin-sliced bacon
  (about 8 or 9 slices)

Mix ¼ cup ketchup or chili sauce, 2 tablespoons light or dark brown sugar and 2 teaspoons cider or white vinegar in a small bowl and set aside.

Preheat oven to 350 degrees. Heat oil in a medium skillet. Add onion and garlic and sauté until softened, about 5 minutes; set aside to cool.

Mix eggs with thyme, salt, pepper, mustard, Worcestershire, red pepper sauce and milk or yogurt. Add egg mixture to meat in a large bowl, along with crackers, oatmeal or bread crumbs, parsley, cooked onions and garlic; mix with a fork until evenly blended and meat mixture does not stick to bowl. (If mixture does stick, add additional milk a couple tablespoons at a time, and continue stirring until mixture stops sticking.)

Turn meat mixture onto a work surface. With wet hands, pat mixture into a loaf approximately 9 by 5 inches.

To bake free-form, cover a wire rack with foil. Prick foil in several places with a fork. Place rack on a shallow roasting pan lined with foil for easy cleanup. Set formed loaf on rack. Brush loaf with glaze. Arrange bacon slices, crosswise, over loaf, overlapping them slightly and tucking them under loaf to prevent curling.

Bake loaf until bacon is crisp and loaf registers 160 degrees, about 1 hour. Cool for at least 20 minutes. Slice and serve.

To bake in a loaf pan, omit bacon and double glaze. Turn meat mixture into a loaf pan with a perforated bottom, fitted with a drip pan. Use a fork to pull mixture away from pan sides. Brush mixture with half of glaze. Bake until glaze is set, about 45 minutes. Brush with remaining glaze and continue to bake until second coat has set and loaf registers 160 degrees, about 15 minutes longer.

Makes 6 to 8 servings.

Basic Muffins

....

If you're short on time, you can melt the butter, mix it with the eggs and stir into the dry ingredients. After the batter is thoroughly mixed, beat in the yogurt and proceed with the recipe.

....

vegetable cooking spray

3 cups all-purpose flour

1 tablespoon baking powder

½ teaspoon baking soda

½ teaspoon salt

10 tablespoons (1 stick plus 2 tablespoons) butter, at room temperature

1 cup minus 1 tablespoon sugar

2 large eggs

1½ cups plain yogurt

Adjust oven rack to lower-middle position and preheat oven to 375 degrees. Coat a 12-cup muffin tin (with standard-size molds that have ½ cup capacity) with vegetable cooking spray. Mix flour, baking powder, baking soda and salt in a medium bowl; set aside.

Beat butter and sugar with an electric mixer at medium-high speed until light and fluffy, about 2 minutes. Add eggs, one at a time, beating well after each addition. Beat in half of dry ingredients. Beat in one-third of yogurt. Beat in half of remaining dry ingredients, alternating with one-third of remaining yogurt and repeat until fully incorporated.

Use a large ice cream scoop to divide batter evenly among muffin cups. Bake until muffins are golden brown, 20 to 25 minutes. Set on a wire rack to cool slightly, about 5 minutes. Remove muffins from tin and serve warm. Makes 1 dozen large muffins.

Gwen Barclay and Madalene Hill

"Be flexible and not afraid to substitute."

They weren't professional chefs and never had a lick of training beyond their own kitchens, but Gwen Barclay and Madalene Hill sold out classes at the Zona Spray Cooking School for their extensive knowledge of herbs and how to best use them in cooking.

The mother-daughter pair from Texas used to travel annually to Ohio, where they would teach in Hudson and also teach classes at the Western Reserve Herb Society in Cleveland. Hill passed away on March 5, 2009, at the age of ninety-five, and Barclay has since retired, but their names remain synonymous with herb growing, particularly in Texas.

Hill was born in Texas, reared in Kansas and then moved back to Texas, where Barclay was born and raised. When Barclay left for college, her parents retired to the country and purchased a small farm north of Houston, near Cleveland, Texas. Hill began growing herbs and the family began a small nursery. The herb business took off and as word spread, more and more visitors would stop by the farm. By 1967, the family had converted an old chicken house into a garden room to accommodate the many garden clubs and civic groups who were visiting their Hilltop Herb Farm. Hill also began serving food to the groups, first lunch and then Saturday night dinner.

By this time, Barclay, an accomplished cellist, was teaching elementary school music. After her children arrived, she stopped teaching and when large groups visited, helped her parents on the herb farm. As the business grew, Barclay and her family moved closer to the farm and she began working there full time. In 1983, the farm was wiped out by a tornado and the family moved to another location, but eventually sold the property and opened a restaurant in Houston. Barclay recalls how the 1980s were difficult economically—the restaurant didn't survive long. But Hill and Barclay's knowledge of herbs by this time was well-known in Texas and the pair produced their first book, *Southern Herb Growing*, in 1987. For herb growers, the book remains an American standard.

The pair began to receive invitations from across the country, and for the next eight years spent about six months of the year on the road, teaching classes on herbs, how to grow them and how to cook with them. They taught at Zona Spray every year during the period, offering two or three classes at a time. The school's files contain dozens of their recipes, for everything from teas and herbal sauces to baked goods.

"Mother would concentrate on the plants and getting them started and I would do the bulk of the cooking," Barclay recalls of their teaching days. The pair never professed to be chefs or to teach strict cooking techniques. Instead, they focused on how to extract the best flavor from the fresh herbs and spices they were using, as well as offering instruction on how to grow and preserve them.

Their advice to students was to always use the herbs that were in season and not to be afraid to substitute one for another to give their dishes new and different flavors. "From the seasoning standpoint, that was the thing that we stressed, to be flexible and not be afraid to substitute. Just because this book or that book says to use so-and-so herb or spice, it doesn't mean that you can't use something else. If it's a classic dish, and you change the seasoning, you probably can't call it that anymore. It's probably not the same dish, but that's not to say that it won't be just as good, it will be different," Barclay said.

In 1993, Barclay took a job as food service director at the Round Top Festival Institute, located in the Texas Hill Country in Round Top, Texas. Her mother moved with her and was instrumental in cultivating the McAshan Herb Gardens there, where she grew more than two thousand different species of herbs and remained active, teaching and giving talks on herbs, until her death.

A Simple Fresh Herb Liqueur

1½ cups sugar
¼ cup water
1 liter vodka or brandy

2 cups, firmly packed, leaves and tender stems from herb of choice: Rose Geranium, Lemon Balm, Lemon Verbena, Mint (especially good with red-stem apple mint)

Combine sugar and water; bring to a boil and stir until sugar is completely dissolved. Pack leafy herbs in a large glass container. Cool syrup to lukewarm and pour over herbs; add vodka or brandy. Cap and store in a cool, dark place at least one month before using; shake occasionally. Strain before decanting into bottles.

Delicious with fruit or as a delicate aperitif.

Sweet Corn Timbales
with Basil Cream

A delicious light luncheon dish inspired by a Fannie Farmer recipe.

2 cups fresh corn kernels,
    cooked and drained

1½ cups milk

4 whole eggs

1 tablespoon all-purpose flour

½ teaspoon salt

⅛ teaspoon ground white pepper

1 teaspoon ground coriander seed

½ cup finely grated Swiss cheese
    (preferably Gruyére or Emmentaler)

2 tablespoons freshly grated
    Parmesan cheese or additional
    Swiss cheese for topping

Basil Cream:

1¼ cups heavy cream

½ teaspoon salt

⅛ teaspoon freshly ground white pepper

2 tablespoons finely shredded
    fresh sweet basil

chopped fresh parsley for garnish

Preheat oven to 375 degrees. Place ½ cup corn in blender bowl; add milk, eggs, flour, salt, white pepper and coriander seed in that order. Blend until smooth. Butter twelve ½ cup custard dishes, soufflé dishes or a muffin pan with 12 holes. Divide remaining corn kernels evenly between them. Sprinkle each with part of the grated Swiss cheese.

Pour blended mixture over corn kernels, stirring each lightly with a knife to mix. Place dishes in a large baking pan; set on oven shelf and pour in boiling water up to halfway up sides of dishes. Bake 15 to 20 minutes, or until a knife comes out clean when inserted in the center of dish. With a large, heavy metal spatula or a hot pad, carefully remove timbales from water bath. Cool to room temperature, up to 2 hours, or cover and refrigerate up to 3 days.

When ready to serve, bring basil cream ingredients to a boil in a small saucepan. Carefully unmold timbales by running a thin knife around the edge. Turn out and place in a large shallow baking/serving dish with 1-inch space between them. Pour basil cream over timbales and sprinkle with Parmesan cheese or additional Swiss cheese. Bake in a preheated 350-degree oven for 10 to 15 minutes (longer if refrigerated) until timbales are lightly browned and have absorbed some of the sauce. Serve immediately, garnish with chopped fresh parsley.

Makes 6 servings as a main dish, or 12 as an accompaniment.

Famous Chefs & Fabulous Recipes

Vietnamese Shrimp Curry with Black Mushrooms and Red Chiles

Our version of a traditional Southeast Asian dish.

8 large dried or fresh black Chinese mushrooms (also known as Wood, Cloud or Tree Ear)

2 tablespoons vegetable oil

1 large yellow onion, cut in half and sliced very thinly

2 large cloves garlic, mashed or minced

1 to 2 tablespoons mild curry powder

2 cups canned coconut milk (not cream of coconut, which is sweetened)

4 Kaffir lime leaves (can substitute lime peel)

2 bay leaves (Daun salaam or Indian bay may be used)

2 pieces lemon grass (each 3 to 4 inches long)

2 tablespoons minced fresh ginger or galangal root

2 to 3 small whole dried red chiles or 1 teaspoon chopped fresh hot chiles, seeds and stems removed (adjust to taste)

1 pound raw shrimp, peeled and deveined

2 small cucumbers or zucchini squash, thinly sliced on diagonal

salt, to taste

¼ cup thinly sliced fresh basil leaves

hot steamed rice or cellophane noodles (rice vermicelli)

chopped fresh basil, cilantro, lemon balm or spearmint leaves for garnish

Rinse mushrooms carefully under cold water. If using dried, soak in hot water for 30 minutes. Remove tough stems and slice caps thinly. Heat vegetable oil in a large sauté pan or wok; sauté onions and garlic until softened but do not brown. Add prepared mushrooms and curry powder; mix well and cook briefly until very fragrant. Stir in coconut milk and bring to a boil. Add lime leaves (or lime peel), bay leaves, lemon grass, ginger or galangal and red chiles; reduce heat and simmer for 10 minutes until reduced slightly.

Add shrimp, a few at a time, cooking only until color changes. Add cucumbers or squash and cook until completely hot and tender, about 1 minute.

Season with salt as needed and add sliced basil leaves. Serve shrimp and sauce over rice or cellophane noodles, garnish with fresh herbs.

Makes 4 servings.

Shirley O. Corriher

"Just enjoy what you are doing and don't panic."

S hirley O. Corriher is every chef's fairy godmother. When
they consult with her, it is as if she waves her magic wand
and their culinary troubles disappear. But it's not magic that
Corriher is dispensing, it's something even more reliable—
chemistry. The fact that she dispenses her science in such a
lighthearted and humorous way makes her all the more endearing and enduring.

Perhaps she is so helpful because she's been in their shoes. While not a professional chef, Corriher still recalls vividly cooking for a living. After working
as a research biochemist at Vanderbilt Medical School, Corriher and her former husband started a boys boarding school, Brandon Hall, where she prepared
daily meals for one hundred and forty students and staff. Her first attempts were
disastrous, but later on, she was able to put her science to the test and figure
out what was behind her cooking failures. She still believes that knowing what
went wrong provides solace to the cook—their dish may have failed, but at least
she can give them an explanation.

After a divorce and with three children to support, Corriher began working
at Rich's Cooking School in Atlanta, run by cookbook author Nathalie Dupree.
Her job was to set up for the cooking classes and clean up after, but it wasn't long
before Corriher began chiming in during class, offering her scientific explana-
tions for the students' questions and the puzzles that chefs could not decipher.

The school taught classic French techniques and Corriher learned a lot about
cooking. Eventually she was able to distinguish herself as the woman with the
answers. Her career blossomed as she began consulting for chefs, food manu-
facturers and kitchen appliance makers.

Her first book, *CookWise: The Hows and Whys of Successful Cooking*, came out
in 1997, after ten years of writing and research. It won the James Beard Foundation Award for food reference and technique books. The follow-up, *BakeWise:
The Hows and Whys of Successful Baking*, was released in 2008, and also won a
James Beard Award for baking.

She has helped Julia Child and Jacques Pepin solve culinary mysteries, has
consulted for major companies, including Maytag and Proctor and Gamble, and
continues to write and teach throughout the world, to groups that range from
home cooks to chemical engineers. Soon after *CookWise* came out, Food Network personality Alton Brown and his wife contacted her; they wanted to create a
cooking show based on the chemistry principals of her book. For a few years, she
was a frequent guest on Brown's show, appearing as the mad scientist character.

Corriher has taught many times at the Western Reserve School of Cooking,
first for Zona Spray and later for Catherine St. John. Her classes typically sell

out and she is beloved for her down-to-earth southern charm and devilish sense of humor. She doesn't get ruffled over mistakes—she's made her career out of them—and she always seems to be able to find the answer to what went wrong.

Mostly, Corriher just doesn't want cooks to be afraid. That is the lesson she tries to teach as often as she can. Corriher remembers her own fear when she had to do something as simple as sautéing a pair of chicken breasts. They would always stick to her pan. "I used to be terrified of sautéing," she recalls. Now she knows that the chicken won't stick if left to its own devices. Her advice to students is to leave it alone. Take a sip of wine. Have a Zen moment and be at peace with the universe and your chicken breasts. Before you know it, through the magic of chemistry, the proteins in the chicken will have coagulated and the chicken will release itself from the pan easily, so you can flip it and enjoy another sip of wine and another Zen moment while the second side cooks.

"A lot of people are just afraid. Little things like that are such an enormous help in cooking," she said. "Just enjoy what you are doing. Don't panic."

Touch of Grace Biscuits

....

These are my grandmother's feather-light, real Georgia biscuits. The secret of light biscuits is a very wet dough. The more moisture in the dough, the more steam created in a hot oven and the lighter the biscuits.

....

1½ cups self-rising flour (if self-rising flour is not available, use 1½ cups all-purpose and 1½ teaspoons baking powder)

⅛ teaspoon baking soda

½ teaspoon salt

1 tablespoon sugar

3 tablespoons shortening

⅞ to 1¼ cups buttermilk or cream

1 cup plain all-purpose flour to shape

2 tablespoons melted butter

Preheat oven to 475 degrees. Spray an 8-inch round cake pan with nonstick spray.

In a medium mixing bowl, combine flour, soda, salt and sugar. With your fingers or a pastry cutter, work shortening into flour mixture until there are no shortening lumps larger than a small pea. Stir in buttermilk. Permit to stand 2 or 3 minutes. This dough is so wet that you cannot shape it in the usual manner.

Pour remaining cup flour onto a plate or pie tin. Flour your hands well. Spoon a biscuit-size lump of wet dough onto flour; sprinkle some flour over dough. The wet biscuit should now have a light coating of flour on the outside. Pick up biscuit, shape into a soft round, at the same time, shaking off excess flour. The dough is so soft that it will not hold its shape. As you shape each biscuit, place into an 8" round cake pan. Push biscuits tightly against each other so that they will rise up and not spread out. Continue shaping biscuits in this manner until all dough is used.

Brush biscuits with melted butter and bake just above the center of oven until lightly browned (15 to 18 minutes). Cool a minute or two in pan. Split biscuits in half, butter or spread with fruit butter while they are hot and eat immediately.

Makes about 10 biscuits.

Adapted from *BakeWise* by Shirley O. Corriher (Scribner, 2008).

Fruit Butter

1 stick unsalted butter

1 package (8 ounces) cream cheese

2 tablespoons Grand Marnier or
    Chambord liqueur

⅓ cup powdered sugar

1 small jar (8 ounces) good preserves
    (cherry, strawberry, peach, etc.)

zest of 1 orange

In a food processor fitted with a steel blade attachment, process butter, cream cheese, liqueur and powdered sugar to blend well. Stir in preserves and zest by hand. Chill well.

Makes 2 to 3 cups spread.

Salmon Fillet with Sweet, Grainy Mustard Crust

Reduced apple juice gives a wonderful sweetness to grainy mustard and fresh dill to make a sweet, spicy crust on a salmon fillet.

2 cups apple juice

½ cup grainy mustard

4 sprigs fresh dill, finely chopped

1 medium (12 ounces) salmon fillet

¼ teaspoon salt

⅛ teaspoon ground white pepper

several sprigs fresh dill to garnish

Preheat oven to 375 degrees.

In a medium skillet, bring apple juice to a boil and boil vigorously, until less than ¼ cup remains. (You really only want about 1 to 2 tablespoons apple juice left.) Stir grainy mustard into reduced apple juice. Heat and stir until mixture is consistency of mustard before you add apple juice. Remove from heat. Stir in fresh dill.

Rub salmon with salt and white pepper and place on a lightly greased baking sheet. Coat fillet with apple juice-mustard mixture. Bake 10 to 15 minutes, depending on thickness of salmon. Garnish with sprigs of fresh dill.

Makes 4 servings.

Country Style Dried Beans

3 slices streak-o-lean (bacon)

2 onions, chopped

1 tablespoon sugar

4 to 6 ounces country ham pieces, chopped

2 small hot peppers, seeded

2 bay leaves

1 teaspoon thyme

1 teaspoon salt

white pepper, black pepper, red pepper

1 to 2 pounds dried beans

2 smoked ham hocks

water or chicken stock

In a heavy soup pot, sauté streak-o-lean until browned. Add onions and cook until soft. Sprinkle with sugar and cook until lightly browned. Add chopped country ham, hot peppers, bay leaves, thyme, salt, white, black and red pepper. Cook together a minute.

Rinse dried beans and pick out any trash. Drain. Add to pot. Add water or stock to cover by 2 to 3 inches. Add ham hocks. Bring to a boil; reduce to a simmer. Simmer until tender but not mushy, about 4 hours (will depend on age and size of dried beans). Remove bay leaves when spooning into serving dish.

Makes 8 servings.

Jane's Golden Tomato Bake

2 pounds canned tomatoes

zest of 1 lemon

salt and pepper

fresh basil, chopped

2 cups bread crumbs

⅓ cup light brown sugar

⅓ cup butter melted

Preheat oven to 350 degrees. Pour tomatoes in baking casserole, sprinkle with lemon zest, salt, pepper and fresh basil. Stir to mix. In a medium skillet, melt butter and stir in bread crumbs. Heat and stir just to mix. Stir in brown sugar. Spread bread crumb-sugar mixture evenly over top. Bake 20 to 25 minutes.

Makes 6 servings.

David Hirsch

"You can really make wonderful meatless meals."

David Hirsch was just beginning his career as an archi-
tect in New York City when he decided that a life
behind a desk was not for him. He headed north to Ithaca,
home of Cornell University, Ithaca College, and a budding
eatery known as Moosewood Restaurant. More than thirty-
five years later, he's still at Moosewood and still happy that he chose a life in a
rural landscape with others who share his vision of the world.

In 1972, Hirsch packed up and moved north to the Finger Lakes, to live
in a commune as part of what he remembers as a "back to the land movement."
He had graduated from City College of New York with a degree in architec-
ture and had worked for a few years at entry-level jobs, but couldn't get used
to the idea of sitting inside all day, working on projects with which he felt no
connection. Communes were typical near college campuses in the 1970s, and
Hirsch remembers the group he lived with as mostly urban types seeking an
escape from big city life.

The following year, Moosewood, which would become an American icon,
opened in downtown Ithaca. The restaurant, which *Bon Appétit* magazine named
one of the most influential restaurants of the twentieth century, continues to
be the standard bearer for vegetarian cuisine. Operated by a collective of members who share work duties, one of Hirsch's neighbors joined in its first year.
In 1976, Hirsch applied for a job there. The kitchen wasn't a foreign place for
him; he had cooked for fraternity houses for two years at Cornell. The kinds of
vegetarian foods that Moosewood was serving up appealed to him.

"This is really the kind of food that I like," he said, "I felt a real kinship with
it." He found the vegetarian food wasn't limiting because it drew from a broad
spectrum of cuisines. "They had a unique way of looking at food and it remains
very multi-cultural and eclectic in a global way," Hirsch said.

More importantly, Hirsch liked the kinship he felt with the other members
of the collective. The kitchen at Moosewood is small, and true to the nature
of a collective, everyone works together and helps each other. "It's very much
about cooperation," he said. Hirsch likes to tell the story of an intern from the
Netherlands who was training in the Moosewood kitchen. He was shocked
to see how everyone helped each other and how willing the staff was to teach
him. He had trained in kitchens in Amsterdam where the environment was
competitive and anything but cooperative.

Of the nineteen collective members who operate Moosewood, some have
been there since 1973; most have been there for at least twenty years. Hirsch
said the group is a bit surprised at how many years the restaurant has survived.
Members stay because they are comfortable there and the collective has diver-

sified, which has keeps things interesting. The collective began producing vegetarian cookbooks with recipes from the restaurant, which now number eleven. Hirsch played a role as co-author of all of the books, and also wrote one on his own, *The Moosewood Restaurant Kitchen Garden*. The collective also markets a line of salad dressings and soups for retail sale.

In the 1990s, Hirsch began to travel, teaching classes on vegetarian cuisine. This brings a new dimension to his work, beyond running the restaurant and has helped keep his interest in Moosewood alive. Hirsch is at ease teaching in front of large groups and enjoys the performance aspect of the classes. He first came to the Western Reserve School of Cooking in 2008. When he teaches, Hirsch said he hopes to show students how vegetarian cuisine doesn't mean giving up good food. While there may be health benefits to eating meatless, Hirsch sees them as an aside. He would rather people eat vegetarian because they know it will be a good meal. "I'd like them to know that you can really make wonderful meatless meals—an incredibly delicious, satisfying, enjoyable meal."

Fennel Vichyssoise

Classic Vichyssoise is a thick and creamy rich potato leek soup. Here is a reduced-fat version made even more elegant with the addition of the fresh, sweet anise flavor of aromatic fennel. Serve it as the first course at a dinner party or accompany it with a flavorful salad for a relaxed midday meal.

3 cups chopped potatoes

3 cups water or vegetable stock (stock is better)

1 tablespoon fresh lemon juice

1½ cups chopped leeks, white parts only

2 teaspoons olive oil

4 garlic cloves, minced or pressed

2¼ cups chopped fresh fennel bulbs (1 or 2 large bulbs, 2½ pounds whole plants with fronds)

½ cup peeled and chopped parsnips (optional)

1 tablespoon dry white wine or water

1 to 1½ teaspoons salt

⅛ teaspoon ground black pepper

½ teaspoon ground fennel seeds

½ cup minced fresh parsley

3 cups 2% milk

minced fresh chives

Combine potatoes, water or stock and lemon juice in a medium pot. Cover and bring to a boil; uncover and simmer until potatoes are tender, about 15 minutes.

Meanwhile, in a soup pot, sauté leeks in oil on medium heat for about 5 minutes, stirring frequently, until softened. Add garlic, chopped fresh fennel, parsnips if using, and white wine or water.

Famous Chefs & Fabulous Recipes

Cover and continue to cook for 5 to 10 minutes, stirring occasionally. Add salt, pepper, ground fennel and parsley. Reduce heat to low, cover and cook until vegetables are very tender, about 5 minutes. Add potatoes to soup pot.

In batches in a blender or food processor, purée soup with milk until smooth and creamy. Serve hot, at room temperature or chilled. Top each serving with a sprinkling of minced chives.

Makes about 9 cups, for 4 to 6 servings.

Adapted from *Moosewood Restaurant Daily Special*, 1999, Copyright Moosewood Inc.

Pasta with Zucchini and Mascarpone

Of course, you can make this pasta almost any time of year, but it's a really lovely, delicate dish when the zucchini is at its seasonal best, small and firm with glossy skin. A large nonstick skillet works best here, but if you don't have one, a large cast iron frying pan will do. However, you may need to add about 3 tablespoons of the pasta cooking water to the sautéing zucchini to prevent sticking.

Accompany this pasta with a chewy bread, tomato salad, a side of green beans and maybe juicy, ripe sliced peaches for dessert.

2 teaspoons olive oil

2 cups finely chopped onions

6 cups sliced baby zucchini, sliced in half lengthwise and cut into ½-inch thick semi-circles

3 garlic cloves, minced or pressed

1 pound farfalle (bow-tie pasta)

2 tablespoons fresh lemon juice

1 cup mascarpone cheese

2 pinches freshly grated nutmeg

¼ cup grated Parmesan cheese

freshly ground black pepper (optional)

Bring a large covered pot of salted water to a boil. Meanwhile, heat oil in a large skillet and sauté onions on medium-high heat for about 5 minutes, stirring frequently. Add zucchini and garlic and sauté, stirring frequently, until zucchini is crisp-tender, 7 or 8 minutes. Cover to keep warm until pasta is ready.

When water boils, add pasta, stir and cover pot. When it returns to a boil, uncover pot and cook pasta until al dente. Drain and transfer to a large warmed bowl.

Stir lemon juice, mascarpone cheese and nutmeg into sautéed zucchini. Add skillet mixture along with pan juices to pasta and toss well. Sprinkle with grated cheese and, if you wish, add pepper. Serve hot.

Adapted from *Moosewood Restaurant New Classics*, 2000, Copyright Moosewood Inc.

Vegan Turnovers

These enticing savory turnovers make an impressive appearance at the dinner table—hot, puffed, flaky and golden brown. The creamy tofu filling is snappy with sun-dried tomatoes, nutritious with greens and full of herbs and spices. Serve two per plate (or one for those with daintier appetites) with a bright colorful vegetable on the side and it's quite smashing. We suggest kale, spinach, chard, collards, mizuna, arugula, or some combination of these for the 4 cups of greens in the recipe. Use fresh dill or basil whenever possible. If you must use their dried counterparts, add them earlier in the cooking process along with the thyme and fennel.

1 cake firm tofu (16 ounces)

⅓ cup sun-dried tomatoes (not oil-packed)*

1 tablespoon olive oil

1 cup chopped onions

¼ teaspoon salt, or less to taste

4 cups rinsed, stemmed and chopped greens

pinch dried thyme

½ teaspoon freshly ground fennel seeds

2 garlic cloves, minced or pressed

1 tablespoon fresh lemon juice

1 tablespoon chopped fresh dill or basil (1 teaspoon dried)

¾ pound phyllo pastry (12 by 17-inch sheets)**

¼ cup olive oil

Place tofu between two plates, weight the top plate with a heavy object and press for 20 minutes. Place sun-dried tomatoes in a heat-proof bowl, cover with boiling water and set aside.

Warm oil in a large skillet. Add onions and salt and sauté on medium heat for 8 to 10 minutes, or until translucent. Add greens, thyme and fennel. Cover, lower heat and continue to cook for another 5 to 10 minutes, stirring often, until greens are tender but still bright green. Drain and set aside.

In the bowl of a food processor, crumble pressed tofu and add garlic, lemon juice and dill or basil. Process until mixture is smooth and creamy. In a bowl combine tofu mixture with drained cooked greens and mix well. Drain and chop sun-dried tomatoes and fold them into filling.

Preheat oven to 350 degrees. Lightly oil two baking sheets.

Unfold 16 phyllo sheets on a clean, dry working surface. Have filling, oil and a pastry brush nearby. Take two sheets from the stack and place them with the short sides facing you. Brush lightly with oil and neatly fold in half lengthwise. Brush strip with oil. Place ½ cup of filling at the end of the rectangle. Fold lower left corner up and over diagonally until the bottom edge is flush with the right side and you have a triangle at the end. Keep folding triangle up, as you would a flag, to make a triangular pastry. Brush both sides with a little oil and place on prepared baking sheet.

Repeat to make eight pastries in all. Bake for 20 to 25 minutes, until turnovers are golden brown and slightly puffed.

Makes 4 to 6 servings.

Notes: If you don't have a food processor, crush the tofu in a bowl with a potato masher and vigorously mash in the garlic, lemon juice and fresh herbs.

Unoiled phyllo becomes brittle once exposed to the air so keep a damp towel on the not-yet-used phyllo while you work. It's also helpful to work in a draft-free spot. A new inexpensive 2-inch paint brush works great as a phyllo pastry brush.

*If you like, replace the sun-dried tomatoes with chopped, pitted kalamata, Sicilian green, niçoise, or Spanish olives.

**You can use puff pastry instead of the phyllo.

Adapted from *Moosewood Restaurant New Classics,* 2000, Copyright Moosewood Inc.

Deborah Madison

"I hope they take away some sense of empowerment and joy."

S he is one of the strongest voices of the American vegetarian movement and her commitment to local foods and farmers markets makes Deborah Madison one of the country's most relied upon writers when the topic is vegetables.

So it may be a surprise to some that Madison is not actually a vegetarian, at least not in the strict sense of the word. She did follow a vegetarian diet when she spent eighteen years living in a Buddhist community at the San Francisco Zen Center. But she doesn't believe in a diet that excludes things.

Madison is not so much anti-meat, as she is exceptionally pro-vegetable. Madison grew up with a father who was a botany professor and a prolific gardener, so vegetables were always a big part of her life and her diet. They didn't eat a lot of meat, so not eating it at all wasn't that difficult for her and vegetables have always captured her attention. "What I really like are vegetables. That's what I have a feeling for and I'm good at working with," she said. "Vegetables are gorgeous things and I can't imagine not being excited by them."

Her enthusiasm has spilled onto the pages of eleven critically-acclaimed books, written mostly on the topic of vegetarian and farmers market cooking. Her 1997 book, *Vegetarian Cooking for Everyone*, won Madison her first James Beard Foundation Award. She earned her second in 2002, for *Local Flavors, Cooking and Eating from America's Farmers' Markets*.

Madison's cooking career began in 1969, when, fresh out of the University of California, Davis with a degree in sociology and city planning, she entered the Zen Center. She sought a job in the kitchen and eventually worked her way up to head cook. It was there that her relationship with vegetables blossomed. "I wanted to cook, and in a vegetarian community, that's what I had to work with," she recalled.

In 1977, she took a job at Alice Waters' Chez Panisse restaurant in Berkley and spent about eighteen months in the kitchen. It was Madison's only formal training in cooking and came just at the right time. When the Zen Center opened Greens restaurant in 1979, Madison was its debut chef. She got started writing when she was approached by a publisher to put together a cookbook from the restaurant.

Over the years, she has traveled the country teaching and speaking, promoting vegetarian foods, farmers markets and the Slow Food movement. Madison made several stops at Zona Spray's Cooking School, and recalls the experience fondly for the intimate setting and the devoted students. These days, Madison devotes nearly all of her teaching time to a program at Rancho la Puerta in

Tecate, Mexico, where she goes four times each year to teach seminars devoted to getting students immersed in the kitchen and garden. Many of her students are professional women who never learned to cook. Often on the verge of retirement or concerned about their health, they want to learn how to cook and eat better foods.

When she teaches, Madison's goal is for her students to return home with skills and confidence. "I hope they take away some sense of empowerment and joy that they can go home and cook something for themselves," she said.

Quinoa Salad with Dried Fruits and Toasted Pine Nuts

The tiny seeds of quinoa are light, nutritious and one of the easiest of the new grains for us to assimilate. Quinoa has a naturally bitter coating which protects it from birds, so be sure to rinse well.

1 cup quinoa

2 cups water

½ teaspoon salt

6 dried apricots

2 tablespoons snipped chives or
   3 small scallions cut in narrow rounds

¼ cup dried currants,
   softened in warm water

3 tablespoons finely diced yellow
   and green bell peppers

3 tablespoons pine nuts

Lime-Cumin Vinaigrette (recipe
   follows)

Swish quinoa in a bowl of cold water. Pour into a fine-meshed strainer and rinse under running water. Bring water to a boil, add salt and quinoa. Lower heat, cover pan and cook 15 minutes. Taste—there should be just a little resistance and the opaque spiral ring of the germ should show. Drain.

While quinoa is cooking, cut apricots and vegetables into small pieces, make vinaigrette and toast pine nuts in a dry pan until they're golden. Toss quinoa with vegetables and vinaigrette while still warm. Add pine nuts just before serving.

Makes 4 to 6 servings.

Lime-Cumin Vinaigrette

1 garlic clove

salt

grated or minced zest of 2 limes

2 to 3 tablespoons fresh lime
 or lemon juice, to taste

2 tablespoons chopped scallion
 or finely diced shallot

½ jalapeño, seeded and minced

½ teaspoon cumin seeds

½ teaspoon coriander seeds

¼ teaspoon dry mustard

⅓ cup olive oil

2 tablespoons chopped cilantro

Pound garlic with ¼ teaspoon salt in a mortar until smooth (or put it through a press). Combine with lime zest, juice, scallion and jalapeño. Toast cumin and coriander seeds in a small dry skillet until fragrant, immediately remove to a plate to cool. Grind to a powder in a spice mill and add to juice mixture. Whisk in mustard and oil. Taste and adjust seasoning if needed. Let dressing stand for at least 15 minutes; add cilantro just before using. Makes about ½ cup.

Adapted from *Vegetarian Cooking for Everyone* (Broadway, 1997).

Baked Olives

What happens to olives when they're baked is a complete transformation of flavors. Though baked, they're served at room temperature.

2 cups kalamata olives

½ cup red or white wine

3 tablespoons olive oil

1 garlic clove

1 tablespoon chopped parsley

1 tablespoon fresh marjoram
 or 1 teaspoon dried oregano

freshly ground pepper

red pepper flakes

Preheat oven to 375 degrees. Rinse olives and put them in a baking dish large enough to make a single layer. Add wine, half the oil and bake until fragrant and swollen, about 30 minutes.

Pound garlic in a mortar with remaining ingredients. When olives come out of oven, stir in this mixture. You may serve them right away, but they are better if left to sit for several hours, as the flavors will develop.

Makes 2 cups.

Adapted from *Vegetarian Cooking for Everyone* (Broadway, 1997).

Betty Rosbottom

"Use the freshest and best ingredients."

You could call Betty Rosbottom the Zona Spray of Columbus, Ohio. In 1976, she established La Belle Pomme Cooking School, which went on to become part of the city's famed Lazarus department store and was in many ways responsible for the city's culinary awakening.

Like Spray, Rosbottom ended up in Ohio when her professor husband accepted a job teaching at the Ohio State University. She too had studied at LaVarenne Cooking School in France, and like Spray, she also was able to attract some of the biggest name chefs of the time to teach at her school. When Jacques Pepin came to teach in 1978, his three-day session was standing room only. The following year, a visit by Marcella Hazan resulted in a *Time* magazine profile of the school and Columbus' growing gourmet movement.

Rosbottom grew up in Memphis and attended Sophie Newcomb College, when it was still the women's arm of Tulane University, where she majored in French. When it came to food, her roots were strongly southern. But a year in France during college opened her eyes to what the food world had to offer. After marrying, she lived in Princeton, N.J. and Philadelphia, where she began taking cooking classes. After becoming a proficient cook, she began toying with the idea that she might like to teach cooking some day.

After the move to Ohio, Rosbottom started teaching classes, first from her home and later establishing the La Belle Pomme. As a young mother, Rosbottom said she was looking for something to do and liked the idea of teaching, having previously taught French. "I like food. I like the creativity of it. I like teaching," she said.

After five years on her own, Rosbottom sold the store to Lazarus and continued to run it for the next fourteen years, until it closed in 1995. Rosbottom says the sale to Lazarus was a benefit and likely would not have happened today. She believes that Lazarus' ownership of the store made it a larger force in the community that it would have been. Rosbottom laments that each year there are fewer people in Columbus who remember the school, particularly since the Lazarus stores have all become part of the Macy's chain.

In addition to running La Belle Pomme, Rosbottom began writing books and traveling to teach and promote her books. She made several stops at Zona Spray Cooking School in the 1990s, promoting her book, *First Impressions*, which focused on entertaining and appetizers. Rosbottom remembers how the school, though small, was packed with enthusiastic students. Her connections to the school don't end there. Tom Johnson, who is currently on the staff at Western Reserve School of Cooking, previously taught for Rosbottom at La Belle Pomme.

Since relocating to Massachusetts in 1995, Rosbottom continues to teach and write. For twenty years, she wrote the syndicated food column, *That's Entertaining*. She directs classes at the Different Drummer's Kitchen in Northampton, Massachusetts and is currently awaiting publication of her ninth book, *Sunday Roasts*, a follow-up to her 2008 *Sunday Soups*. When she teaches, Rosbottom said her lesson is the universal one of cooking teachers: "Use the freshest and best ingredients and at this point, if they can be local, that's great."

French Bread Stuffed with Smoked Salmon and Leeks

A loaf of partially sliced French bread, filled with sautéed leeks and paper-thin slices of smoked salmon, makes an unusual and elegant appetizer.

1 loaf French bread, about 20 inches long and 2½-inches in diameter

6 tablespoons olive oil, or more as needed

6 tablespoons unsalted butter, or more as needed

2 cups chopped leeks (including 2 inches of the green leaves)

1 teaspoon dried dill

salt and freshly ground black pepper, to taste

10 to 12 ounces smoked salmon, thinly sliced

sprigs of dill, for garnish

Slice bread on the diagonal into ½-inch slices, cutting almost but not quite all the way through loaf.

In a medium heavy skillet over medium heat, heat olive oil and butter until butter is melted. Stir to mix well. Generously brush mixture over top and sides of loaf and on each slice. You should have about ¼ cup of the mixture left in the skillet. If not, add an equal amount additional oil and butter to make ¼ cup.

Heat reserved oil and butter in skillet over medium heat until hot. Add chopped leeks and stir constantly until leeks are softened, about 5 minutes. Add dried dill and cook a minute more. Remove and season with salt and pepper. Stir to mix.

Place loaf on a baking sheet. Spoon some of leek mixture between each slice. The bread can be prepared an hour ahead to this point. Cover loosely with foil and keep at room temperature.

When ready to serve, preheat oven to 350 degrees.

Bake loaf, uncovered, on center oven shelf until bread is warm and crust is crispy, about 5 minutes. Remove from oven and insert 1 thin slice smoked salmon between each slice of bread. Return to oven for 2 to 3 minutes, just to warm salmon. Remove from oven.

To serve, place warm loaf on a long, narrow serving plate or wooden board. Garnish with fresh dill sprigs. Cut all the way through loaf to separate slices and serve each slice topped with salmon and leeks.

Makes 36 to 40 slices.

From *First Impressions* by Betty Rosbottom (Morrow, 1992). Used by permission of Betty Rosbottom.

Sherried Cheddar Terrine

Created by Adrienne Badin, a talented caterer from Fort Wayne, Indiana, this appetizer pairs French Roquefort with Cheddar from New England. The cheeses are creamed with a little butter (the Cheddar gets a splash of sherry as well) and layered with walnuts in a terrine. The terrine, which can be prepared several days ahead, makes a striking presentation garnished with bouquets of sage, clusters of red and green grapes and wedges of Granny Smith apples.

nonstick vegetable cooking spray

1 pound Vermont Cheddar cheese, shredded

6 tablespoons unsalted butter, slightly softened, divided

2 tablespoons dry sherry, port, or brandy

8 ounces Roquefort or Stilton cheese

1½ cups coarsely chopped walnuts, divided

3 walnut halves, for garnish

fresh sage leaves, for garnish

3 Granny Smith apples

1 to 2 tablespoons lemon juice

several bunches red seedless grapes

Line a 4-cup terrine or loaf pan with 3 sheets waxed paper so that paper extends over the long sides of pan. Spray top layer of paper with nonstick vegetable cooking spray. Or use an 8-inch cake pan: Line bottom with a triple thickness of waxed paper cut to fit pan. Spray top sheet with nonstick spray.

Place Cheddar cheese, 4 tablespoons butter and sherry in a mixing bowl and beat with an electric mixer or by hand with a wooden spoon until well blended and smooth. Set aside.

Combine Roquefort cheese with remaining 2 tablespoons butter and mix, using an electric mixer or a wooden spoon, until smooth.

Press half the Cheddar mixture into prepared pan. Pat firmly but gently to make an even layer. Sprinkle half the chopped walnuts over this layer. Add all of the Roquefort mixture, again pressing down firmly but gently to make an even layer. Top with remaining walnuts and make a final layer with remaining Cheddar mixture. Cover terrine with plastic wrap and refrigerate overnight or up to 2 days.

To unmold, remove plastic wrap. Run a knife around sides of pan to loosen. Invert terrine onto a serving plate and remove waxed paper. Arrange 3 walnut halves equidistant from each other down the center of terrine. Surround with several sage leaves. The terrine can be unmolded several hours in advance and refrigerated. Bring to room temperature 30 minutes before serving.

To serve, core and halve apples, but do not peel. Cut each half into 8 wedges and toss wedges with lemon juice to prevent discoloring. Arrange bunches of grapes and apple wedges around terrine.

Makes 12 to 14 servings.

From *First Impressions* by Betty Rosbottom (Morrow, 1992). Used by permission of Betty Rosbottom.

Mushroom and Leek Pinwheels

4½ tablespoons unsalted butter

1½ pounds mushrooms, finely chopped

1 tablespoon finely chopped garlic

½ cup chopped leeks

¾ cup chicken stock

12 ounces cream cheese, broken into chunks

½ teaspoon salt

¼ teaspoon freshly ground black pepper

4 tablespoons chopped fresh chives or parsley

1 package (17¼ ounces) frozen puff pastry (containing 2 sheets pastry), defrosted

To prepare filling, melt butter in a large heavy skillet over medium-high heat. When hot, add mushrooms and sauté, stirring for 3 to 4 minutes. Add garlic and leeks and sauté stirring 2 to 3 minutes more. Add stock and cook over high heat until all liquid has evaporated, 5 to 6 minutes longer.

Lower heat and add cream cheese. Cook, stirring constantly, until cheese has melted. Add salt and pepper. Stir in chives. Refrigerate until well-chilled.

Roll each puff pastry sheet out on a lightly floured work surface into a 12 by 14-inch rectangle. Spread half of the filling on each sheet, going all the way to the edges except for a ½-inch border on one of the long sides. Roll up the pastry, tightly into a coil, starting with the long side without the border. Moisten the ½-inch border lightly with water and press to seal the end. Wrap rolls in plastic and freeze to firm, about 45 minutes. The logs can be prepared to this point in advance and refrigerated for up to 2 days. They can also be frozen for 2 to 3 weeks. Cover plastic-wrapped logs tightly with aluminum foil. Defrost in refrigerator for 24 hours before baking.

To make pinwheels, slice ¼-inch-thick slices from each roll. You should get about 40 pinwheels from each roll. Arrange on two large baking sheets lined with lightly greased aluminum foil. The pinwheels can be prepared to this point in advance. Cover baking sheets with plastic wrap and refrigerate for up to 6 hours.

When ready to bake, preheat oven to 450 degrees. Bake pinwheels 12 to 14 minutes. Using a spatula, turn pinwheels over and bake for an additional 5 to 8 minutes, until golden brown and crispy. Watch them carefully as they bake. Remove with a spatula and arrange on a napkin-lined serving tray. Serve hot.

Note: If using a food processor to chop the mushrooms, process in small batches so that the mushrooms are chopped to an even consistency.

From *First Impressions* by Betty Rosbottom (Morrow, 1992). Used by permission of Betty Rosbottom.

Denise Vivaldo

"Let yourself off the hook and enjoy your own party."

You could call her the original party girl, and Denise Vivaldo wouldn't mind a bit. "To get paid for giving parties is a pretty fabulous job," she says. Especially when you consider the parties that she gives. There was the Academy Awards Governor's Ball, the long list of Hollywood movie wrap parties or *Sunset Magazine*'s Taste of Sunset party.

But this party girl is also a savvy businesswoman, whose diverse company offers food styling, recipe development and a host of other culinary consulting services. She has styled food on television shows too numerous to name, has written seven books and is in the business of teaching others how to start their own successful catering businesses.

Catering a party for a thousand people doesn't ruffle her feathers, and yet, it took her a while to be able to host a dinner party for friends without stressing out over it. Vivaldo calls herself the classic hostess. She would be getting ready to have friends over when she would look around and think, "If only I could paint the house tonight. You are out of your mind with craziness," she said. A few years ago, Vivaldo decided to stop putting so much pressure on herself because she realized that her friends didn't care, they just wanted to spend time together. These days the parties she throws may be a little less fabulous, but they are a lot more fun, especially for her.

One of her favorite ways to entertain is to make a simple pasta dish and serve it with bread and a green salad in her back yard. "You have to let yourself off the hook and enjoy your own party. My guests have more fun and I'm not always in the kitchen worrying about stupid stuff," she says.

A native of Northern California, Vivaldo sold real estate for many years before deciding that she wanted to be a chef. She trained at the Ritz Escoffier and LaVarenne in France and at age thirty-three, enrolled at the California Culinary Academy in San Francisco. After graduation, Vivaldo moved to Los Angeles to start her own company, Food Fanatics. With a celebrity clientele in Southern California, Vivaldo is rarely without work, and she's done it all, from small family weddings to movie premier parties. She was hired to be kitchen director for the Academy Awards Governor's Ball for two years running.

For several years, she helped to write other people's books, including Suzanne Sommers, Richard Simmons and Susan Powter, and after a while decided that she had something to say herself and began writing about catering and hosting parties. Vivaldo travels the country teaching seminars on the catering business to those who are interested in getting into that line of work. She first brought her classes to the Western Reserve School of Cooking in 2006.

Increasingly, she is finding her classes filled with a mixture of men and women, young and old, who are looking for a new career or a first-time job. Vivaldo said there are plenty of opportunities out there for people who want to work in food. But her advice is to make sure it's something that you love. "The reason most people survived in food is because they went into it because they have a love of the food. If you love it, it's worth it. Some projects are stinky and some projects, I would have paid them to do it. But I think you should really love it, otherwise there are other ways to make money," she said.

These recipes from Vivaldo's *Do It For Less! Parties* were taken from menus she developed for an "Arabian Nights" theme party and a "Spring on the Terrance" theme party.

Lemon-Caper Potato Salad

3½ pounds small red or white potatoes

½ cup extra-virgin olive oil

juice and zest of three lemons

3 tablespoons minced shallots

2 tablespoons chopped fresh parsley

3 tablespoons chopped fresh dill

salt and freshly ground pepper, to taste

2 tablespoons capers, rinsed and drained

Scrub potatoes and cut into quarters. Place in a stockpot and fill with enough cold water to completely cover by 1 inch. Bring water to a boil, reduce heat and simmer until potatoes are just tender. Drain in a colander.

In a bowl large enough to hold potatoes, whisk together olive oil, lemon juice, lemon zest, shallots, parsley and dill, until well-combined. Season with salt and pepper, to taste.

Add warm potatoes and capers. Toss gently with a wooden spoon or your hands, to coat with the dressing. Serve warm, or refrigerate and serve chilled.

Makes 12 servings.

Marrakech Chicken

¼ cup all-purpose flour

1 tablespoon ground turmeric

1 tablespoon ground ginger

1 tablespoon curry powder

1 tablespoon ground cinnamon

1 tablespoon ground cumin

6 cups chicken stock

12 boneless, skinless chicken breasts
(6 to 8 ounces each)

salt and freshly ground black pepper,
to taste

½ cup olive or peanut oil,
more as needed

6 cups sliced onions (about 3 large)

3 tablespoons minced garlic

¾ cup lemon juice

2 cups sliced black olives, golden raisins
or dried apricots

½ cup honey

2 cups chopped fresh cilantro

Preheat oven to 250 degrees.

Combine flour, turmeric, ginger, curry powder, cinnamon and cumin in a mixing bowl. Slowly whisk in chicken stock until smooth.

Season chicken with salt and pepper. Heat oil in a large sauté pan over medium heat. Cook chicken in batches for 3 to 4 minutes per side, or until cooked through.

Reserve juices in pan, place chicken on a baking sheet and move to oven.

Add onions to pan juices in sauté pan and cook until onions become translucent, about 4 minutes. Add more oil as needed.

Add garlic and sauté for 1 minute. Slowly whisk in chicken stock mixture. Bring mixture to a boil, stirring constantly.

Add lemon juice. Lower heat and simmer, stirring occasionally for 10 minutes, or until sauce thickens. Add more stock or water if sauce gets too thick or starts to dry out.

Just before serving, stir in olives and honey. Season with salt and pepper to taste. Return chicken to pan and simmer until heated through.

Garnish with chopped cilantro and serve immediately.

Makes 12 servings.

Toasted Almond and Feta Zucchini

3 pounds zucchini

2 sticks, unsalted butter

3 tablespoons olive oil

3 pounds onions, thinly sliced

12 ounces feta cheese, crumbled

1 cup, toasted, slivered almonds

salt and freshly ground black pepper, to taste

Trim ends from zucchini and cut in half lengthwise. Cut each half into half-inch thick slices to make a half-moon shape.

Heat butter and olive oil in a large sauté pan over medium heat. Add onions in batches and cook, stirring frequently, for 15 to 18 minutes, or until onions have reduced and become golden brown. Remove onions from pan.

Add zucchini to pan and sauté for 2 to 3 minutes, or until crisp-tender. Stir in caramelized onions.

Remove from heat and toss with feta and almonds. Season with salt and pepper to taste and serve immediately.

Makes 12 servings.

The Recipes

Chapter 7

Locally Grown

"Your goal is taste."

For twenty years, Parker Bosley operated one of the most celebrated restaurants Cleveland, Ohio, has ever seen. When Parker's New American Bistro opened in 1986, Bosley served locally-sourced meat and produce when the idea was still in its infancy in Ohio. It's not surprising that Parker's was sometimes referred to as Cleveland's Chez Panisse.

Even since his retirement in 2006, Bosley continues to be an integral force in the Cleveland area farm-to-table movement. It makes sense, when you consider that Bosley was a farm boy. Born in the late 1930s in Farmington Township in rural northern Trumbull County, the idea of farm-fresh food just makes sense to him.

Bosley didn't start out as a chef. He studied music, French and art history at Baldwin Wallace College and taught grade school in Berea, Ohio. He left Ohio for Okinawa, Japan, and later France, where he taught the children of military personnel stationed there.

By the time he was back in Ohio in the 1970s, Bosley had become a well-seasoned home cook, and it wasn't long after that he began taking classes at the Zona Spray Cooking School. He recalled that at the time, Spray's was the only place of its kind in the Cleveland area.

Bosley later studied at LaVarenne in France, where he counts John Desmond among his favorite instructors. "He was a phenomenal teacher. He taught me how to make fish stock. It is one of the most wonderful things, if done right. I love to make that kind of stuff," he said.

No longer teaching elementary school, Bosley was looking for a job cooking in a restaurant kitchen and found it at the well-known Sammy's in Cleveland. It was through Spray that Bosley was able to meet French Chef Michel Pasquet, and in 1983, Bosley left Ohio again, this time to apprentice at Pasquet's Paris restaurant. Upon his return, Bosley taught regularly at Spray's school for a few years, until 1986, when he ventured out on his own, opening the celebrated Parker's in Cleveland's Ohio City neighborhood.

Bosley recalls the era as a wonderful time in northeast Ohio, with the whole region awakening to the possibilities of new American cuisine. Bosley began to stress the importance of fresh, high-quality ingredients, after he realized that he was doing everything right, but inferior ingredients were holding back the quality of his food. He sought out the kinds of farm-fresh foods that he had grown up with, becoming a pioneer in the city's farm-to-table movement. After the lights went out at Parker's, Bosley ushered in a new career, working as a consultant to encourage entrepreneurial farming and farmers markets. He believes small farms could be a major economic engine in the aging rust-belt region.

Bosley doesn't teach anymore, disappointed in how food television has skewed the kitchen stage for many good chefs, requiring them to be more entertainers and less cooks. "I don't want to have to entertain anyone," he laments, adding that Julia Child's television shows would probably fail in today's market. But his lesson on cooking is still alive and connected to getting the best possible ingredients and presenting them in the best possible way. "You have to know your craft, your technique. But your goal is taste—taste, taste until you get this really wonderful product. You are making food and it has to be exciting to eat."

Stuffed Breast of Chicken

4 boneless chicken breasts, skin on

8 tablespoons cream cheese

⅔ cup carrots

⅔ cup leeks

⅔ cup zucchini

salt and pepper, to taste

butter

Julienne vegetables. Blanch vegetables in a pot of boiling water for 1 to 2 minutes. Remove and drain.

Soften cream cheese and mix with vegetables. Season with salt and pepper.

Pull back skin of chicken breasts and season meat with salt and pepper. Place about 2 tablespoons of mixture on each chicken breast and pull skin back over filling.

Season breasts with salt and pepper on the outside and dot with butter. Run under broiler to brown and blister skin. Finish cooking in a 350-degree oven for about 10 minutes or until chicken is cooked completely.

Makes 4 servings.

Famous Chefs & Fabulous Recipes

Pork Loin Stuffed with Apricots

8 dried apricots

½ cup Madeira wine

1 cup water

1 cup stock (chicken or veal)

2 tablespoons minced shallots

1 tablespoon butter

4 slices pork loin (3 ounces each)

salt and pepper

3 tablespoons butter

Cover apricots with Madeira and water and bring to boil. Remove from heat and cool.

Make a pocket in each slice of pork. Pound pork between layers of plastic wrap, to tenderize. Reshape slices.

Remove apricots from their liquid and return liquid to boil; reduce. Chop apricots with shallots. Season pockets of pork slices with salt and pepper and fill with apricot and shallot mixture.

Season outside of pork with salt and pepper. Melt butter in pan and sauté pork on each side for 1 to 2 minutes. Place in a 350-degree oven to finish cooking.

Pour butter from sauté pan and deglaze with apricot liquid. Reduce and add stock. Continue cooking until sauce has reduced and thickened.

Remove sauce from heat and whisk in 3 tablespoons butter. Check seasoning. Serve sauce over pork.

Makes 4 servings.

Zack Bruell

"Understand that all cooking is layering flavors."

When it came to Cleveland's contemporary restaurant scene, Zack Bruell was the trail blazer. He was there in the 1980s, when Cleveland didn't have much of a food identity in Ohio, let alone nationally, and he helped to introduce the city to the new food culture of the West Coast.

But after ten years and two incarnations of his highly successful restaurant, Z Contemporary Cuisine, Bruell closed up shop and disappeared. He hid out in nearby Akron, where he worked, seemingly in name only, as executive chef at the city's well-regarded Ken Stewart's Grille. It was a period of self-imposed exile brought on by too many twelve-hour days and a desire to spend more time with his young family.

His nine-year low profile ended in 2004, when he opened Parallax in Cleveland's Tremont neighborhood and Bruell returned to a city anxious to welcome him back. Diners still remembered Z, which burst onto the Cleveland food scene in 1985. Today, his portfolio includes four of the most celebrated restaurants in the Cleveland city limits—Parallax Restaurant and Lounge, L'Albatros Brasserie & Bar, Table 45 and Chinato—and Bruell has grown beyond chef into the restaurateur he believes he was always meant to be.

Bruell grew up in the Cleveland suburb of Shaker Heights. After high school, he attended the University of Pennsylvania's Wharton School of Business. His first shock came when he ate in the cafeteria, his first experience with food that wasn't home cooking. The experience inspired him to cook for the first time and he turned to a hot plate and toaster oven in his dormitory to prepare his meals. Another shock loomed; in 1972, Uncle Sam came calling and Bruell was drafted.

He spent a year in the Coast Guard Reserves and then transferred to the University of Colorado Boulder. There he earned a business degree and forged a friendship with Michael McCarty, who introduced him to French cuisine and a new world of food. He was fascinated and knew he wanted to be a part of the cuisine. Acting on advice from McCarty, he enrolled at the Restaurant School in Philadelphia. He graduated in 1977 and ran his first restaurant in Philadelphia. Eventually, he went back to California and helped McCarty launch Michael's in Santa Monica, one of the most significant restaurants in establishing California's nouvelle cuisine.

Bruell was keeping company with some of the country's most celebrated young chefs and Cleveland was definitely a backwards career move. But in 1982, Bruell accepted a lucrative offer to run the Garland at Landerhaven, outside of Cleveland and moved back. "I don't look back. I have no regrets in my life. It was not the easy decision. I worked with the who's who in L.A., and I was the only one who came back to a secondary market," he recalls.

After a few years back home, Bruell was ready to go out on his own and opened Z in 1985, to celebrated reviews and national attention. For the next ten years, Bruell worked ninety hours a week, until one busy Saturday night when he had an epiphany over the grill: he needed a break. He spent the next year golfing, his main passion outside the kitchen, until Akron's Ken Stewart called. Chef Roger Thomas was leaving and Stewart needed a high-profile chef. Bruell agreed to work for a few months, but stayed eight years. He left in 2004, and returned to Cleveland to open the seafood restaurant Parallax.

Bruell was quickly called upon to help the Cleveland Clinic reinvent its formal restaurant, Classics and in 2007, Bruell's contemporary Table 45 opened there. It was a pivotal moment for Bruell, who had always been in the kitchen.

After a few nights, his young staff booted him off the line, telling him, "We can do this, get out of our way," pushing him into the front of the house. It was the first time in his career that he actually had the chance to mix with customers and Bruell found that despite the bruise to his ego, he actually liked being there. "I realized that's what I should have been doing all along. It freed me up to do other stuff. They changed my life," he said. European travel and two other restaurants, the French bistro L'Albatros and the Italian Chinato, followed in 2008 and 2010. "I still am a chef, but I'm not a line cook. I'm a restaurateur. That's what I've turned into. That's what I wanted to be all along."

With four restaurants to manage, Bruell has no time for teaching now. But in the 1990s, he taught numerous classes at the Zona Spray Cooking School. Bruell liked to focus on the basics, in particular sauces, something which has always made his cooking distinctive. He remembers having twenty or thirty students at the school, hovering around the cook top in the school's cramped kitchen to watch, smell, listen and taste. "I want them to understand that all cooking is layering flavors. If you understand the layering of flavors, you can start out with a base technique and start layering things into it. That's the staple of fresh cooking," he said. "I try to make people understand that it's not rocket science. A lot of people are very afraid of it. Once you understand technique, you just let it go."

Sherry Wine Vinegar Sauce

1 cup sherry wine vinegar	2 cups demi-glace (veal, duck or chicken)
1 tablespoon minced shallots	½ cup heavy cream

Reduce sherry wine vinegar and shallots in saucepan to half a cup. Add demi-glace and reduce to sauce consistency. Add heavy cream and reduce to desired consistency. Season with salt and pepper. Serve on duck, chicken, or pork. Makes about 1½ cups.

Madeira Sauce

1 cup Madeira wine　　　　　½ cup heavy cream
2 shallots, finely chopped　　salt and pepper
2 cups demi-glace

Reduce Madeira and shallots in saucepan to ¼ cup liquid. Add demi-glace and reduce to sauce consistency. Let out with heavy cream and reduce to desired thickness. Season with salt and pepper.

Makes about 1½ cups.

Pommery Mustard Sauce

2 cups demi-glace (chicken or pork)　　1 cup heavy cream
2 shallots, finely chopped　　　　　　salt and pepper
2 cloves garlic　　　　　　　　　　　Pommery mustard

In a saucepan, reduce demi-glace with shallots and garlic by one-third. Add heavy cream and reduce to desired consistency. Remove from heat and add mustard. Season with salt and pepper.

Makes about 2 cups.

Tomato Vinaigrette

4 ripe tomatoes (peeled and seeded)　　salt and black pepper
2 tablespoons sherry vinegar　　　　　fresh herbs
6 tablespoons extra-virgin olive oil

Chop tomatoes finely. Place in mixing bowl with vinegar and olive oil. Season with salt, pepper and fresh herbs. Chill.

Makes about 2 cups.

Meredith Deeds

"Taste, taste, taste."

Meredith Deeds is a California girl and she can make a really fine fish taco. So no one was more surprised when her first teaching assignment at the Western Reserve School of Cooking was a class on how to make pierogi. Pierogis are a staple of Northeast Ohio food, but Deeds is neither Polish nor an expert in Eastern European cooking.

Deeds found a friend to help and began intensive pierogi training to acquire the skill before she had to teach about the potato-filled dumplings. But when the time came, she feared that the class would know that she was a pierogi fraud. The class went well and Deeds now considers herself an expert on the subject. "I did enough research on it that I can probably do a dissertation on pierogi," Deeds says.

That wouldn't be her last memorable class at the school. One time, she was teaching a class at a local grocery store with fellow teacher Carla Snyder. One of their portable burners caught on fire and caused the store's sprinkler system to go off. The whole class got soaked and the fire department had to come turn off the alarm. When the water finally stopped pouring, one of the students asked, "Well, aren't you guys going to finish the class now?"

Deeds ended up in Hudson in 1998, when her husband was offered a teaching position at Case Western Reserve University. A native of San Diego, Deeds grew up in a restaurant—her mother operated a diner and she worked there from a young age, waiting on tables, washing dishes and later working as a cook. The pies and the soup were always homemade and Deeds cracked a lot of eggs and poured a lot of coffee.

Her interest in food grew and she studied at the California State Polytechnic University's Restaurant School. Because they moved a lot for her husband's career, Deeds began writing about food and selling her articles to magazines and newspapers. She was always interested in teaching, but never lived close enough to a school to make it happen. Once she discovered Western Reserve, Deeds approached then-owner Carole Ferguson about work.

"I loved teaching at the cooking school, I still have such a warm spot for it," Deeds says. Her time in Hudson was short, but it proved fruitful. She and Snyder forged a writing partnership at the school that continues to this day. Together, they have written six books, including *The Big Book of Appetizers*, which was nominated for a James Beard Foundation Award in 2007.

Between books, she writes a blog, gives food demonstrations and continues to teach. Her most important lesson to her students is to taste their food, and she's always surprised by how many people don't taste a thing until the dish is done. "Taste, taste, taste. You only get one shot at making it great before it gets to the table," she said.

Carla Snyder

"Always want to learn more."

In 1988, Carla Snyder walked through the door of the Zona Spray School of Cooking and begged for a job. With three young children at home, her husband wasn't crazy about the idea. Over the years, though, Snyder's career as a cooking teacher, caterer and most recently as a prolific cookbook author, made him change his mind. "He wasn't really on board with it right away. But it really did turn out to be a really great thing," Snyder said.

Snyder remembers well her first meeting with Spray. "I was scared to death of her. Everybody was. She could use silence like no one else. She just looked at you and you'd started blathering." Spray was reluctant to hire Snyder, preferring to hire people who had been through her cooking program. But Snyder persisted. "I remember telling her that I was a really hard worker and that I loved to learn." Spray agreed and after the first week, Snyder knew she had found her home. "It is such a wonderful venue, and the opportunity to work with all of the wonderful chefs who have gone through that place. You always learned something, every night, not to mention Zona, who was always the source of information. She was a wonderful mentor," Snyder said.

The school is one of the reasons that Snyder moved to Hudson. A native of Weirton, W.Va., Snyder describes her upbringing as "white bread." Her mother's idea of cooking was Mrs. Paul's Fish Sticks and anything else she could make from a box. No one in her family had ever learned how to cook. Weirton, though, was a town filled with ethnic immigrants and Snyder was fascinated by the smells, foods and languages at her friends' homes. Over the years, Snyder taught herself to cook by relying on cooking magazines. After college, she married and lived for a while in Washington, Pa., before her husband's job brought them to Warren, Ohio, where Snyder began to do some catering on the side. A friend from Warren had moved to Hudson and told her about the school. When Snyder relocated to the Cleveland area, she insisted on living in Hudson to be near the cooking school.

Snyder had been working at the school for about five years, taking classes and assisting other chefs, when Spray asked her if she would be interested in teaching. She enjoyed it so much she eventually gave up her catering business. Snyder prefers to teach single technique-driven classes—all sautéing or all braising—because the information is intensive in one area and she believes it stays with the students better. "I'm really technique-driven, that way people know how to cook. If you can cook that perfect chicken breast and change out the sauce forty different ways, then it's the exact same thing to cook a pork chop or a piece of fish," she said.

When Snyder teaches, she tries to encourage her students not to be nervous about trying new things and to always want to learn more. "Do the things you don't know how to do. It's only food and even if you screw it up, it will still probably taste good, and don't apologize if it doesn't taste really good because no one will probably know but you. The worst thing that can happen is that you have to throw it away."

It was also at the school that Snyder met her writing partner, Meredith Deeds. They formed a partnership that, since 2005, has produced six books, including the 2007 James Beard Award nominee, *The Big Book of Appetizers*. They are currently at work on several more and Snyder left the school in 2007, to pursue her writing career full-time. Snyder finds she is most fulfilled by her books. "I really like the writing," she said.

Brie and Pear Quesadillas

When paired up with rich, buttery brie cheese you've created an untraditional, but savory take on a south of the border classic. Roasting poblano chiles gives them a totally different flavor, not so green, but smoky and deep while roasting the pears gives them a concentrated sweetness.

3 pears, halved, peeled and cored

1 large yellow onion, halved and thinly sliced

10 flour tortillas

½ pound brie, thinly sliced

3 poblano chiles, roasted, peeled and sliced into thin strips

4 tablespoons unsalted butter

4 tablespoons oil

salt and freshly ground black pepper, to taste

Preheat an oven to 400 degrees.

Arrange pears cut side down on a baking sheet lined with parchment. Roast pears in oven for about 20 minutes or until they soften and dry on the outside. Remove pears from oven and let cool. Slice thinly.

Meanwhile, heat 3 cups water to a boil in a medium skillet. Add onions and cover and remove from heat. Let stand until onions wilt, about 12 minutes. Drain completely and pat dry on paper towels.

Heat a nonstick or well-seasoned skillet over medium heat and add 1 teaspoon butter and 1 teaspoon oil. Lay down 1 tortilla and quickly lay down some onion, pepper, cheese, pear and more cheese. Be careful not to overfill or it will be impossible to turn the quesadilla in the pan. Sprinkle with salt and pepper; top with another tortilla. Turn heat down to low and cook tortilla until lightly browned on bottom. Using a wide spatula and your hand, turn tortilla to brown other side. (Once turned, cheese will begin to melt and act like glue to make tortilla stick together.) Repeat with remaining tortillas and fillings. Cut tortillas into 6 wedges each. Serve warm.

The quesadillas can be assembled 8 hours ahead of time and kept covered in refrigerator. Once quesadillas are cooked they can be kept in a 200-degree oven for one hour. Slice right before serving.

Makes about 30 pieces.

From *The Big Book of Appetizers* by Meredith Deeds and Carla Snyder. Copyright © 2006 by Meredith Deeds and Carla Snyder. Used by permission of Chronicle Books.

Grilled Prosciutto Wrapped Shrimp

Wrapping seafood in prosciutto makes such good sense. It not only helps keep the seafood from drying out during the cooking process, it also lends a rich, salty flavor to whatever it encases. In this recipe, we've marinated the shrimp in garlic, rosemary and olive oil, which stands up well to the earthiness of the prosciutto.

¼ cup finely chopped garlic	2 tablespoons lemon juice
½ teaspoon salt	24 large shrimp (16 to 20 per pound)
2 tablespoons minced fresh rosemary leaves, plus sprigs for garnish	12 thin slices of prosciutto sliced in half lengthwise
3 tablespoons olive oil, plus oil for brushing shrimp	wooden skewers

In a large zipper lock bag, combine garlic, salt, minced rosemary, 3 tablespoons oil and lemon juice. Add shrimp and toss to coat. Marinate shrimp, chilled, at least 4 hours or overnight.

In a shallow dish, cover skewers in water and soak 30 minutes; prepare grill.

Wrap each shrimp around middle with one strip prosciutto. Thread 4 shrimp on each skewer and brush with additional oil. Grill shrimp on an oiled rack, set about 5 inches over glowing coals, 3 to 4 minutes on each side, or until just cooked through.

Alternatively, brush shrimp with additional oil and grill in a hot well-seasoned ridged grill pan, covered, over moderately high heat, 3 to 4 minutes on each side, or until cooked through.

Garnish shrimp with rosemary sprigs and serve with lemon wedges. Makes 24 pieces.

Notes: The shrimp can be marinated, wrapped in prosciutto, skewered and kept covered in the refrigerator up to eight hours before grilling. Try this technique with other types of seafood as well. We like to wrap our salmon fillets or scallops in the prosciutto and serve them alongside roasted root vegetables for an easy, but impressive meal.

From *The Big Book of Appetizers* by Meredith Deeds and Carla Snyder. Copyright © 2006 by Meredith Deeds and Carla Snyder. Used by permission of Chronicle Books.

Sweet Potato and Leek Pancakes with Applesauce and Sour Cream

Sturdy little pancakes topped with chunky applesauce and sour cream is our idea of the perfect comfort food. We think of this dish as a sit-down appetizer but if you make the pancakes small, it could easily be passed or set out on a buffet table. These are best when served hot from the oven. Make lots—they will disappear fast.

4 cups Braeburn, Gala or Mutsu apples, peeled and cut into ¼-inch dice

⅓ cup light brown sugar

3 tablespoons lemon juice

2 tablespoons unsalted butter

1 cup thinly sliced leeks, white and pale green parts only, washed

salt and freshly ground black pepper

1 cup peeled and grated russet potato

2 cups peeled and grated sweet potato (yam)

1 large egg, beaten

⅓ cup all-purpose flour

1 teaspoon salt

½ teaspoon baking powder

¼ teaspoon freshly ground black pepper

¼ teaspoon grated nutmeg

⅓ cup vegetable oil

½ cup sour cream

2 tablespoons chives, minced for garnish (optional)

To make applesauce, add apples to a medium saucepan and cook over medium heat until apples begin to give off water. Turn heat to medium-low and stir occasionally, cooking until apples break down and become thick, about 20 minutes. (This technique concentrates the flavor of the apples.) Adjust heat as necessary so that apples don't brown or burn. Add brown sugar and lemon juice and continue to cook for another 5 minutes. Remove from heat and keep warm.

Heat a large skillet over medium heat and add butter. When butter has melted and skillet is hot, add leek and sauté, stirring until tender, about 5 minutes. Remove from heat and transfer mixture to a large bowl to cool.

Preheat oven to 250 degrees. Add potatoes and egg to leek mixture and stir to mix. Add flour, salt, baking powder, black pepper and nutmeg and mix thoroughly.

Heat 2 tablespoons oil in skillet over medium heat. Drop batter by ¼-cupfuls into skillet. Using a fork or spatula, flatten each mound to a 4-inch round. If you want to make them smaller, add batter by rounded tablespoons. Cook until brown, about 3 minutes, turn to cook the other side for an additional 3 minutes. Transfer to a baking sheet lined with parchment paper and keep warm in preheated oven for up to 1 hour. Repeat with remaining batter, adding more oil to skillet as needed.

To serve, transfer 1 large pancake to each plate or 2 or 3 smaller ones and top with applesauce and sour cream. Garnish with a sprinkling of chives if desired. The pancakes and applesauce can be made up to 24 hours before serving, covered and refrigerated. Reheat in a 350-degree oven for 7 or 8 minutes. Rewarm applesauce in microwave or on stovetop.

Makes 6 large or 18 small pancakes, to serve 6.

From *The Big Book of Appetizers* by Meredith Deeds and Carla Snyder. Copyright © 2006 by Meredith Deeds and Carla Snyder. Used by permission of Chronicle Books.

Grape Leaves with Rice and Pine Nut Filling

From the many variations of stuffed grape leaves or dolmas, this Greek version is a party favorite. The jasmine rice will perfume the filling as will the lemon and the herbal notes from the chives, tarragon and fennel. The crunch of the pine nuts and sweetness of the currants combine to make these dolmas irresistible.

1 jar (16 ounces) preserved
  brined grape leaves

¼ cup extra-virgin olive oil

1 cup onion, minced

½ cup pine nuts

1 cup jasmine rice

½ cup chopped currants or raisins

¼ cup minced Italian parsley

2 tablespoons chopped fresh chives

2 tablespoons chopped fresh tarragon

2 tablespoons chopped fresh

  fennel greens

½ teaspoon lemon zest

½ teaspoon salt

¼ teaspoon cardamom

⅛ teaspoon cinnamon

2 cups chicken stock

¼ cup lemon juice

¼ cup olive oil

¾ cup chicken stock

1 lemon cut in half lengthwise
  and thinly sliced, for garnish

Separate grape leaves and rinse under running cold water. Soak leaves in cold water while preparing rice filling.

Heat a medium saucepan over medium heat and add olive oil. When oil is hot, add onion and sauté until soft. Add pine nuts, jasmine rice and currants and cook, stirring for 2 or 3 minutes. Add parsley, chives, tarragon, fennel greens, lemon zest, salt, cardamom, cinnamon and 2 cups chicken stock and bring to a simmer. Do not stir. Cover, turn down heat and let rice cook for about 20 minutes or until tender and liquid has been absorbed. Remove rice from heat, fluff with a fork and transfer to a large bowl to cool.

Drain grape leaves and lay them out on a towel to dry.

Working with one leaf at a time, place a rounded teaspoonful (don't overstuff) of rice filling at the base of the leaf where it connects to the stem. Cover filling with tail end of the leaf and roll it. Fold sides of leaf to center, to enclose filling and roll up the package from stem end to tip. Finish with the seam on the bottom. Line a 3-quart lidded saucepan with grape leaves that have ripped or torn. Cover bottom of pan with a layer of stuffed grape leaves. Squirt a little lemon juice on top and lay a few unstuffed grape leaves to cover. Continue to roll grape leaves and layer them in pan. Top rolled grape leaves with more ripped or torn grape leaves to cover.

When you've finished making layers, pour olive oil, ¾ cup chicken stock and remaining lemon juice into pan, cover and place over medium heat. Braise rolls for about 45 minutes at a bare simmer. Remove from heat and cool until the rolls are easily handled. Arrange grape leaves on a tray and garnish with sliced lemons.

Grape leaves are good warm or at room temperature. They can be kept covered and refrigerated for 3 days.

Makes about 4 dozen.

From *The Big Book of Appetizers* by Meredith Deeds and Carla Snyder. Copyright © 2006 by Meredith Deeds and Carla Snyder. Used by permission of Chronicle Books.

Fred and Linda Griffith

"Be really comfortable with the utensils and the ingredients."

I f you're from northeast Ohio, you don't even have to mention their last names. They are simply Fred and Linda—and they are, in many ways, Cleveland's first couple of food. In their more than thirty years together, not only have they managed to write six cookbooks and teach countless cooking classes, but they brought Slow Food USA to Cleveland, founding the Northern Ohio chapter of the sustainable food organization.

Now semiretired, Fred and Linda Griffith live in a Shaker Heights condominium brimming with dogs, cats and memorabilia from their travels, including a photo of them with James Beard, which hangs in the bathroom. They no longer teach, but remain keen observers and active participants in the bustling Cleveland food scene. They talk with excitement and pride about local chefs—Jonathon Sawyer, Michael Symon, Zack Bruell—and how Cleveland has truly blossomed into a food destination city.

This wasn't always the case. When the Griffiths met in 1978, Cleveland was a mish-mash of ethnic foods. Sure, you could get good pierogi in Cleveland and an excellent plate of pasta, but no one was coming just to eat the local fare. The pair helped to promote the city, its chefs and its cuisine and along the way established themselves as nationally-known culinarians. Their book, *Onions, Onions, Onions*, released in 1994, won a James Beard Award for single-subject cookbooks.

The pair taught cooking from their home, but beginning in the 1990s, also made several guest appearances at the Zona Spray Cooking School. Wherever they teach, Linda said she tries to impart to her students to approach food without fear and to learn to be comfortable with the ingredients and the equipment. Don't make a federal case out of it, she says, because it's just food, and even if it's not perfect, no one will know but you.

It was this kind of fearlessness that got Linda cooking to begin with. A Massachusetts native, Linda attended Brandis University before marrying and relocating to Cleveland. She describes her grandmother as a "wonderful Jewish cook," but her mother as, "not an especially wonderful cook." Linda didn't give cooking much thought until after moving to Cleveland, when it became clear that she would have to return the dinner invitations she and her husband received. Even though she had never cooked, Griffith presumed it was easy, so she opened a cookbook and simply started following the directions. She uncovered a natural talent for cooking and a keen sense of taste that has guided the Griffiths through their books.

For Fred, who is best know as the long-time host of the *Morning Exchange* program on Cleveland's WEWS, food was in his roots. His father operated a twenty-four-hour restaurant, McFarland Lunch, in his hometown of Charleston,

West Virginia. It was located about halfway between the city's two compet-
ing newspapers, the *Charleston Gazette* and the *Charleston Daily Mail*. Griffith
worked in the restaurant from the time he was a boy, but says his talents were
scrubbing pots and mopping floors. His early exposure to a host of newsmen,
however, set the tone for his future career as a radio broadcaster and later as a
television news director and on-air personality.

Linda's culinary skills were becoming widely known in Cleveland and in
1978, *Cleveland Magazine* named her one of the city's ten best cooks. She was
director of the Cuyahoga County Hospital Foundation and needed a member
of the media to serve on her board of directors. Around the same time, both of
their first marriages were ending. When Linda approached Fred about serving
on her board, he first turned her down, while he recovered from a broken femur.
Eventually the leg healed and a relationship began. They married in 1981 and
have been writing and cooking together ever since.

Tapenade with Garlic and Sun-Dried Tomatoes

Travel in the south of France and you will often find a crock of this lusty olive paste
on the table of most cafes. It can be as simple as a combination of garlic, black Mediterranean olives and olive oil, or richly enlivened by anchovies, fresh oregano and
sun-dried tomatoes. This makes a great spread for focaccia or a toothsome bread.
Stored in a tightly-covered container, tapenade will keep for weeks in the refrigerator. Just bring to room temperature before serving. If you have an herb garden,
try including oregano flowers. They are especially delicious.

2 packed cups pitted niçoise
   or kalamata olives

12 oil-packed, or water-softened,
   sun-dried tomatoes

5 plump garlic cloves

2 teaspoons fresh oregano leaves

1 teaspoon freshly ground black pepper

¼ cup extra-virgin olive oil
   plus up to 2 tablespoons (if needed)

In the bowl of a food processor fitted with a metal blade, combine olives, sun
dried tomatoes, garlic, oregano and pepper. Pulse until puréed. Taste and add
more tomato, if desired. With motor running, gradually add ¼ cup olive oil.
Scrape and process again. Add more olive oil, if needed to make a thick, spread-
able paste. Scrape tapenade into a clean container and store in refrigerator.

Bring to room temperature before serving. Makes about 2 cups.

Adapted from *Garlic, Garlic, Garlic* by Fred and Linda Griffith (Houghton Mifflin Harcourt, 1998).

Lu-B-Vee Bi Ghan'-Nam

The Shaheen sisters slowly simmer this simple Syrian stew of lamb and green beans in a fragrant and flavorful tomato sauce. While the stew is cooking, they brown some tiny soup pasta and cook it together with rice and beef stock. The tasty stew is served over this luscious rice mixture. All together, this is a very satisfying, but light, dish, well-suited to the summer, when green beans right from the garden are especially delicious.

For the stew:

¼ cup olive oil

1 pound lamb shoulder,
    cut into 1-inch cubes

2 medium yellow onions, finely diced

2 plump garlic cloves, minced

¼ rounded teaspoon allspice

kosher salt and freshly ground
    black pepper

2 pounds green beans trimmed
    and cut in 1-inch pieces

1 can (8 ounces) tomato sauce
    or 2 large fresh tomatoes, chopped

For the rice:

4 tablespoons unsalted butter

1 cup rosa marina or orzo pasta,
    available in Italian markets

2 cups long-grain rice

4 cups beef stock, boiling

Heat half the oil in a large sauté pan over medium-high heat. Add lamb and stir until browned on all sides, about 10 minutes, adding more oil as needed. Add onions, garlic, allspice, salt and pepper. Stir until onions are tender, 3 to 5 minutes.

Add ¼ cup water and simmer for 10 minutes. Stir in beans and tomatoes. Add enough water to cover contents of pan halfway. Increase heat until liquids bubble. Cover and reduce heat to medium. Cook until lamb is tender, stirring occasionally, 20 to 30 minutes.

To prepare rice: In a large saucepan, melt butter over medium-high heat. Add rosamarina and stir until browned, 10 to 12 minutes. Add rice and stir until grains are well-coated. Add boiling stock. When mixture is bubbling, cover and simmer for 30 minutes, or until liquid is absorbed by the rice.

Spoon generous amounts of rice in the center of heated soup plates. Ladle stew over rice.

Makes 4 servings.

From *Cooking Under Cover* by Fred and Linda Griffith (Houghton Mifflin Harcourt, 1998).

Famous Chefs & Fabulous Recipes

Cabbage Onion Flatbread

We adapted this recipe from a Molly O'Neill recipe that appeared in the *Sunday New York Times Magazine* in 2000. If you want to add a bit of heat, substitute minced poblano chile for the minced onion.

1 cup whole wheat flour

1 cup all-purpose flour

½ teaspoon ground coriander

½ teaspoon ground turmeric

½ teaspoon ground cardamom

½ teaspoon kosher salt

2 cups finely shredded green cabbage

2 teaspoons minced fresh ginger

2 tablespoons minced onion

2 plump garlic cloves, minced

2½ teaspoons black sesame seeds

⅔ cup water

2 tablespoons vegetable oil, plus more for frying the bread

Sift flours, spices and salt into a large bowl. Stir in cabbage, ginger, onion, garlic, sesame seeds, water and oil. Using your hands, knead dough on a lightly floured surface for 12 minutes. Let rest under a towel for 15 minutes.

Separate dough into 12 equal balls. On a lightly floured surface, roll out each ball into a round about ⅛-inch thick.

Place a medium skillet over medium heat. Lightly oil skillet and fry each round, turning once, until golden brown, about 1 minute per side. Transfer cooked flatbreads to a platter and keep warm. Continue until all breads are cooked, adding more oil to skillet as needed. Serve breads warm, with tasty kebabs.

Makes 12 flatbreads.

Scot Jones

"Invest in your work."

Perhaps it was times he spent eating out as a child that cemented Scot Jones' desire to become a chef. Maybe it was the fact that his dad, a heating and cooling contractor, knew the kitchens of every restaurant in his hometown of Akron, Ohio, and would send young Scot off to explore the kitchen if he was getting antsy at the dinner table. Or maybe it was the Sundays he would spend cooking dinner with his dad—the one meal his large family actually ate a home. More than likely, it was a combination of all of factors, but Jones knew from the time he was a youngster that he wanted to be a chef.

The youngest of nine children, Jones' mother was a pediatric oncologist, his father a mechanical contractor. With two professional parents, there wasn't much cooking going on in the bustling household. When his mother did cook, Jones says, no one looked forward to it. Mostly, the family dined at restaurants, often five or six times a week. But on Sundays, his father would spend the day preparing elaborate dinners, and Scot was at his side from the time he seven years old. "My father and I would cook every Sunday. That was the one meal we ate at home. My dad cooked with a bottle of Lambrusco. It was in the sauce, it was on the roast, it was in the salad." His family wasn't Italian, but Jones' mother always joked that someone slipped garlic into her son's baby bottle, because of his affection for Italian cuisine. By the time he was twelve, young Scot was cooking meals for the whole family.

By the time he was fourteen, he used his dad's restaurant connections to get a job bussing tables at a local restaurant, the Amber Pub. A year later, Akron restaurateur Joe Iacomini pinched him to work at a new restaurant he was opening. One of his chief duties was driving Iacomini around in his Lincoln Continental, while he smoked his cigar in the back. Jones didn't even have a license yet, but it didn't seem to bother Iacomini, who was more concerned with checking out the parking lots of his competitors to see where the business was.

He stayed with Iacomini for five years and earned a two-year degree at the University of Akron's School of Hospitality Management. From there, he left for the Culinary Institute of America, returning home to Ohio to work at Johnny's on Fulton Road, one of Cleveland's longest-standing Italian restaurants. Ten years later, he came home to Akron where he opened Grappa, an Italian restaurant. He followed that with work in Canton, as executive chef for Fedeli, an Italian restaurant that caught the attention of the Testa family, Akron developers who were in the process of opening a restaurant with rock star Chrissie Hynde of the Pretenders. Well-known for her vegan lifestyle, Hynde wanted to open a vegan café in her hometown of Akron and Jones was tapped as executive chef.

Far from being a vegetarian, let alone a vegan, Jones developed a menu of

Mediterranean-style dishes with vegan ingredients and VegiTerranean was born. Plans are in the works to open branches of the restaurant throughout the country. In the meantime, Jones has submerged himself deeper and deeper into the vegetarian lifestyle and has visited the Western Reserve School of Cooking to teach classes on vegan cooking.

His advice to students is practical and heartfelt: invest in the best equipment for the job and the best ingredients, but more importantly, invest yourself in the people you cook for.

When he teaches, Jones said he tries to pass on everything he knows, in hopes that his students will outshine him in the kitchen some day. "They're taking a little bit of me to add to their spice rack," he said.

Holiday Nutty Party Crunch

I like to have this out while guests arrive to serve with some Prosecco.

2 cups air-popped popcorn

2 cups mini spelt pretzels or other whole grain pretzels

1½ cups puffed kamut or puffed wheat cereal

1½ cups whole grain, lattice-woven cereal squares

½ cup slivered almonds

¼ cup pure maple syrup

2 teaspoons toasted sesame seeds

¼ cup dried goji berries

2 teaspoons toasted sesame oil

1½ teaspoon chili powder

½ teaspoon garlic powder

¼ teaspoon salt

¼ cup cranberries

Preheat oven to 350 degrees, coat baking sheet with cooking spray.

Toss together popcorn, pretzels, cereal squares, puffed cereal, almonds, syrup, sesame oil, chili powder, garlic powder and salt in a large bowl. Spread mixture in a single layer on prepared baking sheet and sprinkle with sesame seeds.

Bake 35 minutes or until toasted, stirring often.

Cool and transfer to serving bowl, stirring in goji berries and cranberries.

Makes about 8 cups.

Root Vegetable Sticks with Roasted Garlic Dip

6 medium carrots, trimmed, peeled and cut into sticks (6 cups)

6 medium red and gold beets, peeled and cut into carrot-like sticks (6 cups)

2½ tablespoons olive oil, divided

1 head garlic

1 can (15 ounces) cannellini beans, drained, with the liquid reserved

1 tablespoon lemon juice

1 teaspoon grated lemon zest

1 teaspoon basil (dried)

Preheat oven to 450 degrees.

Toss carrots and beets with 1½ tablespoons oil. Season with salt and pepper. Spread in a single layer on baking sheet.

Trim papery top from garlic head, wrap in foil and set in corner of baking sheet.

Roast vegetables and garlic 25 minutes or until carrots and beets are tender, but not soft, and garlic feels soft when lightly squeezed.

Remove baking sheet from oven, open foil packet around garlic and cool.

Squeeze garlic cloves from skins and place in food processor with cannellini beans, lemon juice, lemon zest, basil and remaining 1 tablespoon olive oil.

Pulse mixture until creamy and smooth, adding some reserved bean liquid if necessary. Season with salt and pepper.

Serve garlic bean dip in a bowl alongside roasted vegetables.

Makes about 1 cup dip.

Thanksgiving Pot Pie

Filling:

2 medium potatoes, diced (2 cups)

2 large carrots, sliced (1 cup)

3 tablespoons olive oil, divided

1 package (16 ounces) firm tofu, drained (cut into cubes)

1 large sweet onion, diced (2 cups)

¼ cup plus 2 tablespoons San-J-Tamari soy sauce, divided

½ teaspoon granulated garlic, divided

¼ teaspoon cayenne, divided

½ cup all-purpose flour

2 cups wild mushrooms

1 cup chopped broccoli florets

2 cloves garlic, minced (2 teaspoons)

4 cups vegetable stock

½ cup plain soy milk

3 tablespoons red wine

1 tablespoon chopped fresh thyme

1 tablespoon chopped fresh sage

1 teaspoon hoisin sauce

½ teaspoon vegan Worcestershire sauce

Crust:

1¼ cups all-purpose flour

½ teaspoon salt

½ cup vegetable shortening

1 teaspoon chopped fresh rosemary

1 teaspoon chopped fresh sage

To make filling, cook potatoes and carrots in large pot of boiling salted water, 10 minutes or until just tender. Drain and set aside.

Heat 1 tablespoon oil in skillet over medium-high heat. Add tofu and cook 5 minutes or until tofu begins to brown. Stir in onions, 2 tablespoons tamari, ¼ teaspoon granulated garlic and ⅛ teaspoon cayenne and cook until onions begin to soften. Push veggies to the side of a Dutch oven and add remaining 1 tablespoon oil to bottom of pot. Stir flour into oil to make roux.

Stir broth into vegetables once gravy is smooth. Add tofu, potatoes, carrots, soy milk and remaining ¼ cup tamari and wine. Stir gently, add thyme, sage, hoisin sauce, Worcestershire sauce and remaining ⅛ teaspoon cayenne. Remove from heat and set aside or transfer vegetables to large casserole dish.

To make crust, preheat oven to 375 degrees. Mix together flour, salt and shortening with fork or pastry blender until mixture is crumbly. Stir in up to 4 tablespoons cold water, if necessary, for dough to stick together. Gently knead rosemary and sage into dough and shape dough into a ball. Place dough ball into plastic bag and push out from center of ball to shape the dough to size of Dutch oven or casserole dish. Remove dough from bag and lay over vegetable filling in Dutch oven or casserole dish. Poke holes in dough to allow steam to escape.

Bake 45 minutes or until crust is golden brown. Let stand 10 minutes before serving.

Doug Katz

"Be organized, be efficient and be prepared."

Chef Doug Katz isn't the only successful chef in the Cleveland area who started out taking classes at the Zona Spray Cooking School, but he may well have been the youngest. The owner of Cleveland's Fire Food & Drink restaurant, Katz was given a gift of two classes at the Zona Spray Cooking School for his tenth birthday. So it's probably not surprising that by the time Katz was in high school, he was running his own catering company. At fifteen he was working at Zack Bruell's Z Contemporary Cuisine, and at seventeen, he catered a wedding reception for ninety people.

Katz knew early on that food was his future. "My family was all into food. My mom would always make dinner. My parents, brothers and sisters and grandmother—food was always a great time in my family for us," he says of his food-centric upbringing in the Cleveland suburb of Shaker Heights.

After graduating from the University of Denver with a degree in Hotel and Restaurant Management in 1991, Katz moved on to the Culinary Institute of America, where he earned a degree in culinary arts in 1994. After working at restaurants in Boston, Portland, Oregon, and Aspen, Colorado, he returned to Cleveland to work at Moxie when the doors opened in 1997.

By the time Katz opened Fire in July 2001, at the age of thirty-one, he had been cooking and working in restaurants for more than fifteen years. Fire is located in Cleveland's eclectic and bustling Shaker Square neighborhood, where the weekly farmers market is just outside his front door and Katz has handshake relationships with the Ohio farmers who supply his meat, produce and cheese.

His rising culinary star brought him to the Western Reserve School of Cooking as a guest chef and teacher, years after he had been a student of Zona Spray's. When he teaches, Katz said he provides recipes, but really doesn't want to teach from them, preferring to show his students cooking techniques and how to be organized in the kitchen, skills that he believes will take them farther than any recipe. He strives to teach students to "be organized, be efficient and be prepared," the same advice he gives to young chefs who work for him. "I would rather teach as few recipes as possible and the students get an intensive education," and Katz often will teach a full dinner menu from beginning to end, stressing techniques such as braising, roasting or sautéing.

At Western Reserve, the students are down to earth and teaching in the small kitchen setting allows for plenty of questions and interaction. "I've always had a warm and great experience there," he said, adding that over the years, the school has continued to provide a setting that makes students really want to learn.

Parisienne Gnocchi

1½ cups water

8 ounces butter

1 tablespoon salt

1 teaspoon salt

2 cups all-purpose flour, sifted

2 tablespoons Dijon mustard

1 tablespoon chives, finely cut

1 tablespoon parsley, minced

1 tablespoon tarragon, minced

1 cup Gruyere, shredded

6 or 7 eggs

Set up a heavy duty mixer with paddle attachment. Have all ingredients ready before cooking. Combine water, butter and 1 tablespoon salt in a medium saucepan and bring to a simmer over medium-high heat. Reduce heat to medium, add flour all at once and stir rapidly with a stiff, heat-proof spatula until dough pulls away from sides of pan and bottom of pan is clean, with no dough sticking to it. The dough should be glossy and smooth but still moist.

Enough moisture must evaporate to allow dough to absorb more fat when eggs are added. Continue to stir for 15 to 20 minutes, adjusting heat if necessary to prevent dough from coloring. A thin coating will form on bottom and sides of pan. When enough moisture has evaporated, steam will rise from dough and an aroma of cooked flour will be noticeable. Immediately transfer dough to mixing bowl.

Add mustard, herbs and 1 teaspoon salt. Mix for a few seconds to incorporate and release some of the heat, then add cheese. With mixer on lowest speed, add 4 eggs, one at a time, beating until each egg is completely incorporated before adding the next. Increase speed to medium and add another 2 eggs, one at a time, mixing well after each one. Turn off mixer. Lift some of the dough on a rubber spatula and turn spatula to let it run off. It should move down the spatula very slowly; if it doesn't move at all or is very dry and just falls off in a clump, beat in an additional egg. Place dough in a large pastry bag fitted with a ⅝-inch plain tip and let rest for about 30 minutes at room temperature.

Bring a large pot of lightly salted water to a simmer. Pipe gnocchi into salted water, cutting them into water. They will sink. Keep water temperature hot but not boiling. Once gnocchi float to top, poach them for another 1 to 2 minutes. Remove with a slotted spoon or skimmer and drain on napkin-lined sheet tray. Taste one to test timing, it may still seem slightly undercooked in the center, but it will be cooked again. Repeat with remaining dough. Oil and refrigerate.

When ready to serve, heat 2 tablespoons canola oil in a skillet over high heat. Add gnocchi and cook until golden brown. Season to taste with salt and pepper. Set aside until ready to serve.

Makes twelve 2-ounce servings.

Butternut Squash Soup

3 butternut squash, cut in half
   lengthwise and seeded

¼ cup water

kosher salt, to taste

white pepper, to taste

1 stick unsalted butter

1 small stalk celery, diced small

½ carrot, diced small

1 yellow onion, diced small

2 cups chicken stock

3 tablespoons heavy cream

¼ cup hazelnuts, toasted and crushed

¼ cup cream, lightly whipped
   and unsweetened

2 tablespoons maple syrup

2 teaspoons sage, chopped

Preheat oven to 350 degrees. Season squash with salt and pepper. Place flesh side down in a large deep baking dish, add water to reach ⅛-inch up side of squash, cover with foil and bake for 1 hour or until soft. Let cool.

Spoon meat into a bowl and chill until ready to proceed.

In a large saucepot, sweat onion, celery and carrot in butter for 10 minutes. Add squash and chicken stock, season to taste with salt and white pepper. Purée in a food processor or blender until smooth, strain. Chill until ready to serve.

To serve, bring soup to a simmer (use a heavy saucepot to avoid burning) and add heavy cream. Thin with additional stock if necessary. Ladle into bowls and top with a spoon of whipped cream, a drizzle of maple syrup, a sprinkling of hazelnuts and a pinch of sage.

Makes 10 servings.

Braised Chicken Thighs

12 chicken thighs

kosher salt, to taste

black pepper, to taste

3 ounces olive oil

4 cups mirepoix (2 cups yellow onion,
1 cup carrot, 1 cup celery,
all coarsely chopped)

1 tablespoon tomato paste

2 sprigs fresh thyme

2 bay leaves

3 cups red wine

2 cups chicken stock

Preheat oven to 375 degrees. Wash chicken thighs in cold water and dry well. Season with salt and pepper and sear skin side in 2 ounces olive oil in a rondeau pot or Dutch oven. Turn thighs and continue to cook for 3 minutes or until browned. Remove from pan and set aside on a plate.

Pour out any excess grease. Heat 1 ounce olive oil and add mirepoix to pan. Cook vegetables until browned. Add tomato paste, thyme and bay leaf. Stir constantly until tomato paste coats vegetables and starts to brown. Deglaze pan with red wine and reduce by half.

Add chicken stock and bring to a simmer. Add chicken thighs and finish cooking in oven for about 30 minutes or until browned (uncovered). When fork tender, remove thighs to a deep serving platter.

Strain jus into a saucepot. Reduce jus to sauce consistency and pour over chicken, seasoning to taste.

Makes 6 servings.

Bev Shaffer

"Don't forget to have a good time."

W hen you see the photo Bev Shaffer has posted on her Facebook page—wearing a colander for a hat, chili pepper earrings, a tie-dyed chef's jacket and sporting a giant whisk, you know this woman has a sense of humor. So it should come as no surprise that Shaffer's best advice to her cooking school students is: "Don't forget to have a good time."

Cooking, she says, should be enjoyed as much as eating. It's clear that Shaffer has taken her own advice. She followed her passion into cooking and is a self-trained chef whose career branched out into unexpected areas. "I was on the fence between being a psychologist and a lawyer, so food was a natural transition," she chuckles.

In the 1970s, Shaffer was working at IBM in New Jersey when she met her husband, John Shaffer, an Akron, Ohio-native. When IBM transferred him to the company's Cleveland office, Shaffer settled into her husband's hometown and soon became an integral part of the local food scene.

In 1984, she opened What's Cooking, where she sold high-end cookware and began catering and teaching classes. After thirteen years, she grew tired of no vacations and decided it was time to work for someone other than herself. She became the cooking school director at Akron's Mustard Seed Market, Ohio's first certified organic retailer.

Shaffer's love of food (and her sense of humor) comes from growing up in New Jersey, in an Italian-Hungarian family. Food was everywhere and the women were always cooking, particularly during the holidays, when baking was done in large quantities. When Shaffer embarked on her own cookbook series, she naturally choose sweets as her subject matter. "I adore chocolate. I thought that would be a good start, anyway," she said of the series. In 2006, she released *Brownies to Die For!*, followed in 2009 by *Cookies to Die For!* and in 2010 by *Cakes to Die For!*

The books are a bit of surprise, though, when you consider they are the product of a woman who spent many years cooking tofu for a living. Shaffer sometimes jokes that she'll eat tofu as long as she can chase it with a slice of chocolate cake. But she is committed to using the finest, purest ingredients she can find, even if that happens to be butter and chocolate. "You can simplify things, but you have to use the absolute best ingredients," she said.

In 2007, Shaffer released the *Mustard Seed Market & Café Natural Foods Cookbook*, filled with favorite recipes from the store and cooking school. In her spare time, she writes, lectures and teaches in a variety of venues, including the Western Reserve School of Cooking.

Shaffer has taught several topics at the school, including baking, seafood, organic foods and of course, chocolate. Whatever she teaches, Shaffer always tries to teach techniques along with recipes, to make the lessons worthwhile. Because of its small setting, Western Reserve offers an intimacy that is perfect for teaching, she said. The students are attentive, knowledgeable and eager to learn, but also want to have a good time, which suits Shaffer just fine. "Since they are so close to you, you can see it right in their eyes if you say something good," she said.

Bread and Chocolate: A Little Dessert Bruschetta

1 baguette, cut diagonally into at least 25 ½-inch slices

4 to 6 tablespoons unsalted butter, melted

¾ cup coarsely grated bittersweet chocolate

¼ cup coarsely grated semisweet chocolate

½ cup coarsely grated milk chocolate

Heat oven to 350 degrees. Depending on diameter of baguette, you may choose to cut each slice in half. The object is to have slender fingers of bread. Brush butter lightly on one side of slices; put on foil-lined baking sheets and toast in oven just until crispy, 5 to 7 minutes. Remove from oven and let cool on a wire rack.

Combine bittersweet, semisweet and milk chocolates in a medium bowl. Sprinkle mixture generously atop cooled bread slices. Return baking sheet to oven to soften and warm chocolate mixture, about 12 additional minutes.

Serve immediately.

Makes approximately 25 servings.

White Chocolate Mousse

2 cups heavy whipping cream

6 ounces white chocolate, cut into pieces

1 teaspoon vanilla

Strawberry Coulis (recipe follows)

In a medium saucepan, cook and combine whipping cream and white chocolate over low heat, stirring constantly, until smooth.

Stir in vanilla. Pour into a large bowl; cover with plastic wrap. Refrigerate 6 hours or overnight until mixture is very cold and thickened, stirring occasionally.

Using a mixer, beat cream mixture at high speed until light and fluffy. Do not over beat.

Serve chilled, topped with strawberry coulis.

Makes 4 to 6 servings.

Strawberry Coulis

2 cups quartered hulled strawberries (about 12 ounces) or frozen berries, thawed

¼ cup water

3 tablespoons granulated sugar

2 teaspoons fresh lemon juice

Combine strawberries, water, sugar and lemon juice in blender. Purée until smooth. Cover and refrigerate until cold, at least 2 hours.

Makes about 2 cups.

Tilapia Baked in a Pesto Crust with Smoked Tomato Relish

4 (6-ounce) tilapia fillets

½ cup prepared pesto

1 cup bread crumbs

For the relish:

1 cup prepared salsa

2 plum tomatoes, finely diced

2 tablespoons ketchup

1 teaspoon liquid smoke

Heat oven to 400 degrees. Make relish by mixing ingredients together and set aside.

Spread 2 teaspoons pesto over each fillet. Sprinkle 1 to 2 tablespoons bread crumbs over each fillet.

Bake for approximately 10 minutes or until fillets test done. Serve each fillet topped with 1 to 2 tablespoons relish.

Makes 4 servings.

Michael Symon

"Don't learn a recipe, learn techniques."

He is Cleveland's own Iron Chef, but he is the first to admit, he might have stayed only Cleveland's own, if not for Zona Spray. In 1998, Symon was two years into running his flagship restaurant, Lola, when *Food & Wine Magazine* named him one of the ten best new chefs in the country. But what most people don't know is that it was Spray who brought *Food & Wine* officials to Lola's. "Zona was the person that brought them into my restaurant. She would take no credit for it, but she was the one. That was a turning point. It made my career from being known in Cleveland to being known nationally," Symon says of the honor.

Since then, it seems there is no end in sight to the heights Symon's career will take. He's a fixture on the Food Network, where he is one of the Iron Chefs on *Iron Chef America*. He's also on cable's Cooking Channel, where he teaches cooking on his own show. But Symon remains a Clevelander, literally and at heart, which is why he is quick to credit Spray and other locals for the role they played in his success.

There was Carl Quagliata, who he worked for at the former Cleveland restaurants Piccolo Mondo and Giovanni's, and Mark Shary, owner of Players, Symon's first restaurant job after culinary school and where he met his wife, Liz. Symon credits Shary for teaching him how to cook in a restaurant kitchen and how to layer flavors. Quagliata, he said, taught him the business of running restaurants.

They were lessons well-learned by this favorite son and lessons he's been happy to share with others. Symon teaches cooking classes at his restaurant, Lolita, about twelve times a year. He was first a guest teacher at the Zona Spray Cooking School when he was chef at Giovanni's. Quagliata knew Spray and arranged for Symon to give classes there.

Symon remembers the school as ahead of its time in the American culinary landscape, due to Spray's dedication to her craft. "She was very passionate and very knowledgeable. She knew everything about food and was a little bit of a history book about food," he recalled. "Now there are cooking schools all over the place. There was nothing really like it at the time and it preceded by a lot, of the kind of food movement that has happened."

Symon loves teaching and believes the greatest thing a chef can do is to pass on his craft. "My biggest lesson that I try to beat into people, the point that I like to make, is don't learn a recipe. Learn techniques. When I'm teaching a class, I go through techniques very deliberately. The worst thing you can do is to learn to make a single dish. It's so much more valuable to learn the technique of cooking."

For Symon, cooking was something he learned at home from a young age. His mother was half Greek and half Sicilian, while his father's family had Ruthenian roots from the Carpathian Mountains, in what is now the Ukraine. There was plenty of Greek food and typical Eastern European food—pierogis, dumplings and cabbage—as well as Sicilian fare. "Food was huge in my family," Symon recalls. "We never went out for dinner. I had McDonalds for the first time at thirteen and thought, 'I can't believe people eat this stuff.' I was so spoiled by great food."

He worked in restaurants as a teenager and after attending the Culinary Institute of America, Symon worked in New York for a while before returning home. "I came back to Cleveland because I have a Greek-Sicilian mother. I moved to the East side (from where he grew up on the West side) and she thinks I live out of town." Turns out, mother knew best about coming home.

Symon's success includes his Lola and Lolita restaurants in Cleveland, Roast in Detroit, and his B Spot casual eatery, which he plans to expand into more locations. Symon's cooking style was influenced not only by his ethnic heritage, but by Ohio and his home city of Cleveland. "When we opened up Lola, I said it was 'Midwestern' and they looked at me like I was purple. That was what I believe the food was and still is, but with my little interpretation. I built on what surrounded me and what I could always get the best of."

Almond Crusted Lamb

1 rack of lamb, 8 bones
  (about 2 pounds)
4 ounces chopped almonds

1 sprig rosemary
2 cloves garlic, minced

Preheat oven to 400 degrees.

Mix almonds, rosemary and garlic together with a fork. Use mixture to thinly crust lamb rack.

Place rack in skillet and roast for 6 to 8 minutes, or until desired doneness.

Makes 4 servings.

Moussaka

1 eggplant, sliced and grilled

3 red peppers, roasted and peeled

1 pound garlic mashed potatoes

½ pound feta cheese

2 sprigs rosemary, chopped

Preheat oven to 400 degrees.

In a small lasagna pan (9 by 13-inches), form moussaka by layering eggplant, red peppers, potatoes and feta. Season layers with rosemary. Repeat ingredients, ending with eggplant.

Bake for 20 minutes or until golden brown.

Crab Grape Leaves with a Lemon and Tarragon Vinaigrette and Roasted Peppers

¼ pound grape leaves

1 cup short grain rice

¼ pound fresh lump crab meat

4 tablespoons chopped tarragon

zest of 1 lemon

1 ounce white wine vinegar

1 ounce lemon oil

1 ounce extra-virgin olive oil

2 large red peppers, roasted, peeled and chopped

salt and pepper, to taste

Cook rice in salted boiling water until tender and let cool.

Mix rice with lemon zest, 2 tablespoons tarragon and crab meat. Season to taste with salt and pepper. Set aside.

Wrap rice mixture in grape leaves using about 1 tablespoon filling per leaf.

Make a vinaigrette by puréeing vinegar and remaining tarragon, slowly adding oils to make an emulsion.

Marinate grape leaves in vinaigrette for 1 hour with red peppers and serve chilled.

Makes about 2 dozen, depending on size of leaves.

Roger Thomas

"You have to care about what you are cooking and who you are cooking for."

Few chefs talk about care and compassion the way Roger Thomas does. Care for the food, the way it is prepared, the ingredients that are used; compassion for the process of cooking and the diner who will be partaking of the meal.

Preparing food and feeding another is an expression of the heart, a lesson that Thomas said took him a few years to learn. But it is clear his connection to food as an expression of caring began in his childhood and deepened at every turn of his career.

As a young child growing up in West Virginia, Thomas's family never had much money, so they kept large gardens and raised their own animals. Their survival depended, in part, on how well they cared for their food. Of the food on his grandmother's breakfast table, she cured the bacon, churned the butter and baked the bread.

When Thomas was eight years old, his family moved to Akron, Ohio, but every summer he went back to stay with his grandparents. One of his chores was picking vegetables from their garden, a task he hated, but now relishes the memory. "I was given a fantastic gift with that and never realized it at the time," he recalled.

In high school, Thomas dated the daughter of Akron restaurant owner John Piscazzi. He was just a sophomore in 1971, when Piscazzi opened Akron's Wine Merchant restaurant. Piscazzi's mother, Lucia, a native of Bari, Italy, was the cook and Thomas hung around the kitchen so much that she put him to work—for free. Thomas spent his afternoons making bread, butchering meat, cutting fish and helping Lucia make sauces. "It was a tremendous opportunity, but like most seventeen-year-olds, I had no idea how lucky I was," he recalled.

After graduation, Thomas stayed on at the Wine Merchant and it didn't take him long to prove himself. The following year, when Lucia underwent heart surgery, Thomas assumed the role of head cook at age nineteen. He stayed at the Wine Merchant for the next thirteen years, but then felt the desire to stretch himself creatively. Akron restaurateur and French native Pat Martel, who owned Maison Martel, suggested that Thomas head to Europe for training and helped arrange a meeting with French Chef Michel Pasquet. The meeting took place at the Zona Spray Cooking School, where Pasquet was a visiting teacher. With the little English he spoke, Pasquet looked at Thomas and said, "One year, you come in one year." Thomas gave Piscazzi a year's notice and left for Europe in January 1987. He trained for two years, first with Pasquet in Paris, and later with chefs in the Loire Valley.

His trip to meet Pasquet wasn't Thomas's first time at Spray's school. He had taken classes there over the years and had developed a friendship with Spray. "I couldn't believe how much we thought like each other. She resonated with me and took an interest in me," he said.

After his return home from Europe, Thomas quickly began to make a name for himself. He was the chef who helped Akron restaurateur Ken Stewart launch his namesake restaurant, a position that showcased Thomas's talents and solidified his reputation as one of the top chefs in northeast Ohio. He left Stewart's to purchase the Wine Merchant from Piscazzi, following the death of Lucia, but the renamed restaurant, Sixteen Eighty, was short-lived. Thomas worked as a consultant for other restaurants, until 2000, when he opened Piatto in downtown Akron. In 2005, he moved the restaurant to the Sheraton Suites in nearby Cuyahoga Falls and renamed it Piatto Novo.

Over the years, Thomas was a frequent guest at Spray's school, often making dishes that were popular at the Wine Merchant. But more than recipes, Thomas liked to pass on the wisdom of the cooks who shared with him—his grandmother, John and Lucia Picazzi, and Pasquet. "I think what I talk about the most is being comfortable in the kitchen and cooking with compassion for the people you are cooking for and the ingredients you are using, and compassion for the basic, fundamental act of cooking."

Like many chefs, Thomas views the table as a place for more than just nourishment for the body. "Cooking is such a fantastic way for us to connect. When we come to the table, we're a little more civilized and a little more human, especially as the world gets faster. There is an intimacy to cooking for someone. You have to care about what you are cooking and who you are cooking for."

Roasted Potatoes

2 pounds redskin or Yukon Gold potatoes—scrubbed and cut into 1-inch pieces

salt and pepper, to taste

2 tablespoons dried oregano

1 clove garlic, pressed

1 tablespoon paprika

½ cup olive oil

2 bay leaves

Put potatoes in a large mixing bowl. Season with salt, pepper, oregano, garlic and paprika. Stir to distribute seasoning. Pour on oil. Stir to coat potatoes with oil. Pour into a baking pan. Put bay leaves on either side of pan. Bake at 375 degrees until browned and crisp. Remove bay leaves. Serve immediately.

Makes 4 servings.

Family Style Polenta

8 cups water

1½ tablespoons salt

3 cups cornmeal

4 ounces unsalted butter

¾ cup grated Parmesan cheese

tomato sauce

chopped parsley

extra grated Parmesan

In a heavy-bottomed pot, mix water and salt. Add cornmeal, stirring constantly and whisk until smooth. Bring to a boil over high heat, stirring constantly with a wooden spoon. When polenta begins to bubble, reduce heat to medium-low and cook, stirring often, until polenta is creamy and no longer grainy, about 20 minutes.

Remove from heat. Stir in butter and cheese. Pour into serving dish. Drizzle with tomato sauce, sprinkle with chopped parsley and cheese and serve.

Serve along with roasted or grilled meats, sausages, poultry, fish or vegetables in any number of combinations.

Makes 8 main course servings.

Tuscan Style Pork Tenderloin

2 pork tenderloins, (8 to 10 ounces each)

1 ounce pancetta, chopped

1 tablespoon fresh rosemary leaves, chopped

2 cloves garlic

1 teaspoon cracked black pepper

flour

3 tablespoons olive oil

salt, to taste

1 cup Chianti or other dry red wine

2 cups good quality chicken stock

2 tablespoons unsalted butter

Trim visible fat and silverskin from tenderloins and set aside. In a food processor or mortar and pestle, mix together pancetta, rosemary, garlic and pepper until it becomes a paste. Make half-inch slits halfway through tenderloin sides, two per side, and push paste into each slit. Cover tenderloins and cure in refrigerator at least 4 hours or over night.

When ready to cook, preheat oven to 375 degrees. In a large sauté pan, heat olive oil over medium flame, until hot enough to sizzle a drop of water. Roll pork in flour, shake off excess and brown on all sides. Place pan in a 375 oven for 6 to 7 minutes to achieve medium-rare to medium. Remove pan from oven, transfer pork to a plate and cover loosely with foil. Pour fat out of pan and add wine. Reduce to ¼ cup, scraping brown bits from bottom of pan. Add stock and reduce to about ¾ cup. The sauce will thicken slightly—whisk in butter to bring a gloss to sauce. Slice pork, arrange on plates and pour sauce over. Serve with roasted potatoes.

Makes 4 servings.

Tri-Colored Salad

For the vinaigrette:
½ clove garlic
½ cup light olive oil
¼ cup quality red wine vinegar
salt and pepper, to taste

For the salad:
½ head radicchio
2 heads Belgian endive
2 bunches arugula
½ cup toasted walnuts (or more, to taste)
6 ounces Gorgonzola cheese (or to taste)
fresh cracked black pepper

Smash garlic, add oil and steep for 15 to 30 minutes. Remove garlic. Whisk vinegar into oil. Season with salt and pepper. Whisk until salt dissolves.

Slice radicchio into quarter-inch ribbons. Arrange on one side of plate. Slice endive into quarter-inch pieces lengthwise. Arrange next to radicchio. Tear arugula into small pieces and arrange next to endive. Mix dressing and drizzle evenly on salads. Sprinkle with walnuts and Gorgonzola.

Makes 4 servings.

Jeffrey Waite

"Build on your foundations."

When Hudson native Jeffrey Waite went off to the Culinary Institute of America, he took a knife from The Cookery with him. A graduate of Hudson's prestigious Western Reserve Academy, where his father was on the faculty, he went on to Ohio Wesleyan University. After a few years, he dropped out—he realized that he wanted to attend cooking school instead.

Back home in Hudson, Waite worked and saved money for culinary school. He had his eye on an expensive chef's knife at The Cookery and found it under his Christmas tree that year, a gift from his future wife. "A year later, I was off to culinary school," he recalled. "I still have it in my kit."

Waite trained in classical French techniques at the Culinary Institute of America. He graduated to a job at Washington, Virginia's acclaimed Inn at Little Washington, where he began an apprenticeship with Chef Patrick O'Connell. "At the time, it was the up and coming, the destination restaurant for a lot of people. I went as an apprentice and ended up staying there for seven years."

Home visiting Hudson, Waite stopped in The Cookery and struck up a conversation with Zona Spray. When she heard he was working for O'Connell, Spray quickly invited Waite back to teach, realizing the clout that came from the restaurant, which was the winner of two five-star awards from the *Mobile Travel Guide* and from O'Connell, who has been called "the pope" of American cuisine.

Likewise, Waite had equal respect for Spray. Having grown up in the same town as her cooking school, Waite, perhaps more than other guest chefs, has a sense of awe because of what the school means to the city of Hudson and all of Northeast Ohio.

Waite taught a class on desserts, using recipes that O'Connell had developed at the Inn. Waite eventually left the Inn for the executive chef position at the Jefferson Hotel in Richmond, Virginia, where he served for four years, before heading north to the Berkshires to become executive chef at the Old Inn on the Green in New Marlborough, Massachusetts. In 2003, he returned to Ohio. Waite has worked at a variety of restaurants since and is currently the executive chef at Signature of Solon, a private club.

Waite no longer teaches classes, but said he is constantly coaching the younger chefs who work for him and stresses the lessons he learned in culinary school: "Build on your foundations." Even with the simplest sauces, there is chemistry at work in the way they come together and Waite sees them as the place for all chefs to begin learning. "It is very much one step at a time," he said.

White Chocolate Mousse

This same recipe can be used to make a dark chocolate mousse, just substitute semi-sweet dark chocolate.

10 ounces finest-quality imported white chocolate, broken into small pieces

½ cup sugar

¼ cup water

4 egg whites

2 tablespoons dark rum

1 tablespoon vanilla extract

1¼ cups heavy cream

Raspberry Purée (recipe follows)

Melt chocolate in a large stainless steel bowl set over a pot of simmering water.

In a 1-quart saucepan, combine sugar and water; bring to a boil. Allow liquid to boil until it reaches soft-ball stage—234 to 240 degrees on a candy thermometer.

Meanwhile, in the bowl of an electric mixer, begin beating egg whites in a thin stream, whisking constantly. Whip until bottom of the bowl is no longer hot. Pour melted chocolate onto meringue mixture and blend thoroughly, scraping down sides of the bowl with a rubber spatula. Add rum and vanilla; continue beating until all ingredients are incorporated.

In a separate bowl, whip cream just until stiff peaks begin to form. Using a rubber spatula, gently fold whipped cream into chocolate mixture in three batches, until cream is evenly distributed. Pour mixture into a chilled container and refrigerate until set.

To serve: Put mousse into a pastry bag fitted with a decorative tip and pipe into goblets or serving dishes, or use an oval ice cream scoop dipped in warm water to scoop mousse out onto chilled serving plates and place in a pool of sauce, such as a raspberry purée or passion fruit sauce.

Makes 4 servings.

Raspberry Purée

3 pints fresh raspberries

3 to 4 tablespoons sugar

1 tablespoon fresh lemon juice

Purée berries in a food processor. Strain through a fine strainer to remove seeds, pressing hard on solids with a rubber spatula to extract all the liquid.

Add lemon juice and mix well. Add sugar 1 tablespoon at a time, tasting after each addition, until desired sweetness is obtained.

Makes 1 cup.

Note: You may substitute frozen raspberries, but reduce the sugar by one-half.

From *The Inn at Little Washington: A Consuming Passion* (1996), reprinted with the permission of Patrick O'Connell.

Coeur a la Crème

....

The perforated molds allow the excess liquid, or whey, to drip through the cheesecloth, leaving the delicious "heart" of the cream. Coeur a la crème molds are usually available at kitchen supply stores.

....

8 ounces mascarpone cheese, softened

1¼ cups heavy cream

1 teaspoon vanilla extract

1 tablespoon fresh lemon juice

1 tablespoon Chambord or other raspberry liqueur

½ cup sifted confectioners' sugar

For the raspberry sauce:

1 pint fresh raspberries

1 tablespoon granulated sugar

1 teaspoon fresh lemon juice

fresh raspberries and mint leaves for garnish

Cut cheesecloth into four 6-inch squares. Dampen and wring out lightly. Press one square into each of four (4-ounce), perforated, heart-shaped ceramic molds and set aside. In the alternative, prepare one (16-ounce) mold.

In the bowl of an electric mixer, whip mascarpone cheese, ¼ cup cream, vanilla, 1 tablespoon lemon juice and Chambord until thoroughly blended. Refrigerate.

In a small bowl, whip remaining 1 cup cream and confectioners' sugar until cream forms stiff peaks.

With a rubber spatula, fold whipped cream into chilled cheese mixture in three batches.

Spoon finished mixture into prepared molds and fold edges of cheesecloth over tops. Lightly tap bottoms of the molds on the counter to remove any air spaces between mixture and molds. Refrigerate on a tray or baking sheet a minimum of 2 to 3 hours.

For raspberry sauce: In a blender or food processor, purée raspberries, granulated sugar and 1 teaspoon lemon juice. Taste sauce for sweetness and adjust sugar or lemon juice as needed. Strain and refrigerate.

To serve: Unfold cheesecloth and drape over the sides of molds. Invert each mold onto a serving plate. While pressing down on the corners of cheesecloth, carefully lift off mold. Smooth top with back of a spoon and remove cheesecloth slowly. Spoon raspberry sauce onto plate around heart and garnish with fresh berries and mint leaves.

Makes 4 servings.

From *The Inn at Little Washington: A Consuming Passion* (1996), reprinted with the permission of Patrick O'Connell.

The Recipes

Chapter 8
Our Staff

Catherine St. John

"I'm huge into teaching people to cook beyond the recipe."

Catherine St. John could have never known, back in 1994, when she came to the Zona Spray Cooking School "just to check it out," that one day she would be the owner. St. John is the school's fourth owner and is devoting herself to making sure the school remains an active and relevant force in the culinary community of Northeast Ohio.

Her life as a cooking school teacher, let alone the owner of a school, was not exactly what she imagined for herself, but she embraced the opportunity when it came. In 1992, the Palo Alto, California native arrived in Ohio, moving back to her husband Carl's home state shortly after the birth of their first child.

Her own upbringing in California was food-centric, with her father, Larry White, leading the way. "Food was a very, very important part of my growing up," she recalled. She describes her father as a foodie, before that name existed. He did most of the cooking for the family, regularly baked bread and as director of parks and open space management for the city of Palo Alto, helped to establish the first community organic garden.

Some of her best food memories are of family camping trips, where her father would pack more pots, pans, herbs and spices than he would camping gear. It was nothing for him to whip up eggs with capers and pan-fried trout with brown butter over the camp fire, and St. John recalls how the family would typically attract visitors when the smell of her father's cooking spread. "Often we would have people we didn't know for dinner while we were camping," she said.

After high school, St. John attended a local junior college before enrolling at Tante Marie's Cooking School in San Francisco. In 1983, the San Francisco community and the school were at the forefront of the northern California cooking revolution, led by Alice Waters, Jeremiah Tower and others.

After earning her chef's certificate in 1984, St. John took an internship in Crete, where she submerged herself in the Greek culture and learned firsthand the value of fresh ingredients at the open market stalls. She also came to realize how much America has sacrificed in its own food culture for the sake of convenience. "I learned that people express themselves through food," she said.

Upon returning home, St. John worked for the next eight years in restaurants throughout California, in various kitchen settings, including as a cook in a college dormitory. She married and had her daughter Allison, before packing up for Northeast Ohio.

For the first few years in Ohio, she worked as a caterer and a private chef. St. John had worked at enough restaurants to know that the long hours away from home weren't the kind of life she wanted while raising young children—son Lorenzo came along in 1997.

After hearing about Zona Spray's school, St. John investigated and Spray offered her a spot as a teacher. It wasn't something St. John had originally considered, but Mary Risley, owner of Tante Marie, encouraged her. St. John began her teaching career working for Spray and continued at the school when Carole Ferguson purchased the school.

In 2007, St. John purchased the school and is still in the classroom several times each week. She has developed a curriculum that stays true to classic cooking techniques, while at the same time offering classes for the way the community cooks today, including pressure cookers, grilling classes and classes for couples.

When St. John teaches, her goal is to help her students find confidence in the kitchen and to teach them the skills to go beyond the recipes in front of them and to translate the techniques they have learned into hundreds of different dishes, no matter the ingredients they happen to have on hand.

"I'm huge into teaching people to cook beyond the recipe," she said. St. John loves it when she can see that look in her students' eyes when they understand that the chicken breast they just learned to sear could be a pork chop or a piece of fish; different meat, same technique. "I see the light bulb that goes off over their heads and I know they get it," she said.

Grilled Flatbread

2½ cups bread flour	1 package yeast
2 teaspoons salt	2 tablespoons olive oil
1 tablespoon sugar	1 cup hot water

Measure 1 cup flour into a large mixing bowl and stir in dry ingredients. Add oil and hot water. Blend at low speed with a mixer with a flat beater for 30 seconds and increase to high for 3 minutes, or beat vigorously with a wooden spoon for an equal length of time. Stop mixer and stir in balance of flour, ½ cup at a time. Dough should be a rough, saggy mass that will clean the sides of the bowl. If dough is moist, add a small amount of additional flour.

Place dough on a lightly floured work surface, countertop or breadboard and knead for about 6 minutes. If using a mixer, do the kneading on the dough hook.

Place dough into a lightly oiled bowl. Cover with plastic wrap and let rise in refrigerator for 2 to 3 hours.

Remove from refrigerator and divide into 8 pieces. Roll into balls, cover with a towel or wax paper and let rise for 45 minutes.

Preheat grill on high. It is best to have a table next to the grill to roll out dough before grilling.

With palm of your hand, flatten each ball into a disk. Finish with a rolling pin, flattening dough into a disk about 6 inches in diameter and 3/16 of an inch thick. The disk thinness is more important than making them perfectly round.

Brush lightly with olive oil and place over direct heat. Grill on both sides for 1 to 2 minutes, taking care not to burn. Place on indirect side and repeat, until you have 4 to 5 on the other side of the grill. Place lid on grill for another 2 to 3 minutes, to finish baking bread.

Makes 8 pieces.

Apple Raisin Coleslaw

1 medium head of green cabbage, shredded

2 medium carrots, shredded

2 Granny Smith apples, diced

½ cup raisins

1 cup mayonnaise

¼ cup rice wine vinegar, or more to taste

2 tablespoons sugar

dill, to taste (optional)

salt and pepper, to taste

Mix cabbage, carrots, apples and raisins in a large bowl. Mix remaining ingredients (for dressing) in a separate bowl. Pour dressing over coleslaw and mix well. Check seasoning and refrigerate for several hours before serving.

Makes 6 servings.

Grilled Flat Iron Steak with Chimichurri Sauce

1½ pounds flat iron steak

2 tablespoons brown sugar

2 teaspoons kosher salt

1 teaspoon freshly ground black pepper

1 tablespoon smoked paprika

1 tablespoon garlic powder

olive oil, for drizzling

Prepare your grill for indirect heat grilling.

Combine brown sugar, salt, pepper, paprika and garlic powder together to form a dry rub. Rub both sides of steak with dry rub. Wrap tightly in plastic wrap and let stand at room temperature for 30 minutes before grilling.

Unwrap steak and drizzle both sides with olive oil. Place over coals and grill for 2 to 3 minutes per side. Place steak on indirect heat side for another 7 to 9 minutes with lid closed. To cook to medium rare, allow an internal temperature of 135 degrees.

Let steak rest 5 minutes before slicing. Serve with grilled flatbread, grilled onions and chimichurri sauce.

Makes 4 to 6 servings.

Chimichurri Sauce

1 cup olive oil

¼ cup red wine vinegar

2 tablespoons lemon juice

1 bunch of flat leaf parsley, coarsely chopped

1 bunch of basil

1 tablespoon oregano

2 garlic cloves

1 shallot

freshly ground pepper, to taste

kosher salt, to taste

crushed red pepper flakes, to taste

In the bowl of a food processor, combine olive oil, wine vinegar, lemon juice, parsley, basil, oregano, garlic and shallots. Pulse until well-blended, but do not purée. Add black pepper, salt and crushed red pepper flakes. Transfer sauce to a nonreactive bowl, cover with plastic wrap and let sit at room temperature for at least 2 hours or up to 6 hours. Chimichurri sauce will keep for up to 3 days when refrigerated in a well-sealed container.

Makes about 2 cups.

Pork Tenderloin Brined in Beer

2 pork tenderloins, trimmed

1 bottle (12 ounces) dark beer

12 ounces water

⅛ cup salt

¼ cup dark brown sugar

3 to 4 slices fresh ginger root

4 tablespoons fennel seeds

3 cloves garlic, crushed

2 bay leaves, crumbled

3 strips lemon peel

3 strips orange or tangerine peel

Combine all ingredients, except pork, in a pot and bring to a boil; reduce heat and simmer for 5 minutes. Transfer to a stainless steel bowl and cool in refrigerator. Once brine is cold, brine pork in refrigerator for 1 to 2 days, depending upon depth of flavor desired.

Remove from brine and dry with paper towels. Brown in a heavy-bottomed skillet, put into a preheated 375-degree oven and roast until internal temperature of meat is 140 degrees. Remove pork from pan and let rest for at least 10 minutes before cutting. If using for sandwiches, you may also let it cool down completely.

To cook outside, prepare a grill for indirect heat. On direct heat, sear pork on all sides for 2 to 3 minutes per side. Transfer to indirect heat and place lid on grill. Grill/roast for another 15 to 20 minutes or until internal temperature of meat is 140 degrees. Remove from grill and let rest 10 minutes before slicing.

Makes 8 servings.

Grilled Salmon with Asparagus and Sesame Vinaigrette

4 skinless salmon fillets,
  about 6 ounces each

1 tablespoon soy sauce

1 tablespoon brown sugar

2 teaspoons sesame oil

1 teaspoon fresh ginger, grated

1 garlic clove, grated

1 bunch asparagus, trimmed

a few drizzles of sesame oil

a few drizzles of soy sauce

Sesame Vinaigrette (recipe follows)

toasted sesame seeds

Combine soy sauce, brown sugar, oil, ginger and garlic and rub onto salmon. Marinate for 10 to 15 minutes.

Preheat a grill pan on high and brush with canola oil. Drizzle asparagus with sesame oil and soy sauce. Grill asparagus for a few minutes, until just cooked, but still crunchy. Set aside.

Brush grill pan with canola oil again, if needed. Place salmon service side down and grill on medium-high, 2 to 3 minutes. Turn and grill until desired doneness, another 3 to 4 minutes, depending upon thickness. Return asparagus to pan at the end to heat.

To serve, place 3 or 4 asparagus spears on each plate and place salmon on top. Spoon vinaigrette over top and sprinkle with sesame seeds. Makes 4 servings.

Sesame Vinaigrette

1 tablespoon soy sauce

2 teaspoons sesame oil

2 green onions, finely chopped

1 tablespoon rice wine vinegar

2 to 3 tablespoons canola oil

toasted sesame seeds

Mix vinaigrette ingredients together and set aside.

Asian Plum Chicken Wings

24 chicken wings,
  first and second joints

6 cloves garlic, chopped

1 cup Asian plum sauce

½ cup hoisin sauce

1 teaspoon Asian chili paste

1 tablespoon sesame seeds, toasted

2 tablespoons chopped fresh cilantro
  (optional)

1 tablespoon freshly grated ginger

2 tablespoons dry sherry

1 tablespoon rice wine vinegar

Add all ingredients, except chicken wings, to a bowl and mix well to combine. Place chicken wings in a shallow pan and pour ⅓ to ½ of the sauce over top. Set remaining sauce aside. Mix chicken around to distribute sauce. Let marinate for 6 to 8 hours in refrigerator.

Preheat oven to 375 degrees. Place chicken in a single layer on a foil-lined sheet pan. Bake for 10 to 15 minutes, basting with sauce. Turn chicken over, baste again with sauce and bake for another 10 to 15 minutes or until cooked through. Remove from oven and arrange on a platter. Heat remaining sauce in a small pan and serve on the side. Makes 24 wings.

Note: You can also grill wings. The sauce also goes great with ribs and larger pieces of chicken.

Anne Haynam

"Taste everything. The ingredients won't always be the same."

The space between coach and teacher isn't that wide, but the journey required a major career change for Anne Haynam. When she decided to leave coaching for a career as a chef, she gave up her whistle and court time for a chef's jacket and a sharp knife. To her the switch doesn't seem too dramatic. "I transitioned from one hobby to another. It makes so much sense for me," she says.

Both were equal parts of her upbringing. Haynam grew up in rural Kinsman, Ohio, where her father, an excellent athlete in his own right, ran a metal stamping business with his brother. Her mother, who Haynam describes as an excellent cook, was often in the kitchen, and Haynam was most often at her side. "I was always my mother's best little helper in the kitchen," she recalls. "I come from the kind of family that when we get together, we're eating one meal and talking about what the next meal will be."

She excelled at high school sports and went on to Ohio's Hiram College, where she played softball and basketball. After graduate school in Pennsylvania, where she earned a master's degree in history, she took a coaching job at Dickinson College in Carlisle, Pennsylvania. After several years, she returned to Hiram, where she coached and worked in administration. She also taught exercise, sport science and women's studies.

In 2004, she left college life to focus on becoming a chef. Haynam enrolled at the Western Reserve School of Cooking, earning her chef's certificate in 2006. She's been teaching there since 2007, all while working as a caterer and personal chef. "I do a lot of interactive cooking parties and I have very active classes. I feel like I'm coaching," she says. "Taste everything," is what she stresses to her students. "The ingredients won't always be the same; the combination won't always be the same."

After dabbling in pastry for a while, she decided that she's more comfortable with savory food and has crafted a niche teaching Latino cooking—South American, Central American and Caribbean cuisine, which also relates back to her college days. While at Hiram, Haynam took students on tours of Mexico and Guatemala to study marginalized voices. Spending time with the people, she grew in her understanding of the importance of food in other cultures, which only made her appreciate her ingredients all the more.

"To put into context the importance of something simple like corn to the people in those parts of the world, or peppers, cilantro and lime, all of the key ingredients that we pull out of there—it's part of their soul, from the politics of it to the social significance of it. It drives me a little bit more to try to be true to the cuisine," she says.

Haynam teaches her students to respect their ingredients, but also to think beyond traditional uses for new ways to prepare or combine foods. "There is always more food to learn about and try, which is part of what is so exciting to me. There are always more ingredients, more combinations and more cooking traditions to explore."

Cheese and Shrimp Stuffed Poblano Chiles

8 large poblano chiles, about 3 ounces each

8 ounces shrimp, cooked and coarsely chopped

8 ounces cream cheese, at room temperature

1 cup cheese, queso blanco, Monterey Jack or Oaxaca

¼ cup red pepper, chopped

2 tablespoons minced red onion

3 tablespoons chopped cilantro

2 tablespoons chopped fresh basil

salt and pepper, to taste

For the Sauce:

3 red peppers, roasted, skinned and seeded

2 cloves of garlic, minced

3 tablespoons olive oil

balsamic vinegar, to taste

fresh basil, for garnish

Roast poblanos and red peppers over an open flame or under broiler until blackened. Cover and steam for ten minutes. Set red peppers aside. Rub off loose poblano skins and make a slit in side to remove seeds. Set aside.

For sauce: Remove skin from red peppers and place in a food processor with garlic. Blend until smooth. Add vinegar and oil. Pour into a saucepan and heat over medium heat. Add salt and pepper to taste.

Preheat oven to 350 degrees. Mix shrimp with cream cheese, queso blanco, chopped red pepper, onion, cilantro and basil. Season with salt and pepper. Fill poblanos and place on a foil-lined sheet pan. Bake in a 350-degree oven until heated through and cheese melts, about 15 minutes. The stuffed chiles can be assembled a day in advance before baking.

Spoon 3 tablespoons sauce onto each plate, add chile, top with a tablespoon sauce and garnish with fresh basil.

Makes 8 servings.

Sweet Potato and Black Bean Empanadas with Avocado Cream

For the dough:

¾ cup all-purpose flour

½ cup masa harina

1½ teaspoons baking powder

¾ teaspoons salt

1 tablespoon canola oil,
   plus enough for frying

2 eggs

2 tablespoons water

For the filling:

1 large sweet potato, roasted

1 tablespoon olive oil

¼ cup minced onion

2 cloves garlic, minced

¼ teaspoon cumin

¼ teaspoon oregano

1 cup black beans (canned),
   drained and rinsed

1 teaspoon salt

½ teaspoon ancho chili powder

½ cup queso blanco or grated Cheddar

Avocado cream (recipe follows)

For dough, combine flour, masa, baking powder and salt in a small bowl. Add oil and mix by hand until evenly distributed. In a separate bowl, combine eggs and water; gradually add to flour mixture. Knead dough for 3 minutes or until pliable and well-combined. (You may need more flour or water.)

For filling, roast sweet potato in a 400-degree oven until soft, about 30 minutes. Once cool enough to handle, peel and mash or pass through a ricer. In a sauté pan, heat olive oil over medium-high heat. Add onion and cook until translucent. Add garlic and cook until fragrant, about 30 seconds, and add sweet potato purée. Cook for 2 minutes, stirring frequently. Stir in cumin, oregano, beans and season with salt and Ancho chili powder. Remove from heat and stir in cheese.

To assemble, roll out dough to 1/16-inch thickness. Using a 3-inch circle cutter, make 24 circles. Place 2½ teaspoons filling on each. Brush with egg wash (mixture of 1 egg and 2 tablespoons of water, loosely beaten) and fold in half; seal edges by crimping with a fork. Cover and refrigerate until ready to fry (can be refrigerated for up to 24 hours or frozen for 3 weeks at this point).

Heat oil in a deep pan to 350 degrees. Deep-fry until golden brown on both sides, about 4 minutes. Drain and sprinkle with sea salt. Serve with avocado cream.

Makes 8 appetizer portions.

Avocado Cream

1 ripe avocado, peeled, seeded
and roughly chopped

juice of one lime

¼ teaspoon cayenne

¼ teaspoon cumin

1 cup sour cream

salt and pepper, to taste

Purée all ingredients in a food processor until smooth. Season with salt and pepper. Cover and refrigerate.

Makes about 1 cup.

Tom Johnson

"We're all good cooks. We all can do it."

H e is halfway through his seventh decade, but Tom Johnson is still very much an Ohio boy. A Columbus native, he has worked throughout the state for the past fifty years as a restaurant owner, cooking teacher and food marketer. In the 1980s, he was even named Ohio's first "state chef." He is on the permanent staff of the Western Reserve School of Cooking, where he brings years of knowledge about Ohio and its foods to classes on classical techniques.

Johnson is a self-taught cook. After spending time away from Ohio for school—he studied art history at the University of Pennsylvania—and time in the U.S. Navy as a journalist, Johnson returned to Ohio to continue art history studies at the Ohio State University. In the 1970s, Johnson began pursuing his interest in wine, eventually doing radio broadcasts on wine for the university's station, WOSU, under the name the Table Fare Chef. He traveled to New York and Europe, broadcasting about wine and eventually becoming a restaurant critic. That led to a career working in the wholesale wine business, while teaching creative arts at Ohio State. The wholesale wine business brought him into close contact with Columbus' many restaurant owners and when the wholesale business closed, job offers from area restaurants came quickly.

He worked for Shaw's in Lancaster, Lindey's in Columbus, and later, in the 1980s, the acclaimed L'Armagnac in Columbus, where he was chef and owner for four years. At the same time, Johnson began teaching at Betty Rosbottom's La Belle Pomme Cooking School, a post he held for eighteen years. During his time at La Belle Pomme, Zona Spray invited Johnson to teach at her school, and he became a regular guest, teaching three or four times each year.

After L'Armagnac, Johnson began working as chef at Galatine's in Westerville, outside of Columbus. At the French bistro, Johnson began to promote Ohio-raised produce, meats and wines, showcasing them alongside French wines. His local movement was twenty years ahead of its time and it caught the attention of state officials under then-Governor Richard Celeste's administration, who hired him in the marketing department of the Ohio Department of Agriculture. He started the Heartland Cuisine program at the Ohio State Fair to promote Ohio-made products and was given the title of state chef for Ohio.

With the change of administration, however, Johnson was out of work. He eventually moved north to Cleveland, where he accepted a job as corporate chef for Paramount Distillers, helping set up cooking schools at Ohio wineries and developing recipes using Paramount's products.

Now semiretired, Johnson is on the permanent faculty at Western Reserve, where he teaches classes on French techniques, and still promotes Ohio foods.

A big fan of the late British cookbook author Elizabeth David, Johnson likes to paraphrase her when he gives advice during his cooking lessons. "She said, 'The French woman stands at the stove cooking the world's best ingredients, paying careful attention to what she is doing.' Those are wonderful words for anyone because they talk of paying attention, having confidence and not being afraid to do it," he said. "We're all good cooks and we can all do it."

He tells his students not to try to cook like restaurant chefs, and to ignore television entertainers, who pretend to be chefs and only want to sell products. Instead, he advises, students to look around and see what is grown in their own backyard. Start with the finest ingredients. "A fresh tomato, right off the vine, is about as good as it gets," he said. If that tomato happens to be Ohio-grown, it's even better.

Cheap Chops!

Cotes d'Agneau Boulangere, or lamb chops in the style of the baker's wife, is a warm and winning dish from the French countryside. But first, the etymology! In France, there are two distinct types of bakeries, a patisserie, or pastry shop and a boulangerie, or bread bakery. Traditionally, bread is produced in two shifts, lunch and dinner. This leaves ample time when the bread rises and the ovens are empty. Long ago, before the advent of ovens in the rural French kitchen, covered earthenware or enameled cast iron casseroles were readied on the hearth or on simple stoves, and taken to the bread bakery for a leisurely braise in those unoccupied, wood-fired ovens. These splendid cooking vessels nicely retained the heat when the bread moved into its baking phase. In return for oven space, the housewife, or bonne femme, gave the baker a penny, bought the completed bread from him and marched home with the precursor of our chic little take-home meal, a win-win situation for all concerned and a milestone in customer relations.

For those who are bewildered by cuts of lamb other than leg and the more costly loin or rib chops, know that many wonderful parts of the lamb are yours for the braising, or moist cooking under a tight lid. They are economical and wonderful, but merely require a little time.

The French emphatically do not garnish their lamb with the very sweet American mint jelly, or the vinegary English mint sauce, which throws the wine off. If you like the combination of lamb and mint, sprinkle on fresh mint leaves as a garnish, as I do, or substitute its first cousin, marjoram. However, the French, always pretending innocence, do have their culinary vices: many Frenchmen love a good dollop of Dijon mustard with their lamb. However, as a Cleveland Indians fan, I am honor-bound to use Bertman's Original Ball Park Mustard, the pride of Progressive Field!

4 (8-ounce) shoulder lamb chops, trimmed of peripheral fat

2 tablespoons unsalted butter, plus 1 additional tablespoon

2 tablespoons peanut oil

½ teaspoon sugar

sea salt and freshly ground black pepper

2 large onions, coarsely chopped

½ teaspoon dried herbes de Provence blend or dried leaf thyme

4 carrots, peeled and bias-cut in 2-inch pieces

1 small turnip, peeled and diced (optional)

3 large russet potatoes, peeled and sliced

1 bay leaf

3 cloves garlic, peeled and crushed

⅔ cup dry white vermouth, or dry white wine

1 teaspoon demi-glace (a concentrated meat jelly) or ¼ cup low-sodium beef or chicken stock (both optional, to give a bit more depth to the dish)

¼ cup fresh mint leaves, snipped in shreds

Preheat oven to 325 degrees. Pat chops dry. In a lidded ovenproof, enameled cast iron casserole or heavy sauté pan, add butter and peanut oil and heat until butter is melted. Add chops and brown until they are nearly colored. Sprinkle with sugar (which will give broth a nice dark color) and turning them once or twice, continue browning for an additional minute or two to caramelize the surface. Remove to a plate and discard remaining grease. Lightly salt and pepper chops.

Return pan to medium heat and add additional tablespoon butter. Add onion and sauté with herbs for 5 minutes. It should not brown. Add sliced carrots and turnip, if used. Lastly, stir in sliced potatoes, bay leaf and crushed garlic. Season with salt and pepper and bury chops in the mixture.

Add dry white vermouth or wine and optional demi-glace or stock, stirring to scrape up any encrusted meat juices, incorporating them into liquid. Cover and bake 1 hour in preheated oven.

Serve, either on a warmed platter or from casserole, sprinkled with chopped mint leaves. Accompany with Dijon-style mustard. I customarily serve a light, fruity dry red wine, such as a Beaujolais, a Pinot Noir, or a simple red Cote du Rhone, all lightly chilled for about an hour. Serve with crusty bread from your obliging French baker or your own kitchen.

Makes 4 servings.

Ohio-Style French Onion Soup

This recipe was created while I served as the state chef in the Ohio Department of Agriculture, during the governorship of Richard Celeste. From the standpoint of linking together as many diverse commodities as possible, this was the birth of my professional fusion cuisine! It's also pretty yummy!

For the soup:

5 pounds globe onions, peeled and sliced or chopped

1 tablespoon dried leaf thyme

3 tablespoons butter, corn oil, soybean oil or canola oil

2 quarts homemade chicken stock or salt-free commercial chicken stock

1 bay leaf

6 to 8 tart Ohio apples such as Melrose, peeled, cored and chopped into medium dice

½ cup 3-Islands Madeira or Ruby Port, or Meier's Ruby Port

1 tablespoon Worcestershire sauce

½ teaspoon ground clove

½ teaspoon ground allspice

sea salt and freshly ground black pepper, to taste

For serving:

toasted thin slices (croutons) of French bread

thin slices of Jersey jack cheese, for topping

grated Holmes County, Ohio, baby Swiss cheese, plain or smoked

In a large covered heavy-bottomed soup kettle, slowly cook onions and thyme in butter or oil until soft and transparent. The onions will release a considerable amount of liquid; this is the onions' natural water and contains their residual sugar.

Uncover soup kettle and increase heat. Continue to cook, stirring constantly, as water evaporates and sugar caramelizes. Take care that this does not scorch or burn.

When onions have caramelized to a robust gold, add chicken stock and bay leaf. Bring contents to boil, reduce heat to simmer. Simmer gently for 30 minutes. Discard bay leaf and skim off any grease that has risen to the surface. Continuing to simmer, add apples, 3-Islands Madeira (or Port) and Worcestershire sauce. Simmer an additional 10 minutes.

Stir in ground cloves and allspice. Season to taste with salt and pepper. Adjust seasonings until perfect for your taste.

To serve, ladle soup into individual flame-resistant, ovenproof crocks. Top each crock with a toasted French bread crouton, a thin slice Jersey Jack cheese and a tablespoon Baby Swiss cheese. Glaze under your stove broiler.

Makes 8 servings.

Mary Jones

"You don't have to follow a recipe."

Growing up in a family of twelve children, there was no way that Mary Jones could escape the kitchen. All of the kids were assigned regular chores and Jones, who was number four of the twelve, always looked forward to kitchen duty, where she worked alongside her mother preparing daily meals for fourteen in their Hartford, Connecticut, home.

"Every night we had a full meal, including a homemade dessert. We never ate out. How could you take twelve kids to a restaurant?" So it's probably no surprise that Jones came to make a career not only of cooking, but also of teaching others, particularly children, how to mind their manners. She is an etiquette expert and teaches everyone from young executives to high school hockey players the importance of keeping elbows off the table and a napkin securely on one's lap.

She came to food and manners by way of an accounting career. After several relocations for her husband's job, Jones was living in California with two young sons and started looking for a home-based business. She began delivering lunches to nearby office buildings, with her kids in tow. It was mostly sandwiches and salads and Jones taught herself as she went along, reading cookbook after cookbook and piecing ideas together from various recipes.

Another move in 1993 brought the family, now up to three boys, to Hudson, where Jones found the Zona Spray Cooking School. She was strolling through downtown Hudson with one of her sisters when they stopped inside The Cookery to look around. Her sister announced to the woman behind the counter that Jones wanted to wash dishes at the school and inquired about openings. A few months later, Jones was doing just that. But after her first night of washing dishes, Spray asked her if she was interested in being a chef's assistant. Jones accepted and eventually began taking classes. Six years, and another baby later, Jones had worked her way through the professional program, but continued on as a chef's assistant. With four kids at home, she wasn't interested in working full-time. When Spray retired, new owner Carole Ferguson convinced Jones to consider teaching, and she has been on the staff since 2000.

Over the years, Jones has cultivated specialties, including teaching fresh pasta, knife skills and basics like soups and stews, which appeal to her love of comfort foods. For Jones, her classes are about teaching others how to cook without a book. Learning that it's okay to swap apples for pears, and to change up a salad dressing based on what you have on hand, similar to the way she would disassemble recipes back in her lunch-lady days. "You don't have to follow a recipe. I live by the mantra that cooking should be fun and if you are not enjoying it, you are not going to be a good cook. If the recipe says mushrooms and you hate mushrooms, leave them out," she said.

Jones is responsible for the school's roster of day-time classes, which she created to fit around the schedule of drop-off and pick-up times at local pre-schools. But it is probably her etiquette classes for which she is best known. A strict disciple of manners with her own sons, Jones was growing increasingly tired of the lack of social graces she witnessed—guests who don't RSVP for parties, gift-recipients who didn't send thank you notes. It frustrated her, so she developed a course in which she teaches old-fashioned basics—holding doors for women, assisting others with their chairs, removing hats inside—all practices that once were common-place and now are mostly forgotten. Often her class is a group of young boys, but she is often asked by companies to teach the same skills to adults, whom Jones believes need the lessons as much as the children. Jones sends home with the children in her classes a packet of information on everything they have learned. Her ulterior motive is that their parents will read it and perhaps learn a little something too. "I'm changing the world, one eight-year-old at a time," Jones said.

Basic Pasta

1 cup flour	1 tablespoon oil
1 egg	scant ¼ cup water

Dump flour onto a clean work surface and make a well in the center down to the counter. Mix egg and other ingredients in a small bowl. Add egg mixture to well and with tines of a fork, begin incorporating flour into center until a smooth paste forms.

Using a bench scraper, fold mixture over itself until all flour is incorporated. Knead dough until smooth.

Roll out dough to desired thickness and with a pizza wheel, cut into ¼-inch wide strips. Pasta can be cooked immediately or dried for later use.

Makes 1 serving.

Spinach Pasta

4 ounces fresh spinach
  or 2½ ounces frozen spinach
1 cup flour

1 egg
1 tablespoon oil
scant ⅛ cup water

Cook spinach in salted water to enhance color. Squeeze out excess water and finely chop before using.

Dump flour onto a clean work surface and make a well in the center down to the counter. Mix egg and other ingredients in a small bowl. Add egg mixture to well and with tines of a fork, begin incorporating flour into center until a smooth paste forms.

Using a bench scraper, fold mixture over itself until all flour is incorporated. Knead dough until smooth.

Roll out dough to desired thickness and with a pizza wheel, cut into ¼-inch wide strips. Pasta can be cooked immediately or dried for later use.

Makes 1 serving.

Tomato Pasta

1 tablespoon tomato paste
1 cup flour
1 egg

1 tablespoon oil
scant ¼ cup water

Dump flour onto a clean work surface and make a well in the center down to the counter. Mix egg and other ingredients in a small bowl. Add egg mixture to well and with tines of a fork, begin incorporating flour into center until a smooth paste forms.

Using a bench scraper, fold mixture over itself until all flour is incorporated. Knead dough until smooth.

Roll out dough to desired thickness and with a pizza wheel, cut into ¼-inch wide strips. Pasta can be cooked immediately or dried for later use.

Makes 1 serving.

Farfalle with Fresh Salmon and Peas

1 pound farfalle, made from Basic Pasta Dough (enough for 4 servings)

½ pound salmon, cut in ½-inch dice

½ pound frozen peas, cooked

¼ cup olive oil

1 garlic clove, minced

¼ teaspoon red pepper flakes

1 can (16 ounces) diced tomatoes, with juice

1 cup heavy cream

2 tablespoons fresh basil

salt and pepper, to taste

¼ cup Parmesan cheese

To make farfalle: Cut a sheet of pasta into 1½-inch squares using a fluted pastry cutter. Pinch squares in middle, with one fold on top and two on bottom. Cook pasta to al dente while making sauce. Drain pasta and toss with sauce.

For sauce: Add olive oil to a large heated skillet. Over medium-high heat, add garlic and red pepper flakes and cook until garlic begins to change color. Add tomatoes and season with salt.

Turn heat to medium and cook until tomatoes have reduced by half (about 20 minutes). Add salmon, cream, peas and a pinch of salt. Cook over medium-high heat until cream is reduced by half. Adjust seasonings.

Top with cheese and serve immediately.

Makes 4 servings.

Penne with Sausage, Tomato and Ricotta

1 pound penne, made from Basic Pasta Dough (enough for 4 servings)

½ pound sweet Italian sausage, casings removed

1 large can (28 ounces) diced tomatoes, with juice

8 ounces ricotta cheese

1 clove garlic, minced

1 small onion, diced

2 tablespoon olive oil

¼ cup Parmesan cheese

salt and pepper, to taste

2 tablespoons fresh basil

To make penne: Roll out 1½-inch squares of pasta onto a pencil, starting at a corner. Cook pasta to al dente in boiling salted water while making sauce. Drain pasta and mix with sauce.

For sauce: Heat a large skillet and add oil. Add onions and sauté until translucent. Add sausage and break up with back of a spoon. Scramble sausage until browned and cooked through.

Drain grease from skillet and add garlic, sautéing 1 minute. Add tomatoes, salt and pepper. Bring to boil, then simmer 15 minutes until thickened.

Remove from heat, add ricotta and basil. Top with Parmesan and serve immediately.

Note: You can also boil sausage and slice into ½-inch rounds rather than scrambling. Balance of cooking directions remain the same.

Tri-Color Linguini Frittata with Onions

½ pound linguini, cooked al dente

½ cup chopped red onion

½ cup chopped white onion

2 scallions, thinly sliced

1 clove garlic, crushed

6 eggs

¼ cup grated Parmesan cheese

2 tablespoons minced parsley

salt and pepper, to taste

Heat oil in a 10-inch nonstick skillet. Add onion and sauté until translucent. Add scallions and garlic and sauté 2 minutes more.

In a large bowl, beat eggs and add sautéed onion mixture, half the cheese, parsley, salt, pepper and linguini.

Reheat onion skillet over low heat until a drop of water sizzles and evaporates immediately upon contact. Add linguini mixture. Cover and cook over low heat for 5 minutes. Shake pan to prevent sticking. Cook covered until eggs are set and frittata is well-browned, 10 to 15 minutes.

Invert onto a large plate. Sprinkle with remaining cheese. Cut into wedges and serve.

Makes 6 servings.

Christina Körting

"I don't teach recipes."

A chef's jacket wasn't exactly the kind of white coat Christina "Tina" Körting thought she would wear one day. Born in the Philippines, Körting's family moved to Cleveland when her physician father accepted a position there. Like her father, Körting thought she would one day be a doctor. But in 1978, a twist of fate set her on a course in food and she has never looked back.

Körting's grandmother had registered for a puff-pastry class at the Zona Spray Cooking School. When her grandmother became ill and couldn't go, she encouraged Körting to take her place. "I got hooked," she said, "After that I just started taking more and more cooking classes at Zona Spray."

After high school, Körting enrolled at Case Western Reserve University and began working toward a degree in pre-med. But after a while, it became clear to her that she enjoyed cooking class more than her university classes. She put her course work toward a bachelor's degree in nutrition and after graduation Spray arranged an apprenticeship for Körting with Chef Michel Pasquet, at his Paris restaurant. At the time, the only female chef in Pasquet's kitchen worked in pastry and Körting spent a lot of time with her. She then spent several years in New York, where she took classes at the French Culinary Institute and began to focus solely on pastry.

Körting worked for a number of notable New York chefs, including Daniel Boulud and Eric Bedoucha, before moving to Japan, where she worked as a pastry consultant. When she came home, Körting always visited Spray and taught classes at her school. She remembers Spray as a pioneer of food in Cleveland. "I could look at her as our very own Julia Child. She brought the world to us through food," she said.

In 1990, when Spray asked Körting about setting up a pastry program, the timing could not have been better. Körting had just met her future husband and decided to stay in Cleveland instead of returning to Japan. She worked as pastry chef for a number of Cleveland restaurants, but after the birth of her two daughters, Körting accepted a position with the Swiss culinary supply house Albert Uster Imports.

Körting teaches one week each month at the Western Reserve School of Cooking, focusing on pastry techniques and the basics of pastry. "I don't teach recipes. A lot of people read a recipe and don't know what they are doing and why they are doing it," she said. "Technique is my number one thing." That way, if Körting's students see a recipe that starts with butter and sugar, they know instinctively that those two items are meant to be creamed together, even if there aren't any instructions.

Körting has seen pastry work change a lot over the past twenty years, as cake bakers now find glory on their own television shows and the public's interested in baking is booming. "When I first started, pastry chefs were down in the dungeon, in the basement, or the cave where the wine would be. Now, pastry chefs are superstars," she said.

Rochers

....

The rocher has a long and esteemed history in European confections.

....

2¾ ounces (75 grams) sugar

1 ounce (25 grams) water

5 ounces (150 grams) slivered almonds

3½ ounces (100 grams) pine nuts

¾ ounces (20 grams) butter

6¼ ounces (175 grams) bittersweet chocolate, melted and tempered or compound coating, melted

Place granulated sugar and water in a 4-quart heavy-bottomed saucepan and bring mixture to boil over medium-high heat. Add almonds and pine nuts and stir to coat evenly in sugar syrup. Sugar will turn sandy and change to a clear liquid. Keep stirring until sugar turns golden brown and nuts are caramelized.

When nuts begin to caramelize, lower heat to medium-low and continue stirring until all nuts are evenly caramelized. Remove from heat, add butter and stir to stop the cooking of the caramel and prevent nuts from sticking to each other.

Spread nuts on a parchment-lined baking tray and let cool completely. When completely cooled, break apart any clusters that may have formed.

Place a quarter of the cooled nuts in a small, warmed bowl. Slowly add a quarter of the melted, tempered chocolate or compound coating and immediately mix to entirely cover caramelized nuts with chocolate.

Working quickly, so chocolate does not set, use a spoon to deposit tablespoon-size mounds of chocolate-coated nut mixture on a sheet pan. Try to make attractive shapes with a little height to them for nicer-looking rochers.

Repeat in one quarter increments with remaining nuts and chocolate. Allow rochers to set and cool completely.

Makes 35 to 55, depending on size.

Tuiles

In French, tuile means tile, and it refers to the shape of the classic tuile, which is baked and then molded while still warm and pliable. When cool, it resembles a tiny roof tile.

2½ ounces (70 grams) bread flour	4 egg whites
¼ ounces (7 grams) cornstarch	½ teaspoon (2½ milliliter) vanilla
3½ ounces (100 grams) sugar	3½ ounces (100 grams) noisette butter *see note

Combine flour, cornstarch and sugar into a small mixing bowl. Add egg whites, vanilla and noisette butter. Whisk to combine. Set batter aside for 1½ hours before using, or cover and refrigerate for up to 3 days.

Preheat oven to 375 degrees. Spoon batter onto a baking sheet lined with a silicone liner. Using an off-set spatula, spread each cookie into a 3-inch round. To insure even baking, make sure edges are no thinner than centers.

Bake for 8 to 10 minutes, or until edges are golden and centers are just beginning to color. Immediately remove from baking sheet and drape around a rolling pin or wine bottle. If cookies become too cool and stiff to bend, return to oven to become pliable.

Makes approximately 18 cookies.

Note: Noisette butter—the term in French literally means hazelnut butter, although no hazelnuts are used to make this butter. The melted butter takes on a nutty flavor in addition to changing color. To make, melt unsalted butter until it starts to turn light brown, remove from heat.

Sabayon

A sauce based on a foamy mixture; a cousin to Zabaglione, the egg-based Italian dessert.

3 egg yolks	4 ounces (112 grams) dry white wine
4 ounces (112 grams) sugar	

Whisk to blend yolks, sugar and white wine in a stainless-steel bowl. Place bowl over large saucepan of simmering water. Keep heat on medium-high.

Whisk constantly for 4 to 5 minutes or more. Cook until consistency of lightly whipped cream. Sabayon should never be warmer than body temperature or it becomes grainy. When thick, foamy and tripled in volume, remove from heat. It can be served hot, warm or cool. Serve as a topping over fresh fruit.

Makes about ½cup.

Crème Caramel

A French baked custard.

For the caramel:
2½ ounces (70 grams) sugar
water

For the custard:
16 ounces (500 milliliter) whole milk
3½ ounces (100 grams) sugar
4 whole eggs
¼ vanilla bean

To make caramel: Place sugar in a small saucepan with enough water to saturate. Boil on medium-high until syrup starts to brown. Do not stir while cooking. Once browned, pour caramel into 8 ramekins. Set aside and let cool.

To make custard: Heat milk and sugar to a simmer. In a small bowl, whisk eggs for a minute and slowly whisk in hot milk. Mix completely. Divide custard into caramel-lined ramekins.

Place ramekins in a large ovenproof baking dish. Fill dish with water, about ⅔ height of ramekins. Carefully place in a 300-degree oven. Bake for 35 to 40 minutes, custards are done when they set. Water should not boil during baking.

Allow custards to cool completely, then cover and refrigerate ramekins until serving time. To serve, run a knife along the outside of each crème, then turn over onto a dessert plate.

Makes 8 servings.

Black Forest Cake

Originating from the German Schwarzwälde or Black Forest, this is a chocolate cake with layers soaked in cherry liqueur syrup, filled with cherries and sweetened whipped cream.

For the chocolate sponge cake:

6 eggs

8 ounces (225 grams) sugar

7 ounces (195 grams) cake flour

1 ounce (30 grams) cocoa powder

Preheat oven to 375 degrees. Grease and flour a 10-inch diameter cake pan and set aside.

In the bowl of an electric mixer, combine eggs and sugar. Place bowl over large saucepan of simmering water. While whisking constantly, heat mixture to between 110 and 120 degrees.

Place mixture on mixer and whip on medium speed for 15 more minutes, until volume triples, to stabilize mixture.

Sift together cake flour and cocoa powder. Gradually fold sifted dry ingredients into egg mixture by hand. Fill cake pan with batter and bake immediately.

Bake for 25 to 30 minutes. Let cool completely; slice cake horizontally into three layers.

For the Kirsch syrup:

16 ounces (400 grams) sugar

10 ounces (300 grams) water

2 ounces (60 grams) cherry brandy

For the filling:

16 ounces (or 300 grams) cherries soaked in brandy

28 ounces (700 grams) heavy cream

2 ounces (60 grams) sugar

chocolate shavings, for garnish

For syrup: Combine sugar and water in a saucepan and bring to boil. Remove from heat and add brandy. Set aside to cool.

For filling: Whisk heavy cream and sugar together until stiff peaks form.

To assemble: Take one chocolate sponge layer and soak with Kirsch syrup. Spread a layer of whipped cream on top and top with brandied cherries. Place second layer on top of cherries and repeat. Top with final layer. Frost cake with remaining whipped cream and garnish with cherries and chocolate shavings.

Makes one 10-inch layer cake.

Famous Chefs & Fabulous Recipes

Kathy Lehr

"Take the formula and make anything from it."

There is a commonality among bread bakers, something almost spiritual happens when they first put hands to dough. Much in the way that yeast reacts when mixed with flour and water, they are transformed.

Kathy Lehr understands the transformative powers of dough. A native of Cuyahoga Falls, Ohio, she attended Kent State University during the political tumult of the 1970s and was there on May 4, 1970, when four students were killed by Ohio National Guard troops during student protests.

She earned an education degree and by 1977, she was married to a building contractor, teaching elementary school and entertaining a lot in the evenings. She started taking classes at the Zona Spray Cooking School to sharpen her skills. Lehr enjoyed cooking and started with classes on appetizers and entertaining. Eventually, she took a three-day bread-baking course taught by Californian Danielle Forestier, the first American and first women to receive a master bread baking certification in France. Forestier was Julia Child's bread consultant.

The evening's assignment was to bake the breads Forestier had taught that day and to bring one in for critique the following day. Forestier was extremely critical and Lehr vividly recalls being the last student in class to bring her loaf forward. Forestier stood there and stared at the small, French bâtard and said nothing. She cut into it, smelled it, put it down, looked up and finally said, "This is a magnificent loaf of bread."

In that instant, a career was born and Lehr's life was transformed. She continued with her studies, earning her professional chef's certificate from Spray's school and over the years has honed her bread baking skills to the point that she is now considered one of the country's expert teachers.

When Lehr teaches a bread class, she sees the same look in the eyes of her students that she had when eating Forestier's bread for the first time. "When I tasted her bread, it was the same thing that I see when people in my class taste French bread for the first time. It just blew me away. I had to learn how to make it," she recalled. "Bread is the staff of life. To me, when you can take salt, water, yeast and flour and create what you can create with that, that's amazing. I have a passion for it."

It was Spray who pointed out to Lehr that she needed to teach and pass on her passion to others. In 1987, Lehr began teaching at Spray's school and continues on the staff of the Western Reserve School of Cooking, offering intensive courses in bread baking several times a year.

"My main lesson is that people will take a formula for the bread and be able to walk away from there and be able to create any bread in the world without having to use a book or a recipe. I want to give them the foundation to be able to create anything with the knowledge and the chemistry. It's just a basic formula, but they can take the formula and make anything from it," Lehr said.

It is a lesson that was inspired by Spray and the way she taught Lehr an understanding of food and cooking techniques and how to put them into practice by intuition. "What I got from Zona was that once you understood food and cooking, you should be able to go and pick items from the garden or from the store and just create based upon your knowledge."

Classic French Bread

Adapted from a recipe by Danielle Forestier.

35¼ ounces (1000 grams) bread flour	1 tablespoon (20 grams) salt
1 tablespoon (20 grams) cake yeast OR dry yeast	23.1 ounces (660 grams or about 3½ cups) water

With a stand mixer: Place flour and cake yeast in bowl of a stand mixer. (If using dry yeast, proof in about ½ cup of 94-degree water with a pinch sugar). When you add water in the next step, it should be done rather quickly so that clumps of dry flour do not form. (If you add water rather slowly, use the paddle rather than dough hook to begin incorporation.) Add two thirds of water while using dough hook on speed 2. Add more water to reach desired consistency; it should be quite wet. Mix on low speed for about 2 minutes after reaching desired consistency. Knead on medium speed for about 3 more minutes. Add salt and knead on same speed for another minute. Remove from bowl and finish kneading by hand.

By hand: Place flour in a bowl. Crumble cake yeast into flour and stir with hands. Add about two thirds water and mix with one hand. Continue to add water until flour is mostly incorporated; it will feel quite wet.

Turn dough out onto a floured surface. Flour hands, including palms. Using palm, press out lumps of dried flour. Do this in rows until you have attacked all of dough. Roll into a ball with scraper, smooth side up. Do this process again. Repeat 3 to 4 times until all lumps are removed; this will eliminate much of the kneading time.

Roll into ball and begin kneading. Pick up dough at left or right open end. Slam dough against table with smooth side hitting table. Do a jelly roll on dough with other hand. Repeat about 100 times. Dough will become quite smooth and you will begin to seeing air bubbles. It will feel quite elastic. This is because the gluten has developed.

Add salt by sprinkling on table and rolling dough in it. After dough becomes wet, finish off by kneading a few more times.

First rise: If doing a cool rise overnight in refrigerator, place in bowl, cover with plastic wrap and a towel and place in refrigerator. You may want to punch dough down or pull dough before you go to sleep. This will tighten dough.

If rising on counter, it is wise to do a "tour," which gives more power to dough. The dough temperature should be 78 degrees. Let dough rest on counter, covered with a towel, for 20 minutes. Turn dough over and, assuming dough ball is a clock face, pull at 12 o'clock and 6 o'clock towards center and press ends into center. Pull dough at 3 o'clock and 9 o'clock and press ends into center. Place in a bowl with tucked ends toward bottom of bowl, cover and let rise 1 to 2 hours.

Shaping and second rise: Remove dough from refrigerator and punch down. Set on counter, covered with a towel, for about 30 minutes.

If using second method in rise, remove from bowl and punch down.

Divide dough into 6 equal portions, trying to make them rectangular in shape and cover with towel.

Begin forming into loaves (*see diagram, following page*) doing 2 envelopes and at least 3 "thumbs" for tension in dough. Roll loaf into a cigar shape and place on floured towels on back of a cookie sheet. Seam side should be up. Cover and let rise 50 minutes to 1 hour.

Baking: Oven should be set at 475 degrees. Line oven middle shelf with unglazed bread-baking tiles. Leave 1-inch air space around outer tiles or you'll burn the bottom of the loaves.

Before turning loaves over and slashing, using a turkey baster, inject ¼ cup water into oven bottom. You may also place an aluminum pan with unglazed tile in it on oven bottom when preheating oven. Throw water on tile to create steam.

Slash loaves as directed and immediately slide onto tiles. Your blade should be at a 30 degree angle and form a slight "happy face." Inject steam one more time into oven bottom.

At 7 minutes, begin checking for caramelizing. Loaves should be fairly into caramelization at 10 minutes. The bâtards should take 24 to 28 minutes to bake. The internal temperature should be 210 degrees. Let cool completely before cutting.

Makes 6 (300 gram) loaves.

Envelope (Do 2 times)

1

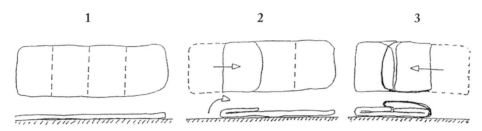

2

3

4

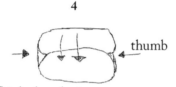

thumb

Stick thumbs in on seam and fold dough down over.

5

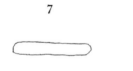

Seal new seam with base of palm.

6

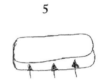

Remember to elongate, too, as you use your thumbs.

7

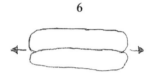

8

9

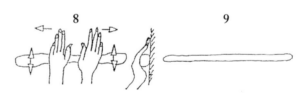

Place on floured towel on cookie sheet (seam side *up*).

Ciabatta

Ciabatta means slipper (or slippery) in Italian and is rightfully named after seeing this short, stubby loaf. After working with the dough, you will understand the slippery aspect! It is a remarkable combination of rustic texture and tantalizing taste. The crunchy crust encases a porous, chewy interior. Everyone who tries this bread falls in love with it, whether toasting it for breakfast or breaking off bits to eat with salami and cheese.

3 grams instant yeast

7½ cups (1000 grams) unbleached flour*

1 tablespoon (20 grams) salt

2 cups (500 grams) biga (recipe follows)

2 tablespoons (28 grams) olive oil

4 cups (776 grams) water

¼ cup medium grind cornmeal (for dusting bottoms)

extra-virgin olive oil

additional unbleached flour, for dusting hands and loaves as needed

coarse salt

Kneading dough: Put flour and yeast in a mixing bowl. Stir with fingers and add salt. Combine biga, olive oil and three cups water. Mix on low speed with paddle. Begin adding remaining water. If you want a very chewy texture, you will want to make dough extremely soupy; you may want to add extra water. Dough should be liquidy and very sticky. Knead about 5 minutes with paddle.

Put in a bowl rubbed with olive oil and cover with plastic wrap. Let rise, covered, overnight or two days in refrigerator.

Shaping dough: Remove dough from refrigerator and let rest on counter for about 30 minutes.

Rub 2 baking dishes, about 8 inches square or 2 rectangular dishes, with a generous amount of olive oil. Place half of dough in each dish, cover and let rise at room temperature for about 1½ hours.

Place oiled parchment or Silpat on a cookie sheet. Sprinkle with cornmeal. Try to shape dough by lifting and curling ends under. This is as close to shaping that you will come to with this dough. Do this a few times over baking dish. Do it a final time over baking sheet and set down on parchment. Oil top of each loaf and dimple loaf vigorously. Let rise at least 1 hour.

Baking dough: Preheat oven at 450 degrees with baking tiles on center rack. Before putting into oven, dimple again and sprinkle with coarse salt and herbs (if so desired). Inject water into oven bottom using a turkey baster. Repeat 3 times in the first 5 minutes of baking.

During the last 5 minutes of baking, remove bread from baking sheet and finish baking directly on tiles. Bake for 30 to 35 minutes or until internal temperature is 200 degrees. Remove loaves and let cool completely on a rack.

Makes 2 loaves.

*I prefer King Arthur all-purpose unbleached flour. If an unbleached flour is unavailable, use bread flour.

Biga

The universal starter, known as biga in Italy, gives strength and force to flour. It also produces a secondary fermentation, which gives the bread a natural flavor and a special porosity. A starter dough is very close to natural yeast. Breads made from this have a much slower rise than those made with commercial yeast. Starters also extend the shelf life of a bread. In many European bakeries, a piece of salt-less dough is saved to use in the next day's bread.

pinch (2 grams) instant yeast
500 grams (17½ ounces) unbleached
   bread flour or all-purpose flour

500 grams (17½ ounces) water

Mix yeast with flour; stir in water. Mix for 2 minutes using a wooden spoon.

Put in bowl, cover with plastic wrap and let rise for 3 to 6 hours. Put in refrigerator until ready to use; can be stored for 2 to 3 days in refrigerator.

*Traditionally, bigas are stiff, but if you like yours wet, add more water. If you prefer it drier, add less water.

Pecan Caramel Sticky Buns

Adapted from a recipe by Julia Child.

Sweet Yeast Dough (recipe follows)

For Caramel:

½ cup (114 grams) unsalted butter

1 cup (215 grams) brown sugar

¼ cup (86 grams) light corn syrup

2 tablespoon (24 grams) water

1 cup (200 grams) whole pecan pieces

For Pecan Filling:

5 tablespoons (72 grams) unsalted butter, melted

¾ cup (170 grams) brown sugar

1 tablespoon (9 grams) ground cinnamon

1½ cups (200 grams) chopped pecans

Preheat oven to 350 degrees.

To make caramel: In bottom of two 9 by 9-inch (or 8 by 8-inch) baking dishes, divide butter, brown sugar, corn syrup and water equally. Melt over low heat on stove top, stirring constantly. When melted, remove from heat. Place ½ cup whole pecan pieces in each pan. Set aside.

To make pecan filling: Combine butter, brown sugar, ground cinnamon and chopped pecans in a bowl.

Forming dough: Weigh sweet dough into 2 pieces, each weighing 550 grams. Roll each piece into a 10 by 12-inch piece about ¼-inch thick. Leaving a ½-inch border on 2 long sides, sprinkle evenly with butter, brown sugar, ground cinnamon and chopped pecan mixture. Roll up jelly-roll fashion from long end and pinch seam to seal or use egg wash.

Cut each log into 9 equal portions, about 1½-inches thick. Set slices in pan, spiral side down. Cover and let rise for 30 minutes. Bake in center of oven for 30 to 35 minutes or until tops are golden brown.

Remove from oven and immediately invert onto a cooling rack with a pan underneath to catch excess caramel which you, of course, must eat as soon as it cools.

Makes 18 rolls.

Sweet Yeast Dough

2 large eggs

⅓ cup sugar

3 cups bread flour

Sponge (recipe follows)

finely grated zest of 1 lemon (optional)

2 teaspoons salt

¾ cup unsalted butter, cut into small
   pieces, at room temperature

egg wash (mixture of 1 egg and 2
   tablespoons water, loosely beaten)

Place 2½ cups flour in a mixing bowl. Add eggs, sugar, sponge and zest. Beat with paddle until smooth. Add salt. Beat 1 minute. Add butter a few pieces at a time. Dough should be very soft. Using hook, knead for about 4 minutes. If needed, add remaining flour. (The flour is the variable because I don't want to waste milk.)

Let rise for 1 hour at room temperature. Deflate dough, cover with plastic wrap and refrigerate overnight.

Makes 2 braids or coffee cakes.

Sponge

1 tablespoon active dry yeast
   (20 grams cake yeast)

1 tablespoon sugar

½ cup water

1¼ cup scalded milk

2 cups bread flour

Proof yeast with sugar and water. Place flour in stand mixer bowl. Add yeast mixture and milk. Using paddle attachment, mix for about 1 minute. Let rest for about 30 minutes.

Mary Ann Napolitano

"There is really no excuse for not having good food."

W hen Mary Ann Napolitano looked at other people's garbage cans on trash night, she often wondered, "What could they possibly be throwing away in those bulging cans?" At one point, she came to the realization that it must be all of the packaging from prepared foods. It was the kind of food that was unheard of in her home.

The grandchild of Italian immigrants who settled in Youngstown, Ohio, Napolitano grew up in a family that cooked everything from scratch. Bread and pasta started out as flour, not in boxes and bags. Vegetables came from the backyard, as did fruit. Fruit trees were cultivated in pots and brought in for the winter or bent over and buried in the ground to preserve them through the cold northeast Ohio winters.

It's no surprise then that Napolitano eventually grew into a career as a baker, caterer and teacher at the Western Reserve School of Cooking. "I grew up with food. It was around all the time. It was one of those things you just did. When people came over, you fed them. It was what we did. I was in the kitchen all of my life."

Napolitano followed a very traditional path in life. In college she studied to be an elementary school teacher. It was her father's dream that his sons would be doctors and his daughters would be teachers, so they would have work schedules conducive to raising children. Napolitano taught for several years, but gave up teaching to be a stay-at-home mom.

After her kids were nearly grown, Napolitano mulled getting back into the workforce. Her route to take her daughter to dance class took her past the Western Reserve School of Cooking. She began taking classes, working her way through a series of pastry and bread classes before enrolling in the professional level courses. She graduated in 2007, and school owner Catherine St. John offered her a teaching job the following year. With Napolitano's background in the classroom and her upbringing with food, it was the perfect match.

She teaches a variety of subjects, including children's classes, crepe making and of course, Italian cuisine. "I'm really happy and comfortable teaching Italian cuisine, it is second nature to me," she said.

Even with four years experience teaching others how to cook, Napolitano continues to be amazed by how much others rely on packaged, prepared or frozen foods for their meals. "I guess what surprised me the most was that people bought food ready made," she said, which is why Napolitano tries to show her students just how easy it is to cook from fresh ingredients.

Cooking and especially baking from scratch is more labor intensive, but Napolitano believes the end product is worth the extra effort. She even prefers to make her own puff pastry than buy the frozen variety and stresses the need for purity in her foods.

"The one thing I like to convey is that it's really not that complicated and there is really no excuse for not having good food. Even a batch of chocolate chip cookies are so much better for you knowing exactly what's in them, instead of when you read those labels and you can't even pronounce the ingredients, the artificial flavorings and colorings," Napolitano says.

Cavatelli Dough

1 cup all-purpose flour	¼ cup water
¼ teaspoon salt	1 tablespoon olive oil

Mound flour on a counter or cutting board and shape into a well. Add salt, a tablespoon water and olive oil to center. Using a fork in a circular motion, pull flour into center of well. Gradually add remaining water, adding more if dough is too dry. When dough becomes too heavy to blend with a fork, use a bench scraper.

Once all flour is incorporated, start kneading dough, using palms of your hands. When you have a cohesive mass, remove from board, scraping and discarding any left-over crusty bits. Lightly reflour board and continue kneading until dough feels smooth, elastic and slightly sticky. Cover with an inverted bowl and let rest 15 minutes.

Using a bench scraper, cut off a piece of dough. Re-cover larger piece of dough with inverted bowl. Lightly flour your work surface. Roll cut piece into a long snake, roughly diameter of your ring finger. Cut strip into ¾ to 1-inch pieces. Using your index finger or thumb, press down and push each piece, rolling it into a scroll. Place cavatelli on floured sheet pans and repeat until all dough is used.

Makes 1 serving per 1 cup flour.

Tomato Sauce

1 tablespoon olive oil

1 large onion (chopped)

1 large pepper (seeded and quartered)

1 large carrot (peeled and halved)

2 cloves garlic (minced)

2 cans (28 ounces) tomato sauce

¼ can water

3 leaves basil (whole)

In a 4 to 6-quart saucepan, sauté an onion in olive oil. Add pepper, carrot and garlic. Avoid burning garlic to keep it from becoming bitter.

Add tomato sauce, rinsing out cans with water and adding to sauce. Stir in basil.

Allow sauce to cook on low. Simmer 45 minutes to an hour for flavors to develop.

Makes enough sauce for 1 pound of pasta.

Wedding Soup

3 quarts chicken stock, preferably homemade or low-sodium

1 head escarole, cleaned, chopped and blanched

¼ head Savoy cabbage hearts, cleaned, chopped and blanched (optional)

2 carrots, cleaned and cut into ½-inch pieces

1 stalk celery, cleaned and cut into ½-inch pieces

1 medium onion, peeled and chopped

2 tablespoons olive oil

Mini meatballs (recipe follows)

kosher salt and freshly ground pepper

Parmesan cheese, freshly grated

Clean loose escarole and Savoy cabbage leaves and blanch them. Drain greens in a colander and chop into bite-sized pieces. Set aside.

Prepare mini meatballs (see recipe). Prepare mirepoix of carrots, celery and onions. Set aside.

In a large kettle on a medium heat, add olive oil. Add mirepoix, salt and pepper. Sauté until onions are translucent.

Slowly pour strained and defatted stock into kettle and add cooked greens and mini meatballs. Stir to combine. Taste and adjust seasonings. Serve hot, with freshly grated Parmesan cheese.

Makes 12 to 15 servings.

Meatballs

3 slices bread, crusts removed

1 egg, slightly beaten

1 pound ground chuck meat

1 cup Parmigiano-Reggiano
  cheese, grated

1 tablespoon fresh parsley, chopped

1 tablespoon kosher salt

1 teaspoon peppercorn, ground

1 teaspoon olive oil

3 cloves garlic, pressed or finely minced

Soak bread in water or milk to soften. Gently squeeze out liquid. In a large bowl, combine ground meat, softened bread, beaten egg, cheese, salt, pepper, garlic and parsley. Mix gently until incorporated; over-mixing can lead to tougher meatballs. If you would like to taste for seasoning, take a small amount, make a patty and fry it in a skillet until cooked. Add more salt, pepper, cheese and parsley for additional seasoning if needed.

In sheet pan with sides, drizzle olive oil and spread to coat. Use a scoop to obtain uniform sizes or gently roll out a portion in the palms of your hands. Wetting your palms with water or oil will help keep meatballs from sticking to them.

Place in oven and bake at 350 degrees for 15 to 20 minutes for the large meatballs (roughly 5 to 10 minutes for the mini-meatballs). Remember, they will continue to cook in sauce or soup. Let cool. Gently place cooked meatballs into pot and stir very gently, trying not to break your meatballs.

Makes 24 regular meatballs or 60 mini-meatballs.

Pizzelles

1½ cups sugar

½ cup oil

6 eggs

1 teaspoon vanilla, lemon,
  or anise extract

1 teaspoon baking powder

3 cups all-purpose flour

Cream together sugar and oil with an electric mixer. Combine eggs into dough one at a time, making sure to crack each egg individually in a separate container before adding. Add extract of your choice.

In a separate bowl, either sift flour and baking powder or stir with a whisk to break apart any lumps. Add to creamed mixture a little at a time. If dough is too runny, add more flour to achieve desired consistency. Drop batter by spoonfuls onto hot pizzelle iron, press and bake until all batter is used. Makes 48 pizzelles.

Nancy Neal

"You get organized before you start and you don't waste a thing."

Folks in Hudson, Ohio, might not be able to recognize a famous chef if one cooked for them, but they probably know Nancy Neal. She's been a fixture at the Western Reserve School of Cooking, and before that, the Zona Spray Cooking School, for nearly twenty years.

Most days, she's behind the counter of The Cookery, the school's retail store, and has performed nearly every role there is at the school, from student, to teacher, to manager, to dishwasher. In fact, washing dishes is how she started out at the school and she did it for free.

In 1992, Neal was a homemaker with four young children. She needed a way to get out of the house once in a while and Spray accepted volunteers who helped with chores in exchange for auditing classes. So dedicated was Neal, that it wasn't long before Spray hired her as an assistant, where her duties were helping the chefs get ready for their classes and assisting them during classes. It was an exceptional world for Neal to enter.

Food was always a part of Neal's life. Her mother was a lover of "fancy food" and liked to experiment with foreign cuisine. She made quiche before it was fashionable and made her own polenta years before it was on restaurant menus. "She really was well ahead of her time. I knew more about food than some people might because of her," Neal recalls.

Now, accomplished chefs came through the door on a regular basis and Neal was able to learn from them. She saw first-hand the best and worst the food world had to offer: the chefs who shared their knowledge freely and kindly and the uber-divas who screamed at the staff and didn't hesitate to embarrass assistants in front of a full classroom. She watched some blossom from budding chefs to celebrity chefs with a shelf of books to their credit.

It was Spray who perhaps had the strongest impact on Neal. She remembers Spray as "a tiny woman with a huge personality." Neal learned two invaluable lessons from Spray. The first was be organized—make sure all of your ingredients are available and measured before beginning to cook. The second was to not waste anything. Spray's frugality was well-known and she insisted that her staffers follow her example. "You get organized before you start and you don't waste a thing," Neal said. They are lessons that Neal learned well and has passed on to many of her students, including her four children, all of whom are accomplished cooks. "She's totally brilliant. She expected a lot out of people and she got it," Neal said.

Aside from her classroom experience, Neal began formal studies at the school and graduated from both the professional series and its pastry course.

Neal attributes her background in graphic design for the passion she developed for pastry. She worked as a pastry chef for a while, making desserts for local restaurants and also working at a local bakery. But she always kept coming back to the school.

Under owner Carole Ferguson, Neal began teaching classes in 1997, and when Ferguson passed on the school to her accountant Ed Schiciano, he asked Neal to run the day-to-day operations. She became its full-time manager, scheduling chefs, arranging classes, teaching and keeping the school running. When Catherine St. John took over in 2007, Neal began to run The Cookery retail store full time.

Linzertorte

This is one of Neal's favorite desserts, which she adapted from a recipe by Rose Levy Beranbaum.

1¼ cups blanched hazelnuts	1¼ teaspoons vanilla extract
15 tablespoons unsalted butter	1¼ cups seedless raspberry jam
2½ cups all-purpose flour	1 egg white, lightly beaten
¾ cup sugar	2 tablespoons sliced almonds
1¼ teaspoons baking powder	1 tablespoon coarse sanding sugar
1¼ teaspoons cinnamon	confectioners' sugar, for dusting
2½ egg yolks	

Preheat oven to 350 degrees. Cut butter into small pieces, wrap in plastic wrap and refrigerate until needed.

In a food processor with a metal blade, process nuts and ½ cup flour until finely ground. Add remaining flour, sugar, baking powder and cinnamon and process until evenly combined. Pulse in cold butter until you have a fine crumb.

Add egg yolks and vanilla extract and pulse just until dough starts to hold together.

Remove dough from processor and gather into a disc. Divide into two pieces, one slightly larger than the other. Flatten smaller dough, wrap and refrigerate.

Press remaining dough into an 11-inch fluted tart pan, including up the sides. If there is excess, add it to refrigerated dough. Spread jam over bottom of torte.

Make a lattice by rolling refrigerated dough between parchment paper to about 10½ inches by 5½ inches and cutting into ¾-inch strips. (It helps to use a metal ruler.) Cover and freeze on a sheet pan for 5 minutes until firm.

Remove top sheet of parchment and, using a long metal spatula, slide it under each strip and lay them onto torte, starting with the longest in the center and working out to each edge, leaving a gap of jam in between. Trim excess as you go with a sharp knife.

Make a quarter turn and repeat, chilling dough and rerolling as necessary. Put left over dough around edge.

Brush lattice and edges with egg wash. Sprinkle almonds around edge and sugar on lattice.

Bake for 35 to 45 minutes, until pastry is golden brown. Let cool to warm before removing from tart pan. Dust with powdered sugar before serving.

Makes 8 to 10 servings.

Barbara Snow

"It's okay to make mistakes."

B arbara Snow was a second-grade teacher before she became a cooking teacher and while the subject matter has changed, her students have not. Snow is one of the most well-known teachers of childrens' cooking classes in Northeast Ohio.

She loves it when children come to class convinced they won't eat half of what they are cooking and end up enjoying foods they swore they would never even try. "The whole time, they're saying, 'We're not eating this, we're not eating that.' Then they all come back for seconds. That's what's fun," she said.

Snow's goal is for children to have a positive experience in her classes so they will want to return to the kitchen. "Even if you make a mistake, it's okay to make mistakes because that makes you learn faster and better." Spills and ruined recipes don't bother Snow—it's all part of the learning process. "Some kids don't have success in a classroom or with sports, but you get them in a kitchen and they just take off."

Growing up in Lakewood, Ohio, Snow learned her appreciation for food from her mother and grandmothers. She became an elementary school teacher and later worked in marketing and sales.

In 1991, she signed up for a class at Zona Spray's cooking school and was hooked. "Once I got my hands in that brioche dough, I never looked back," she said. Snow started taking more classes and after Spray sold the school to Carole Ferguson, Snow came on board as a teacher, eventually taking over most of the childrens' classes. In addition to Western Reserve School of Cooking, Snow has taught for Young Chefs Academy and Sur La Table.

Through her involvement with the International Association of Culinary Professionals, Snow was hired as a brand ambassador for Honeysuckle White Turkey and began developing recipes for them and traveling the country to represent the company.

As important as the lessons she teaches are the lessons she learned from Spray and the other teachers at the school. (She took pastry classes from Tina Körting, whom she had taught second-grade science to years earlier.) Snow remembers Spray's keen sense of food and food trends and her attention to economy. She eschewed fancy equipment when something simple would do—a fork was Spray's favorite lemon reamer. "If a fork would do it, you don't need the tool," Snow recalled.

"I learned how to make really, really good food, easily and as fresh as possible, at very little cost. That's what I remember most from my classes there," Snow said.

Crepes

There is nothing like the look on the face of a junior chef the first time they are able to flip a crepe in mid-air and land it in the pan!

2 large eggs	1 cup flour
¾ cup milk	3 tablespoons melted butter
½ cup water	more butter, for coating the pan

Combine all ingredients in blender and pulse for 10 seconds. The batter should have the consistency of cream.

Place batter in refrigerator for 1 hour; this helps flour absorb liquid so that crepes will be less likely to tear during cooking. You can chill batter up to 24 hours before making crepes.

Place a small amount of butter in a pan and heat. Pour enough batter into center of pan once it is hot enough and swirl to spread evenly. Cook for 30 seconds, turn over with a fork and cook for another 10 seconds. Remove to a plate. Lay them out flat so they can cool.

Continue until all batter is gone. After crepes are cool, you can stack them and store in sealable plastic bags in refrigerator for several days or in freezer for up to two months. When using frozen crepes, thaw on a rack before gently peeling apart.

Fill crepes with any kind of cooked pie filling (fresh or canned), ice cream, Nutella and bananas, or just about anything. Top with whipped cream.

Makes 16 to 20 crepes.

Tacos

This is one of the most popular classes for teens and children. They are always amazed how great these tacos taste.

1 pound ground beef

1 package taco seasoning mix (or 4 tablespoons of Secret Taco Seasoning, recipe follows)

1 cup water

lettuce (iceberg is best), shredded

8 ounces shredded Mexican-style cheese blend

diced tomatoes (canned whole tomatoes are fine if you drain them well after dicing)

1 container (16 ounces) sour cream

8 taco shells

Brown (cook until there is no more pink inside) ground beef in a large skillet over medium-high heat. Add taco seasoning and water, stir, reduce heat and simmer for 30 minutes.

While meat cooks, line up all your other ingredients—this allows you to make your tacos just like they would in a restaurant. Remember: meat will go in first, then lettuce, cheese, tomato and sour cream, so that is how you want to line them up.

Once meat is cooked, put in a bowl and place at the head of your line. Gently hold your taco shell and put a layer of meat in the bottom. Add lettuce, tomato, shredded cheese and finally sour cream.

But part of the fun of being a cook is improvising so if you want tomatoes on top of sour cream, you can do that. Or if you want cheese on the bottom, or sour cream under lettuce...you decide...after all you are the cook!

Makes 8 servings.

Secret Taco Seasoning

6 tablespoons chili powder

4 tablespoons paprika

1 tablespoon garlic powder

3 tablespoons onion powder

2 tablespoons cumin

1 teaspoon cayenne (this is very spicy, so you may want to add a little less or maybe a little more!)

Place all ingredients in a small freezer bag. Seal bag and shake. You can store this in freezer to keep it as fresh. Be sure to mark the bag "Secret Taco Seasoning."

Makes 1 cup.

Gazpacho

....

This is from a class I taught during the height of tomato season in both the Teen Camps and the Passport to Good Eating Camps for eight to twelve-year-olds.

....

3 cloves garlic, peeled

1½ pounds (6 large) fresh tomatoes or 1 can (28 ounces) whole tomatoes (with liquid)

½ cup cold water (if using fresh tomatoes)

1 small white onion, peeled and cut into pieces

1 medium green pepper, washed and cut into pieces

1 large cucumber, peeled and cut into pieces

4 tablespoons red wine vinegar

¼ teaspoon tarragon

1 teaspoon sugar

Place ingredients in a blender or food processor and blend until almost smooth. Transfer to a bowl, cover with plastic wrap and chill at least 2 hours, but overnight is better.

Serve in small bowls. You can garnish your gazpacho with diced avocado, croutons, or diced cucumber. Served with a crusty roll, gazpacho makes an excellent summer meal or first course.

Makes 6 servings.

Jill Wolf

"It's just cooking, not rocket science."

It's always been hard to get Jill Wolf out of the kitchen. Perhaps she inherited her love of cooking from her grandmother, whom she counts among the great cooks she has known. Perhaps it just became a way to shake off the stress of her job as a social worker.

Wolf, a native of Maumee, Ohio, studied social work at the Ohio State University and spent more than eighteen years in the field, often working with or on behalf of disabled adults. Cooking was her outlet after a long day at work.

"I just really enjoyed being in the kitchen. It was therapeutic for me. I would come home from work and just be in the kitchen cooking." It was also a place she spent a lot of time with her children, working on creative cooking projects, and she is proud of the fact that all of her children enjoy cooking.

Wolf moved to the Cleveland area for her husband's job and eventually settled in Hudson. She started taking classes at the Zona Spray Cooking School in the 1970s, while working full-time as a social worker and raising her children.

Once her children were grown and out of school, Wolf began to consider whether she could make a career of cooking. She had finished the professional level courses at the cooking school and had found an affinity in pastry work. "I thought it would be fun to do something different and see if I could make a living cooking instead of in social work."

She was hired to work for the pastry chef at the Intercontinental Hotel on the Cleveland Clinic campus. It was trial by fire and Wolf's eyes were opened to the life of a professional chef. She learned much on the job and used it as a springboard to jobs as the pastry chef at a number of Cleveland area restaurants, including Luxe Kitchen & Lounge.

Wolf has been teaching at the Western Reserve School of Cooking for about six years, mostly pastry classes, but also some savory cooking as well. She remembers Zona Spray for her vast knowledge of food and for being impeccably organized. "Wow, she knew a lot," she recalled.

Wolf is continually amazed by the number and caliber of chefs who come to teach at the school, many of them asking for the chance to return, even though the school is small and so are most of the classes. "There's an uncanny attraction there. We've had some really, really wonderful chefs, who are always more than happy to come back and teach."

She counts food chemist and recipe diagnostician Shirley Corriher and wedding cake designer Colette Peters, as well as fellow staff Kathy Lehr (breads) and Tina Körting (pastry), among her most valuable classes and teachers.

Now, when it's her turn in the kitchen, she draws on her years of culinary schooling, her professional experience and her time spent in social work, as she gets to know her students and helps them to learn. "I like to impart to the students that they should definitely have fun with it. It should be an enjoyable outlet, and not to take it too seriously. It's just cooking, not rocket science. It should be enjoyable, just the way eating is. I think sometimes we take ourselves too seriously," Wolf said.

Herb Rolls

Prepare this the night before you are planning to make the rolls—it develops the flavor that makes these rolls so good.

3 cups bread flour

2 teaspoons salt

Poolish (recipe follows)

8 tablespoons soft butter

6 tablespoons sugar

1 package instant yeast (about 2 teaspoons)

3 beaten eggs

¾ cup warm water

3 to 4 tablespoons fresh chopped herbs, such as rosemary, parsley, or dill

In a standing mixer bowl, mix flour and salt. Add poolish to mix. In water, add yeast to proof, let stand about 5 minutes and add flour mixture. With mixer on low, add butter, sugar, eggs and herbs. Knead with mixer until dough pulls away from sides, 6 to 8 minutes. Place dough in large greased bowl until doubled, about 2 hours.

Spray muffin tins with oil, divide dough onto 24 equal pieces—pieces can be further divided, such as into three small pieces per muffin cup. Shape pieces into ball shapes and fill muffin cups, let rise about 1½ hours more. Bake in preheated 400-degree oven for 10 to 12 minutes or until golden brown. Remove from oven, brush rolls with melted butter.

Poolish

3 cups bread flour

1 teaspoon instant dry yeast

1 cup warm water, may need more to make a smooth poolish

Mix all ingredients together until well combined, cover bowl with plastic and leave on counter overnight. In the morning it should have expanded and be slightly bubbly.

Almond Pear Tart

For frangipane filling:

⅓ cup sugar

⅔ cup almonds

6 tablespoons butter,
    at room temperature

1 egg

¼ teaspoon vanilla

¼ teaspoon almond extract

1½ tablespoons flour

For pears:

3 large pears, peeled and cut into halves

1 quart water

1 pound sugar

½ lemon, cut into wedges

1 teaspoon vanilla

3 to 4 tablespoons apricot jam

Sweet Tart Dough (recipe follows)

For filling: Place almonds and sugar in food processor and grind until sandy. Add butter and mix. Add egg, vanilla, almond extract and flour. Mix until smooth, set aside.

For pears: Combine water, sugar, lemon and vanilla in a saucepan and bring to boil. Add pears and cover with parchment circle topped with a plate to weigh fruit down into liquid. Boil gently for about 5 minutes, reduce heat and simmer until tender.

Roll dough and place in tart pan. Spread thin layer of jam over dough to keep it from becoming soggy. Spread frangipane on top. Remove pears from poaching liquid, blot dry, slice thinly and fan on top of frangipane. Bake at 375 for about 35 minutes. After baking, brush pears with additional jam. Serve with lightly sweetened whipped cream.

Makes 1 tart, serves 8.

Sweet Tart Dough

½ pound unsalted butter,
    at room temperature

½ cup granulated sugar

2 large egg yolks

3¼ cup all-purpose flour

pinch of salt

Combine butter and sugar in mixer bowl, using paddle, until combined. On low speed, add yolks, one at a time. Add flour and salt, mixing just until incorporated. Remove dough, wrap in plastic and chill for about 30 minutes. When chilled, roll and place in tart pan with removable bottom. If dough tears, patch it—there may be extra dough.

Makes 1 tart crust.

Apple Cream Pie

Wolf adapted this recipe from Julia Child's Apple Cream Tart in *Mastering the Art of French Cooking.*

5 to 6 cups peeled, sliced apples (a mix of Honeycrisp, Granny Smith and Golden Delicious works well)

1 cup granulated sugar

1 teaspoon cinnamon

3 tablespoons all-purpose flour

1 tablespoon rum

1 tablespoon vanilla extract

3 tablespoons butter

½ cup heavy cream

Flaky Pie Dough (recipe follows)

In large sauté pan, melt butter and add apples, stirring to coat. Cook several minutes until apples begin to soften. Mix sugar, flour and cinnamon together. When apples are slightly soft, add sugar/flour mixture, stir. When mixture thickens, add vanilla, rum and heavy cream. Cook for another 2 to 3 minutes, remove from heat, cool for 10 minutes. Fill prepared pie dough with apple mixture, top pie with lattice or as desired. Bake at 375 degrees for 30 to 40 minutes until crust is browned and filling is bubbly.

Makes 1 pie, serves 8.

Flaky Pie Dough

2 cups all-purpose flour

¾ teaspoon salt

⅓ cup cold unsalted butter

⅓ cup cold lard

1 teaspoon sugar

4 teaspoon ice water

1 teaspoon apple cider vinegar

In food processor, mix flour, salt and sugar. Add butter and lard, pulse until shortening resembles pea-sized pieces. Pulse in ice water and vinegar just to mix; do not over process. Put dough on lightly floured surface, knead lightly, flatten into a disc, cover with plastic wrap and chill for about 30 minutes. Roll out dough and place into 9-inch pie pan, chill again for 30 minutes before filling.

Makes 1 pie crust.

Jennifer Wolfe Webb

"You can do this."

Whether she's teaching university English or pizza dough, Jennifer Wolfe Webb has known for sometime that she belongs in a classroom. Teaching comes naturally to her and she has always felt completely comfortable leading a group of students. The transition from English to English toffee, however, took some time.

Webb had been an English professor at the University of Kansas when a move for her husband's work landed her in Canton, Ohio. It was 1992. Content to spend a few years as a stay-at-home mom, Webb looked around for someplace to take cooking classes, one of her favorite hobbies.

Cooking had been a passion since age thirteen, when she made her first batch of English toffee. She was blessed with a mother who was a culinary adventurer, trying recipe after recipe for her Kansas City family when Webb was growing up. Her father used to joke that he would have been happy if he had just been able to have the same meal twice.

Webb started taking classes at the Zona Spray Cooking School and by 1997, had worked her way through the professional program. She recalled Spray as "passionate," "no nonsense" and "rigorous."

Webb had great admiration for Spray and also a healthy dose of fear. She remembers a class where her custard failed and Spray stood behind her, asking, "Are you curdling that on purpose?" While the environment was intimidating, Webb also felt forced to stretching herself for the better. "I really felt privileged to have learned from her. She was awe-inspiring."

Along the way, she discovered that food allowed her an outlet for creative expression. "In my case, I'm able to bring my whole self into the kitchen with me. It's also very relaxing."

After she earned her degree, Webb started teaching classes out of her home and eventually at the Western Reserve School of Cooking. "I don't think cooking is rocket science. You can do this. This is fun. It's creative. Nobody is standing in your kitchen behind you criticizing everything you do. Even on your worst day, something you make yourself is better than something you're going to get out of a box or a package. And this isn't even the best you can do yet," she said.

At the same time, she developed a thriving culinary consulting business, putting her master's degree in library science to work conducting market research for food companies, including More Than Gourmet, an Akron, Ohio-based company which makes nationally-recognized classical French sauces and stocks. In her newest endeavor, she directs the food and wine education center at Gervasi Vineyard & Italian Bistro, in Canton, where she also helped develop the kitchen. Her consulting business leaves less time for teaching these days, but she still maintains a position on the staff at Western Reserve. She likes to focus her classes on a single subject or ingredient, such as pizza dough, pie crust, or pumpkin, which allows her to delve deeply into one area. "I'm really just a research nerd," she said.

Chocolate-Dipped Lemon Cream Puffs

For the puff shells:

1 cup water

2 tablespoons unsalted butter

¼ teaspoon salt

1 cup all-purpose flour

4 eggs

4 ounces milk chocolate, chopped

For the filling:

¾ cup strained freshly squeezed lemon juice

8 tablespoons (1 stick) unsalted butter

¾ cup sugar

6 egg yolks

1 envelope powdered gelatin, softened in water

1 cup heavy whipping cream

For the lemon glaze:

2 cups confectioners' sugar, sifted

3½ tablespoons freshly squeezed lemon juice

peel from 1 to 2 lemons, cut in very thin strips, for garnish

For shells: Preheat oven to 400 degrees. Combine water, butter and salt in a saucepan over medium heat and bring to boil, stirring occasionally. As soon as it comes to boil, remove from heat and sift in flour, stirring with a wooden spoon to combine smoothly.

Return to heat and cook, stirring constantly, until paste dries slightly and begins to leave pan sides. Transfer paste to a bowl and stir with a wooden spoon for 1 minute, letting cool slightly. Add eggs, beating each until absorbed before adding the next.

Spoon or pipe (with a pastry bag) batter onto parchment-lined baking sheets, forming 1½-inch mounds. Wet finger with water and smooth top of each mound. Bake puffs about 15 minutes, lower temperature to 350 degrees and continue baking for 10 to 15 minutes, until puffs are firm, golden brown and crisp. Cool on a rack.

Place chopped chocolate in a small metal mixing bowl. Bring 3 inches of water to boil in a small saucepan, remove from heat and place mixing bowl on top. Let sit for 5 minutes. Whisk melted chocolate smooth. Dip tops of puffs in melted chocolate and refrigerate until set.

Shells should be used the day they are made or frozen.

For filling: Combine lemon juice, butter and sugar in a medium saucepan. Bring to a simmer over medium-low heat, stirring occasionally. Whisk yolks in a bowl and whisk in ½ cup lemon mixture. Return remaining lemon mixture back to a simmer and whisk in yolk/lemon mixture. Whisk in gelatin and continue whisking for 3 to 4 minutes, until mixture has thickened. (Do not bring to a boil.) Pour mixture into a bowl, cover with plastic wrap and refrigerate for at least 3 hours.

Whip cream until thick and smooth. Gently fold into lemon mixture until blended. Store covered with plastic wrap in refrigerator. May be made 1 day ahead.

For glaze: In a medium-size mixing bowl, combine confectioners' sugar and lemon juice, mixing with a wire whisk until smooth.

To serve: Up to several hours before serving, transfer filling to a pastry bag fitted with a small, plain tip. Insert tip into side of each puff shell and fill. Drizzle with lemon glaze and serve garnished with lemon peel.

Makes 35 to 40 cream puffs.

Wild Mushroom Risotto with Sliced Steak and Gorgonzola

6 to 7 cups mushroom or chicken stock	2 cups arborio rice
2 tablespoons olive oil	1 cup dry white wine
1 pound fresh wild mushrooms, sliced	2 tablespoons canola oil
2 small onions, diced	4 (6 to 8 ounce) strip steaks
salt and pepper	½ cup crumbled Gorgonzola cheese
2 cloves garlic, minced	2 tablespoons chopped fresh parsley

Bring stock to a simmer in a saucepan and keep at a simmer over low heat.

Heat oil in another saucepan over medium heat. Add mushrooms and onion, season with salt and pepper and sauté until lightly browned and just tender, about 5 minutes. Add garlic and cook for another minute. Add rice to pan and cook, stirring to coat, about 3 minutes.

Add wine and cook, stirring frequently, until absorbed. Ladle 1 cup of hot stock into rice and cook, stirring frequently, until stock is absorbed. Adjust heat to maintain a gentle simmer. Continue adding stock a ½ cup at a time, cooking and stirring until each addition is absorbed, until rice is al dente. (Cooking time is usually 15 to 20 minutes after addition of wine.) Add more stock for a creamier consistency.

Remove pan from heat and season to taste with additional salt and pepper. Cover and set aside.

Warm oil in a heavy skillet over medium-high heat. Sprinkle steaks lightly with salt and pepper. Sear steaks in skillet until cooked to desired doneness, about 3 minutes per side for medium-rare. Let steaks sit for a few minutes, then slice.

Divide risotto among four plates. Top risotto with steak slices, sprinkle with Gorgonzola and parsley and serve.

Makes 4 servings.

Baked Brie with Caramelized Onions, Pecans and Raspberry Coulis

1 two-pound wheel brie cheese,
  top rind trimmed off

4 onions, sliced and sautéed until
  caramelized

⅔ cup toasted pecans, chopped

raspberry coulis (recipe follows)

Preheat oven to 300 degrees. Place cheese on a baking sheet and top with caramelized onions and pecans. Bake 10 to 12 minutes until cheese is warm and softened. Transfer to a serving platter and drizzle with raspberry coulis. Serve with crackers.

Raspberry Coulis

1 package frozen raspberries in light
  syrup, thawed

balsamic vinegar, to taste

powdered sugar, to taste

Drain raspberries in a sieve placed over a bowl, reserving juices. Purée raspberries in a food processor or blender. If desired, strain out seeds by pouring purée through sieve over a second bowl. Add balsamic vinegar and powdered sugar to taste, thinning coulis with reserved juices if needed.

Index

Famous Chefs & Fabulous Recipes

Index by Recipe Type

Entrees

Fruits and Vegetables

Sauces, Jams and Fruit Butters

Soups and Salads